Knowledge Based Systems Methods

BCS Practitioner Series

Series editor: Ray Welland

Knowledge Based Systems Methods

A Practitioners' Guide

Christopher Harris-Jones

Prentice Hall

London   New York   Toronto   Sydney   Tokyo   Singapore
Madrid   Mexico City   Munich

First published 1995 by
Prentice Hall International (UK) Limited
Campus 400, Maylands Avenue
Hemel Hempstead
Hertfordshire, HP2 7EZ
A division of Simon & Schuster International Group

Typeset in 10/12pt Times
by Pentacor

Printed in Great Britain by Hartnolls Ltd, Bodmin.

Library of Congress Cataloging-in-Publication Data

Harris-Jones, Christopher.
    Knowledge based systems methods: a practitioners' guide/
Christopher Harris-Jones.
    p. cm. -- (BCS practitioner series)
    Includes bibliographical references and index.
    ISBN 0-13-185315-5
    1. Expert systems (Computer science) I. Title. II. Series.
QA76.76.E95H358   1995
006.3'3--dc20 95-3381
    CIP

British Library Cataloguing in Publication Data

A catalogue record for this book is available from
the British Library

ISBN 0-13-185315-5

1 2 3 4 5   99 98 97 96 95

To my wife Vivienne

Contents

List of Figures and Tables

Figures

Tables

Preface

For many years I have been involved in the development and use of a wide range of Information Systems methods, both for conventional and for knowledge based systems. During this time I have been promoting the view that knowledge based systems (KBS) should be viewed simply as another approach to the development of computer systems of increasing sophistication. To meet this requirement the methods used to build KBS need to be understandable to the whole of the IT community. They also need to be integrated into conventional development methods.

Commercial audience

The primary audience for this text is that large group of individuals in IT departments now contemplating the prospect of developing KBS within their own organisation. There are a number of methods widely known within the KBS community and some which are known to a relatively small group of commercial KBS developers. Unfortunately, much of the literature on these methods tends to be couched in complex language which at best makes comprehension difficult, and at worst makes it impossible. I have attempted to carry out two main tasks in this book. The first is to provide a framework for understanding how KBS technology can be used to increase the range of Information Systems currently being developed. This is done by providing a conceptual framework to show how the various elements of KBS fit into the development of 'conventional' software systems. The relationship between conventional and knowledge based systems and the need to integrate the two permeates the whole book. Practical advice is also given on how methods integration can be achieved.

The second aim is to describe a set of the main KBS methods currently available in sufficient detail for readers to understand the essentials of these methods. Some of these are currently in the public domain, some have been developed purely for use by individual companies, and some are proprietary and available only from the organisations responsible for their development. Once an appreciation of the methods has been gained, readers can follow two main paths. One is to develop an in-house KBS method as an integral part of existing IT approaches, perhaps as part of a repository as suggested in Chapter 8. A second route is to use the understanding gained to go to one of the suppliers of KBS methods and talk confidently and knowledgeably about the content and structure of a detailed method for the reader's own organisation.

This book is not intended to be yet another 'Introduction to KBS' text, of which there are many. Consequently, it does not describe the technical details of KBS such as, for example, how rules and frames work, backward and forward chaining, uncertainty, and so on. There are many books available which do this and a selection of these is given in the Bibliography (Appendix A). It is not necessary to have a detailed understanding of technical issues such as these to gain benefit from the book. However, some appreciation of the issues of KBS development will permit a deeper understanding of the reasoning behind the shape and content of the methods.

Academic audience

In addition to the commercial audience, many in education and research will find this text useful. It provides a view of KBS methods from someone who uses them to run development projects which must provide a commercially viable solution to real business problems. In this environment the more theoretical ideas of knowledge are not nearly as important as the ability to use the methods effectively in the average IT department to produce sound systems. In particular, those individuals teaching on, or taking, conversion courses aimed at moving into IT, and in particular KBS, will find the contents useful.

Structure

Part I: Background

The first chapter provides an introduction to the commercial aspects of KBS development and sets them in the context of current Information Systems development. The second chapter looks at the history of software engineering and KBS to provide a background for the descriptions of methods in the following chapters. Together the two chapters build a framework for viewing KBS as a very powerful extension to existing IT.

Part II: KBS methods

Chapters 3 to 7 describe the main methods used to develop KBS. The first two chapters look at a number of conventional methods which have been extended to cater for the development of KBS. Chapter 3 describes several methods providing a broad view of the range of approaches available. Chapter 4 then looks in considerable detail at one adapted conventional method and describes how the adaptation was carried out. It then discusses the shape of the final method.

Chapter 5 looks at a number of KBS methods that have been developed, once again to provide a broad view of the range of approaches. Chapters 6 and 7 look at two of these in detail – the KADS method and the GEMINI guidance respectively.

As well as providing a view on the published information on methods, these descriptions have been supplemented with considerable practical experience of developing, integrating, and using KBS methods on projects. A set of references for the methods has been provided in the Bibliography (Appendix A) for further reading.

Part III: Methods in action

The final two chapters, 8 and 9, discuss how KBS methods can be integrated into IT departments and the actions necessary to gain full benefit from the exploitation of KBS technology.

Conventions

One of the objectives of this book is to demystify some of the terminology and so I have tried to keep it to a minimum. However, it is inevitable when discussing a technical subject that jargon creeps in. Wherever possible terminology has been used that is familiar to people working in IT. Whenever more esoteric terminology has been introduced, as tends to happen when discussing the academic origins of KBS methods, it has been explained where it first occurs in the text and is cross-referenced in the index.

There is a long-running debate within IT circles on the use of the terms *methodology* and *method*, and when each is grammatically and semantically correct. It was necessary to select one to ensure consistency throughout the book. It was decided that the use of the term *method* is more appropriate when discussing specific approaches to building computer systems such as SSADM, KADS or Jackson, and this is used throughout.

As this book looks at methods that have been developed to describe the construction of KBS, it was necessary to define a term to refer to software which does not contain KBS components. I have chosen to refer simply to 'conventional' systems in contrast to 'knowledge based' systems.

References

To make the book more readable, the number of references included in the text has been deliberately kept to a minimum. A comprehensive set of references, both for material in the chapters and for additional follow-up reading, can be found in the Bibliography (Appendix A). This has been annotated to indicate the type of material references contain. Wherever possible, references have been included for the most easily available source as well as, where applicable, the original academic sources which could prove more difficult to track down.

Influences

There have been many influences on my work in the area of KBS methods and methods integration and only the most significant can be mentioned here. The main influence has been the many years of practical experience in developing computer systems and implementing development methods. I am essentially a practical person who regularly solves real commercial IT problems. There has also been a significant research element as part of the work.

Almost a decade was spent in conventional IT carrying out all roles from programmer to project manager before moving into KBS. Since then work has focused on consultancy on many commercial KBS projects, lecturing widely on KBS, involvement in the development of GEMINI and KBM, and project management of the IEATP project outlined below.

The other main influence on the integration issues of KBS and conventional methods has without doubt been a research and development project run by BIS which was part-funded by the Department of Trade and Industry under the Information Engineering Advanced Technology Programme (IEATP). The project has now been completed and software to support the construction, configuration and metrication processes has been prototyped and routes for the exploitation of this work are being explored. The project members were BIS Information Systems Ltd (the lead partner), Expert Systems Ltd, and Aston University. References for the work can be found in Appendix A.

It is important to note that since much of the work outlined above was initiated, BIS has been taken over by ACT. Where relevant, references to BIS refer to work carried out entirely by BIS Information Systems before mid-1993, and references to ACT are subsequent developments. Although possibly confusing at times, this dual nomenclature has been necessary since the earlier publications referenced mention BIS, and later publications reference ACT.

Acknowledgements

I would like to express my thanks to all my colleagues at BIS/ACT, Expert Systems and Aston University who have provided information and support during the writing of this book. It is not possible to mention everyone by name but a few must be picked out for their particular support, both with writing the text and on projects which have led to parts of the book. Three people who worked on the IEATP project already mentioned and who provided invaluable material were Toby Barrett (BIS, now with British Rail), Dick Broughton and Ted Walker (both of Expert Systems Ltd). Toby also provided some initial drafts for sections of this book before moving on. Other important colleagues at ACT include Nick Hardie and David Hannaford. Last, but most definitely not least, I would like to thank Trevor Moores (Aston University, now Hong Kong Polytechnic) and Dr John Edwards (Aston University). To those who developed the methods reported herein, I have provided references in the Bibliography and acknowledge their contributions to the field. To those I have unwittingly omitted, apologies and many thanks for your unnamed contribution.

Part I Background

1 Introduction

1.1 What are Knowledge Based Systems?

Knowledge based systems have been the subject of considerable attention during the last decade. Their merits and problems have been discussed widely in the media. This publicity seems to have been divided into several camps – those who believe that KBS are the greatest thing since the invention of computers, those who believe it is all a flash in the pan, and those who have accepted the technology and used it. What is the commercial practitioners' view rather than the media's view? How can businesses gain from the technology – indeed is there anything there at all from which the average company can benefit? This chapter sets out to examine these questions by looking at the way in which knowledge based systems fit into the view of conventional Information Technology and can be exploited successfully in businesses.

1.1.1 Terminology

Before looking at knowledge based systems in detail, some terminology needs to be defined. The names *knowledge based system* and *expert system* are used very widely, often apparently interchangeably. There are no definitions of the two terms that are universally accepted in the business community. A danger with the use of 'expert systems' is that the term 'expert' can be somewhat misleading. People often insist that they are not experts but merely do a particular job; experts are the gurus who sit in a corner and whom the world recognises as being head-and-shoulders above everyone else. When considering the use of KBS in business this view can be very dangerous since many organisations would then claim, probably rightly, that they have no experts and therefore cannot use this technology. However, many individuals would agree that they possess some degree of knowledge which is essential for the performance of their job. While aspects of this knowledge can occasionally be captured in a conventional computer system, for example in accounting or stock control systems, many have knowledge which cannot be captured in this way, typically where a decision has to be made, such as whether or not to extend credit to a customer. This is the type of knowledge typically captured using this technology rather than the guru expertise; hence the term knowledge based systems (or KBS) will be used in preference throughout.

It is not the intention in this chapter to describe in detail what KBS are and how they work; there are many texts available which do this at considerable length (some are listed in the Bibliography in Appendix A). Instead, this chapter concentrates on putting KBS into the context of conventional Information Technology, compares important issues of KBS with conventional systems, and looks at the major issues which are of significance in the development of commercially viable KBS.

1.1.2 Origins of KBS

The discipline of Artificial Intelligence (AI) has existed under that name since the late 1950s. The purposes of people pursuing this subject have been manifold. Initially, many were attempting to model exactly how people solved problems and their ultimate goal was an intelligent machine with some or all of the abilities of a human. This goal has been tempered somewhat over the decades as this venture has seemed increasingly difficult. There were claims during the 1960s that we would have truly intelligent software within twenty years. This has clearly not come true and many have moderated both their claims and their aims. The school of *hard AI* still believes that it is possible, within a sensible period of time, to build genuinely intelligent systems. The aim of this school of thought is to model the way in which people actually think. The *soft AI* school is more intent on systems which mimic the behaviour of humans in solving problems and is not concerned whether such systems actually represent models of how people really think.

The study of AI covers many topics such as artificial vision, robotics, natural language understanding (both written and spoken), as well as problem solving. KBS have risen from AI as one of the more immediately practical areas and are definitely part of the soft AI branch. People in industry and commerce with real business problems are interested in finding answers to those problems. If the solution happens to model the way in which a person actually thinks, it is no more beneficial to a business than a system which simply solves the required problem. The key is that the problem is solved.

1.1.3 KBS and IT

One way in which KBS fit into the view of conventional IT can be illustrated very simply. The pyramid shown in Figure 1.1 represents value as the height and volume as the width.

At the bottom are data – the raw data with which the organisation deals and that are usually held in one or more databases. The width indicates that there are large volumes of the data and the position at the base indicates that each element of the data is individually of a relatively low value. For example, in banking this level will include customer details and account details. These data are manipulated by computer systems such as those that produce bank statements. At this level, the data are simply stored and reorganised. Typical enquiries might be 'What is the balance on account x?'. Data may be transformed to the next level up through the use of Management Information Systems (MIS). These take the

Figure 1.1
Volume versus Value:
view of conventional
systems.

raw data and convert them into 'information'. MIS will typically allow its users to enter queries that are not pre-programmed in accounting systems, perhaps such as 'How many private customers have overdrafts of more than £500?'. This process has reduced the volume of raw data considerably and added value by providing information which individuals in the organisation can use to make decisions. This information is taken by individuals, such as the branch managers, to provide support for making decisions about the running of the organisation. This moves to the top level – Decisions. The decisions have the highest value and the lowest volume. Questions posed at this top level could include 'Which company accounts are in a potentially dangerous state and need investigating?'. Such enquiries cannot be made of a conventional database since it requires considerable expert interpretation of the data. MIS may be able to tell the bank manager which accounts have large overdrafts, or which loan accounts have fallen behind in repayments, but MIS will not say 'look at this account — it appears to have serious problems'. This interpretation is the job of an individual knowledgeable in banking.

The way in which KBS fit into this scheme is illustrated by the variation of the pyramid shown in Figure 1.2. In this, an extra layer has been inserted between

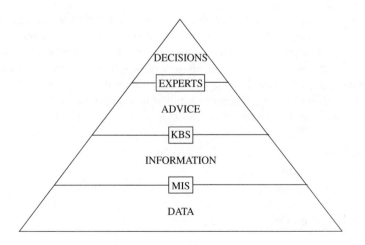

Figure 1.2
Volume versus Value:
KBS

Information and Decisions. KBS can be used to take the information gathered from the corporate database and can then assess this based on its knowledge and produce appropriate advice. A KBS can be used to provide support for decision makers or to devolve the decision making process by allowing someone less senior to make a decision. To continue the banking example, a further illustration is a KBS which examines the details of loans to customers and generates advice for the bank manager on the state of the loan – for example 'the loan is being serviced well', 'there could be problems with the loan repayment', or 'there are major problems with the loan repayment'. In fact a system of this nature has already been implemented by one of the high street banks. It is also important to note that many very successful KBS use information that is provided directly by a user rather than data stored on another computer.

An alternative way of viewing the integration of KBS into mainstream IT has come as a side product of a new way of looking at business organisations. Business Process Automation, also known as Business Process Design, Business Process Reengineering and by many other similar names, is another of those phrases that has appeared during the early 1990s. The move behind the buzz phrase is a shift away from the organisation of businesses as large hierarchies, which are often legacies of older ways of working, into a much simpler flatter structure. This is seen as an innovative move attempting to get away from the traditional structures to improve factors such as communication. For example in a hierarchical organisation it is not unusual for the processing of a single order to be carried out by a whole series of departments with the inevitable potential problems of communication, lost paperwork and so on. One organisation recorded a total of 28 separate departments involved in the placing of one order. In a reengineered company, the objective is to ensure that what is logically a single function, such as placing an order, is carried out by a single department and preferably by just one person. One of the results of this reorganisation is to reduce the number of communication links and thus provide a faster, more accurate, more reliable, more efficient service to the customer. This also has the effect of reducing costs.

An essential element of this is a change to the way in which technology is used within the business, towards being a servant of the business rather than the master, and as an enabler rather than a straitjacket. The way in which KBS fit into this approach is similar to that already described – it fits towards the top of IT providing high value decision support rather than processing large volumes of data. The range of potential support identified by one organisation, McDonnell Douglas, as part of a BPR exercise as being appropriate for KBS development includes:

- finding the customer;
- making the right offering;
- defining the product;
- scheduling production;
- making the product;

- preparing the product for delivery;
- using the product;
- maintaining the product.

As with all general principles, there are many exceptions. There is one very well publicised exception to the view that KBS support the higher end of information processing rather then being in direct contact with the simple business data. Barclays Bank has developed a system known as 'Fraudwatch' which examines Barclaycard transactions for potentially fraudulent cases. Through the use of a mixture of conventional and KBS techniques, this system scans over 1,000,000 transactions every night and generates an exception report of the very small number of potentially fraudulent cases. The input to this system is the raw data, the base of the pyramid, and yet the output is of very high value, running into millions of pounds of savings every year through the early detection of fraud.

1.2 The rise of KBS

To see how KBS have reached their current status it is worth looking back briefly at the emergence of KBS from universities and considering the changes that have taken place since their initial appearance.

1.2.1 Early systems

In the early 1960s, workers in AI believed that it would be possible to build general problem solving systems and a number of attempts were made to do this. The main problem with these was that the problem had to be redefined very precisely in such a way that the computer program could accept it. This reformulation actually solved a significant part of the problem and all that tended to remain was largely algorithmic. The program therefore did not actually do anything significant in terms of intelligent behaviour. It was also realised that in making specific problem solving approaches more generally applicable, the approaches tended to lose much of the power that made them of interest in the first place. This search for general problem solving mechanisms then lost much of its momentum and attention was turned to solving more specific problems. Systems which solved problems in very tightly defined areas started to appear over the following ten years. One of the very earliest 'expert systems', the first version appearing in the mid-1960s, was DENDRAL which analysed the output from a variety of chemical analysis equipment such as mass spectrometers and nuclear magnetic resonance machines and inferred plausible structures for the chemicals of unknown compounds. The system was a great success and has been used by many chemists over a period of several decades. Another area tackled by many researchers was medical diagnosis. The most famous of these systems is MYCIN which addressed the problem of diagnosing and generating treatments for blood infections. Although this has been regarded as a success and has become notorious from its appearance in almost every textbook on expert systems and KBS for the last 15 years, it has never been deployed for the general use of doctors. One of the most well known of the early commercial applications of the technology was built initially by DEC for configuring their computers. Known variously as R1 and XCON, it has been carrying out this task in a live environment since the early 1980s. DEC says that it would now be impossible to operate without the system. It is interesting to note that most of the other major computer manufacturers have followed suit and now use configuration computer systems that contain at least some element of KBS.

The majority of successful KBS have been based on rules. In a sense this has achieved some of the objectives of a generic problem solver since the same type of rule inferencing mechanism can be applied to a wide range of problems. It is, however, by no means universal and there are KBS which employ different forms of knowledge representation.

1.2.2 *KBS into IT*

KBS started to filter into the mainstream of computing during the 1980s and were accompanied by a flood of PC products claiming to allow the users to encapsulate the expertise of their experts very quickly and easily. Although some successful systems were written in the mid-1980s, many were simply experiments to see what the technology could do. This had an unfortunate result. Many people built systems using PC shells to support areas of the business that were not critical – usually because of the risk of failure they perceived in what was commercially a relatively new technology. Consequently, as the systems did not support anything important, it was inevitable that they would never be used. In many people's eyes, KBS then gained the reputation that they were interesting toys but not for solving real business problems. However, a small number of organisations pressed on and built successful systems and these were often widely publicised. As the technology matured, and the KBS development tools became available on a wider range of hardware platforms, an ever increasing number of organisations came to appreciate that KBS had the potential to solve significant business problems. These problems had often been known about for many years but no computer solution had been possible for them. The position in the early 1990s is that KBS are now becoming recognised as very powerful tools within IT. It is also interesting to note that some KBS software is now very successfully marketed as prototyping, windowing or object oriented tools, having mysteriously lost their KBS badge.

1.2.3 *KBS generations*

Just as computer languages are often described as belonging to five different generations, so KBS are now recognised as falling into two generations – no doubt there will be many more in the years to come. First generation KBS are still very much in the majority, with very few commercially successful second generation systems.

First generation systems can be characterised according to a number of attributes:

- Their problem solving is very inflexible. There is usually one method of reasoning used, usually forward or backward chaining, and the system is unable to plan its own reasoning strategies. Consequently their performance tends to be 'brittle' – that is, they usually fail catastrophically when problems fall outside their particular restricted domain but do not flag any errors.
- The systems can only be used for one very specific purpose, for example as a Decision Support tool, and not to act as a training system for the same decisions even though there is much overlap between the knowledge required for the tasks.
- User interface. The user interface is fairly primitive, usually consisting of a simple sequence of questions and answers, often generated dynamically by the tool being used. There are very few explanation facilities and the reasoning behind the sequencing of questions is usually hidden in the coding of the rules. Any explanations are usually simply traces of the rules which have been executed. While this is often useful for debugging, it does not really represent anything approaching a real explanation that is understandable by the non-experts using the system.
- The vast majority use rules as the only means of representing knowledge. This means that the strategies tend to be coded in rules in the same way as the basic domain knowledge. Consequently there is often confusion between that which is knowledge about the domain, and the problem solving knowledge. It also means that it is not possible to make explicit use of the problem solving knowledge by reasoning about the strategies themselves.
- The use of a large set of rules (occasionally broken down into rulesets or modules) and the need to code procedural and strategy elements in the same rule format makes the maintenance of the system very difficult.

The majority of these systems have been written using relatively simple shells, usually PC-based, and are small applications rarely with more than a few hundred rules. Over the last few years, the level of sophistication of tools has been considerably enhanced and many are now marketed as 'development environments' rather than as shells. In some cases this appears to be more of a marketing ploy than evidence of significant improvements in the software. However, there are significant differences between the more advanced development tools and their simpler relatives. The more sophisticated tools now allow the use of multiple methods of representation, typically now rules, frames and/or objects and procedures. This has allowed more complex systems to be built with characteristics attributed to a second generation of KBS. These include:

- Much deeper knowledge of the domain is captured within the system. This allows the problem solving strategies to be adapted by the system, depending on the nature of the problem being solved. It may be possible to use the knowledge base for several purposes, for example both as a decision support system and to support training.

- The deeper knowledge allows it to generate much more acceptable explanations. These are constructed from the knowledge base rather than simply being a trace of the rules.
- More sophisticated problem solving strategies can be coded in the system because of the greater expressive power available in the tools. This permits a more coherent questioning strategy to be employed by the system, which, together with the greater detail in the explanations, allows a more usable system to be generated.
- The separation of the different types of knowledge (i.e. a knowledge base can be held separately from the problem solving structure) allows the logical design to be transformed to a physical design with fewer changes. It also makes the maintenance of the system much easier.

It would appear from this brief outline of the differences that second generation systems will win out every time. However, all these benefits do not come free. The penalty of second generation systems is that they are much more difficult to construct. Although they bring significant benefits to the more complex systems, it is likely that the simpler first generation approach will be with us for many years because they are capable of providing satisfactory solutions to many business problems.

The difference between the level of expertise modelled by first and second generation systems is also reflected in the methods that have been developed. The simpler methods, often based on conventional approaches, can provide satisfactory first generation solutions. The more complex methods, often from academia, are more suited to second generation systems where complex models of deep knowledge are required. This can present a problem for KBS builders. It may seem sensible to go for the more advanced methods on the basis that if they can deal with complex cases they must be able to handle simple cases. However, the more complex methods can apparently demand that extensive knowledge engineering is carried out to build a set of very complex models. This can be totally unnecessary for the simpler types of systems. This problem of scalability is touched on in many of the chapters on the individual methods.

1.3 Is KBS development different?

Throughout the lifetime of commercial KBS, many have stated that the development of KBS is fundamentally different from that of conventional systems so that it is not possible to use conventional development methods. Some even went as far as saying that it was not possible to use structured methods at all. This section raises some of the issues that gave rise to this belief and that have resulted in the work that has gone into the development of KBS methods, and offers some initial thoughts on their possible resolution. These topics will return frequently during many of the subsequent chapters which discuss the methods themselves.

1.3.1 Development approach

In the early days of commercial development, it was widely believed that KBS could only be built through prototyping. This often meant eliciting some knowledge from the expert and then going away and coding it into a KBS tool. The belief behind this was that it was not possible to build a knowledge model entirely on paper in the way that data and process models are built for conventional systems. While this prototyping approach may sometimes produce useful systems when built by a single person, it has many problems. The most notable difficulty occurs in controlling the number of iterations (and therefore the cost and timescales), and in the quality of the end product, in particular the maintainability of the code and its reliability. There has now been a general acceptance that KBS development needs to be controlled in a similar fashion to conventional systems development since in a commercial environment KBS are bound by the same constraints of cost and time. This has resulted in the more formal prototyping approaches found in a number of development methods and in the use of 'rapid development' approaches. The issue of life cycles, and in particular the use of prototyping, is a topic that will appear repeatedly in the more detailed examination of methods in the following chapters.

1.3.2 System types

KBS tend to address slightly different areas of a business to conventional systems. IT systems can generally be divided into three categories according to their primary objective within the organisation – efficiency, effectiveness, and competitive edge.

Efficiency systems are aimed at developing systems (not surprisingly) to increase the efficiency of the organisation, often by speeding up one or more relatively straightforward but often lengthy or tedious tasks, often handling large volumes of data. Examples of these are the more common type of number-crunching systems such as payroll, order processing and stock control. The justification for these systems is usually straightforward and is achieved through cost/benefit analysis. Cost reductions may occur by reducing the number of people required to carry out the relevant tasks and measurable benefits accrue by ensuring that fewer mistakes are made and by increasing the speed of processing.

The second category of systems is those concerned with increasing the effectiveness of the organisation, typically improving the quality and service that the organisation gives to its customers. Typical examples of this are making stock and ordering information available on-line so that potential customers could simply telephone an organisation, find out the current stock position and place an order on the spot. This information would then be passed immediately to the despatch department, ensuring rapid despatch of the order. This type of system can be more difficult to justify since, although there may be obvious advantages such as reducing the paperwork necessary, there are also advantages in that customers may have more loyalty to an organisation that can process their orders quickly. KBS can contribute significantly at this level by providing expertise where it is most needed. An example can be taken from an organisation which produced a large number of complex products, often bespoke, for the specific requirements of customers. However, although customers knew the use to which the product would be put, they were usually unable to identify the specific product required. A KBS was built which led the person taking the order through a series of questions to be put to the customer to identify the most appropriate product for their requirements. This permitted customers to place orders immediately by telephone even though they did not know which product they required. This type of system also has significant elements of the next category.

The final category is competitive edge systems. This is the most difficult of the three to quantify. These systems are usually innovative since, by definition, competitors do not have them, or at least do not have a particularly effective system. KBS play a major role in this area along with other advanced technologies. One of the most significant sets of justifications for this type of system can arise from the analysis of competitive forces such as:

- threat of new entrants coming on to the market;
- bargaining power of suppliers;
- bargaining power of customers;
- threat of substitute products or services;
- rivalry between competing businesses.

These types of threats can be countered through the use of IT. For example, an insurance company could offer cover for unusual risks by using a KBS at each branch, thus circumventing the need to refer to experts in head office. If this is installed before any competitors have developed similar systems then the ability to provide quotes on the spot provides a significant competitive advantage.

1.3.3 Difficulty of specifying the requirements

It is often claimed that the specification of requirements is very difficult for KBS. However, this problem is not limited to KBS. Many conventional systems have been developed where the requirements were defined by the systems analyst to 'help' an uncertain user. When designing a new software system, most people have great difficulty in understanding how it will work and what impact it will have on their normal procedures before seeing the system itself. The consequence is that most system requirements expressed by users are vague. This in turn leads the analysts who have to develop a detailed specification of requirements for the proposed system to assist the users to define the requirements. Once these have been defined, the users are expected to sign-off the requirements. It may then be many months, or even years, before the users see the system to which they have agreed. In this time it is very likely that their requirements (however vaguely expressed initially) will have changed. This may be because they carry out their job in a different way or perhaps because the way in which the organisation works has changed – either because of different corporate policies or because the world in which the organisation operates has changed. The result is a system which is no longer very appropriate. The fault here lies not with either the users or the analysts, but with the way in which the requirements were specified. The problem of requirements specification is often compounded by KBS since the elicitation of the knowledge is even more difficult than conventionally and the person with the knowledge (the expert) is unlikely to be the end user. However, the overall problems are by no means unique to KBS.

1.3.4 Unclear boundaries

It is claimed that the boundaries of KBS are not clear whereas those for conventional systems are well defined. To some extent this is a misunderstanding by KBS workers who have no experience of commercial IT. As has already been seen, users often do not fully understand their requirements and this can mean that the boundaries are unclear. Consequently it is not unusual for relatively arbitrary boundaries to be fixed for a system with the intention of adding functions in the future.

The difference between KBS and conventional systems really relates to the *possibility* of defining clear boundaries; it is generally much easier in conventional IT (even if they may be arbitrary) than it is for KBS. One major reason is that since KBS can deal with incomplete information, it is less simple to define clear boundaries. For example, the output from a KBS which assesses applications for loans or insurance is typically one of three answers – accept, reject, or refer to a higher authority. The first two are precise answers which can be used by the business. The third is effectively the bucket category that means 'I am not sure what the answer is'. Systems of this nature can be prototyped very simply with early versions giving definitive decisions only for the simplest possible cases at either extreme, rejecting the rest into this bucket category. As the knowledge is refined, the refer category shrinks. In theory, work can continue until it has disappeared altogether but this will tend to run into a situation of diminishing returns. Under these circumstances, what are the boundaries of the knowledge?

Even with this apparently trivial example, there can be major problems in defining the knowledge base. It is often essential in this type of system that an application is not classified wrongly and that if there is any doubt it should be put into the refer category. However, because of the need to handle incomplete and possibly erroneous data, the system needs to know when applications are beyond its expertise, i.e. beyond the boundaries of its knowledge base, so that they can be rejected. A problem with some KBS is that they 'don't know what they don't know' and so can easily give a wrong answer. This is particularly problematical in medical diagnosis systems where a wrong classification of a problem could have fatal consequences. It is in this way that the boundaries of KBS are hard to specify.

1.3.5 Knowledge is private

Whereas the information needed to build conventional systems is usually freely available, the knowledge required by KBS is often referred to as private. Analysis of conventional systems usually involves discussing the tasks to be automated with the people who carry them out and making extensive use of existing documented procedures. However, during this process it is not uncommon to discover that someone takes a slightly different approach from the formal procedures simply because it is more efficient. Automating the procedures rather than the way in which tasks are actually carried out is an area which causes many conventional systems to perform less efficiently than the manual approach. The problem is caused by the so-called *private* procedures. While this sometimes generates difficulties for the development of conventional systems, it is a very much larger problem with KBS.

Returning to the example of the bank manager identifying customers who may be having financial problems, the process that the manager goes through in trying to identify such accounts may not be formalised anywhere; it is simply knowledge acquired though years of experience. It is this that should be captured in a KBS.

In attempting to record this expertise, many techniques have been developed for KBS aimed at eliciting information that is private. It is interesting to note that many of the techniques are now moving from KBS development into the interviewing techniques for conventional systems development.

1.3.6 Partial or incomplete information

Conventional systems have fixed requirements for data. For example, an accounting package cannot generate an invoice without access to all of the information needed for an invoice. On the other hand, experts are expected to solve problems with incomplete information, information which may not be wholly accurate, spurious information, and even information that is wrong. If KBS are to provide an expert service, then they must be capable of dealing with these situations. Many techniques have been developed, often based on probability theory, which allow KBS to operate under these conditions. This is probably one of the major features that currently distinguish KBS and conventional systems – conventional systems handle only fixed information, whereas KBS are expected to have the ability to handle less well specified information.

1.3.7 Feasibility

There are a number of important issues related to feasibility. The one usually discussed in academic circles is whether or not a potential KBS is technically feasible. This is obviously also a significant consideration for commercial applications but the issues of organisational and business feasibility are also of major importance.

Organisational feasibility is concerned with whether the business is in a position to take advantage of the proposed system. The corporate philosophy, the organisation of the workforce and the availability of computers and/or terminals are all major issues. KBS have been built which successfully addressed the problem at which they were targeted but failed to be implemented because of organisational issues, such as a poor fit with working practices or an inappropriate environment. It is necessary to address these issues before attempting to build any software.

Business feasibility is concerned primarily with assessing the cost/benefit justification of the proposed system. The commercial return of a system must be sufficient to justify the cost of its development. This is where a major problem lies with commercial KBS. Many of the perceived benefits, such as increased availability of knowledge, more consistent results, and so on, can be extremely difficult to quantify. Most businesses require details of benefits in financial terms and these can be almost impossible to calculate. In the early days of the exploitation of KBS within an organisation, many systems receive approval because they have a champion who believes in their value. As the experience in the development and use of KBS grows, expertise in assessing the commercial value will increase.

1.3.8 Verification and validation

It has been said that the verification and validation (V&V) of KBS is substantially different from conventional systems. One of the most common problems in KBS V&V is that the number of potential solutions can explode into untestable volumes. While it is possible to test the majority of paths through a conventional system, it may be impossible to do so for KBS. A classic example of this is that a system which creates a timetable cannot be exhaustively tested simply because there are a large number of input variables and an enormous number of possible solutions. It may also be that there is no 'right' solution; for example in a timetable there is simply a solution which is acceptable. The use of uncertainty raises further problems. If it is acceptable for an expert to be wrong, it is acceptable for a KBS? If so, then how wrong can it be allowed to become before its performance becomes unacceptable?

1.3.9 Knowledge representation vs data representation

The ways in which data can be analysed and represented are well understood. The position is not the same for knowledge. While it is accepted that data need to be normalised for use within a conventional system, there is no equivalent for KBS. Some researchers in KBS say that it is impossible to normalise knowledge since it is always attached intimately to its usage. Data analysis strives to make the data completely independent of its use, an essential feature if the data are to be held in a database and used by a large number of applications.

1.4 KBS and conventional methods

In the light of the issues raised in the previous section, it is now relevant to consider the relationship between conventional and KBS development methods. The relationship, similarities and differences, have changed significantly over the last decade, the period in which KBS started to move into serious commercial exploitation.

1.4.1 Method differences

Factors causing changes in the approach to the development of conventional systems include:

- Completion of the automation of many of the basic computer-based tasks such as accounting, payroll and so on; and the increased availability of packaged solutions. This has precipitated many organisations to look at other ways in which IT can support their activities.
- Increase in the rate of change in business. A significant factor in this, somewhat incestuously, has been the increased use of IT. One effect has been to reduce the timescales available for system development. The long timescales of several years, common for development in the past, can now mean that the business has changed significantly between the initial specification of requirements and the delivery of the resulting system. Consequently the delivered software no longer matches the information requirements of the business.
- Advances in hardware and falling costs have meant that it is now possible to distribute very powerful PCs widely. This means the frequent delivery of facilities such as sophisticated and visually attractive user interfaces using colour and graphics. Many users now often demand these facilities in all new systems.

These have caused a change in the way conventional systems are built, often bringing them nearer to the ways KBS have traditionally been developed. These changes have included:

- the appearance of rapid development life cycles and prototyping;
- prototyping with the user;
- ensuring the user is deeply involved, possibly even to the extent of designing and building part or all of the system.

Much early commercial KBS development took place in a spirit of experimentation, the developers often not knowing whether the system was possible. Methods were rarely used, partly because it was believed that KBS were significantly different and therefore that conventional methods were not applicable, and partly because many early experiments were outside the immediate pressures normally placed on commercial IT projects. The applications selected tended to be of a low business priority so that failure did not have a significant impact on the business. However, this often also meant that success was not significant either. Of the relatively few systems that did see the light of commercial use, a frequent problem was that they rapidly became unmaintainable because they were poorly documented or because the original developer had left the organisation. One high profile system that has already been mentioned, the DEC computer configuration system, grew incrementally for several years and eventually had to be completely rewritten because of maintenance difficulties.

The problem of system maintenance was one of the factors that led people to start thinking about the use of more formal methods to support the development of KBS. Another major factor was simply the view that as conventional development methods appeared to be useful, then perhaps methods for KBS development would prove equally useful.

Development methods for KBS, or at least outlines of methods, started to appear in the first half of the 1980s. These tended to adopt one of two approaches which are still seen in KBS methods development today. The two contradictory premises on which these are based are:

1. Software Engineering has already developed methods so KBS methods should be an extension of these.
2. KBS development is sufficiently different from conventional systems development for KBS methods to need a completely new approach.

The former approach has resulted in methods such as STAGES and KBM (described in Chapters 3 and 4), the latter in methods such as KEMRAS and KADS (Chapters 5 and 6). This split is not as clearly defined as might be thought. Many of the conventionally based methods have taken on ideas from the KBS-based approaches, and many of the KBS-based methods have, sometimes unwittingly, taken on aspects of conventional software engineering. This difference of approach has been used to divide the methods chapters into two groups. This division is intended more for convenience than as a serious classification since, as is noted in the individual chapters, it is debatable where some of them should be placed.

The methods based on these approaches have their own particular advantages and disadvantages and these are summarised in the following discussion.

1.4.2 Software Engineering based methods

The major advantage of basing KBS methods on conventional Software Engineering (SE) is that it can draw upon a huge body of practical experience stretching back over several decades. The aim of software development of any kind is to provide a system that has advantages over the current manual approach (if one exists) or the current Information System. KBS are no exception. Many software engineering approaches and techniques can be used unchanged by KBS methods. Some, however, do need modification. Cost justification of systems, for example, is a complex task that has been tackled by conventional software engineering. While largely applicable to KBS, it does need to be tempered with the KBS-specific difficulties described in the previous section. However, the use of standard software engineering approaches provides a very sound basis for KBS methods development. It is also an approach which is generally understood and accepted by the level of management likely to be approving KBS projects.

Moving further down the life cycle, one of the major advantages is that a conventional approach is well understood by IT departments and so is more easily accepted than a totally new approach with different terminology. Despite being involved in a rapidly changing area of technology, most members of IT departments are as resistant to change and the introduction of new ideas as any department in an organisation.

One of the biggest disadvantages of an SE approach is the perceived rigidity of the conventional life cycle. KBS development demands a very flexible approach to systems development and the structure of conventional methods can cause problems. The second of the major disadvantages is that conventional methods largely model data and process only – not surprisingly knowledge is not considered and behaviour modelling is generally confined to handling events. These two problems are circumvented in KBS methods adopted from SE methods in a number of ways:

- Additional flexibility may be added through the use of prototyping as a technique to support the knowledge engineer during analysis and design. This automatically adds multiple feedback loops to the life cycle.
- A Rapid Development approach may be taken as the basic life cycle rather than the monolithic waterfall. This immediately provides a much shorter time between the beginning of a development and its installation and also demands much closer contact with the users.
- A knowledge modelling approach can be grafted on to the more conventional data and process analysis but based firmly on accepted analysis techniques.
- A more complex knowledge modelling approach based on detailed research into the structure of knowledge can be incorporated into an SE method. This is likely to introduce significant new terminology.

All of these approaches can be seen in the chapters which describe SE-based KBS methods.

1.4.3 KBS-based methods

The major advantage of KBS methods developed independently from SE-based approaches is that they come to software development untainted by many of the more restrictive practices of conventional software engineering. Conventional SE has had its share of disasters; it has been reported that as many as 80% of systems initiated are never installed as intended. IT departments have a poor reputation in many organisations for failing to produce the required systems on time and to budget. There are therefore those who say that KBS should break completely with conventional SE and so discard all the approaches which have caused so many problems in the past. However, it seems that most KBS developers view this rather as throwing the good out with the bad. A compromise of some sort is often sought by taking the better aspects of SE and using them in appropriately defined KBS methods.

The flexibility needed to develop KBS resulted in many early approaches espousing a prototyping approach. Consequently substantial elements of prototyping, or iterative development, can be found in many KBS methods. It is interesting to note that SE has now taken on many of the ideas formerly associated with KBS development such as the need to have a short lead time and substantial involvement of the users throughout the development. These features now often appear in Rapid Development approaches. This is one way in which SE and KBS have converged, the root of this movement probably lying in the identification of a common problem of specification of requirements rather than in a conscious borrowing of ideas. A similar convergence can be seen in the parallel but largely separate development of the ideas of frames in AI/KBS and object oriented approaches.

The area in which KBS-specific methods tend to score over SE-based methods is inevitably that of knowledge modelling. KBS methods are usually grounded in significant research into the structure and function of knowledge. Consequently they take a much purer approach to its analysis and representation. A major obstacle to the acceptance of this approach by IT departments is that in nature it is intrinsically abstract and uses many alien terms and concepts. However, this problem is by no means insurmountable. Structured analysis and design also introduced many new concepts to IT and these gradually became accepted through training and education. There is no reason in principle why this should not also happen with the terminology of KBS methods.

1.4.4 Which is best?

Both approaches have their attractions and it is difficult to give a categoric judgement that one is always the best approach. The range of conventional methods exists, at least partly, because each has its own characteristics that suit it to particular development environments and specific projects. Much the same can be said of approaches to KBS development. However, an SE approach tends to be accepted more readily by the average IT department. This usually needs to be tempered by prototyping and a rapid development approach to cater for KBS. Detailed knowledge modelling can be useful in the more complex developments and can be introduced gradually as KBS are used to tackle increasingly difficult problems. The complexity of comprehensive knowledge modelling can present more problems than it solves in simple straightforward KBS and needs to be used cautiously. However, care needs to be taken to ensure that the initial simple approach is structured so that it can incorporate detailed knowledge modelling incrementally without discarding any of the modelling approaches taken for simpler systems. The Perspectives Model introduced in the next chapter provides a framework for this incremental approach.

1.5 Major issues

A number of differences between KBS development and conventional systems development have already been discussed. This section looks at some of the issues that are becoming increasingly important in attempts to use KBS technology to deliver workable solutions to business problems. Some of these issues have been addressed by the methods described in later chapters while others are still a topic of research. Where topics are raised which have been directly addressed by methods discussed in later chapters, forward references are given to the appropriate sections.

1.5.1 Integration of KBS and conventional methods

An increasing number of organisations are now building KBS which they want to interface to new or existing conventional systems or embed totally in conventional systems. This becomes very difficult where IT departments are expected to use a conventional method for the conventional aspects, and a KBS method for the KBS elements. One problem is that it is not always clear at the beginning of a project which aspects are conventional and which are KBS. Where there is uncertainty, or the proposed system has both components, it may appear that it is necessary to use two methods at the beginning of the project. There are many problems associated with trying to use two methods on one project, including the obvious one that it can be difficult to use one method, let alone two. Different approaches to development and disparate terminologies complicate their successful use. Some methods were originally designed to be extensions of conventional methods and overcome the problem in this way. However, these tend to be appropriate only for the simpler KBS and are not easily extensible to allow for very complex knowledge modelling. Some SE-based methods are outlined in Chapter 3. The necessary power and sophistication required for complex knowledge modelling is usually only found in methods with more academic origins such as KADS (Chapter 6).

Some attempts have been made to model methods in such a way as to permit the conversion of constructs from one method into another, and to allow the integration of methods. These are discussed in Section 4 of Chapter 2.

1.5.2 Skill reusability and portability

Many commercial IS developers have expressed concern that some KBS methods appear to be going their own way in terms of major issues such as life cycles, techniques, and terminology. Organisations which believe methods are a good thing have usually invested substantial sums of money in taking on methods; for larger organisations this can run into hundreds of thousands of pounds. In addition to these take-on costs there are the continuing expenses of training new staff and maintaining the level of expertise of existing staff through update and refresher courses. Not surprisingly, commercial users do not want a wide range of different methods with no common core since this exacerbates the cost of taking on and using methods. The preferred route is to have a set of KBS techniques that are reusable with different methods and can be used on a wide range of projects. IT traditionally has a fairly high turnover of staff and constant retraining of new staff in unusual methods is an expensive option. This issue is to some degree being addressed by the UK government's GEMINI initiative which is attempting to define a guidance for the development of KBS. It provides a framework for the development of KBS by discussing the major issues facing KBS developers, outlining the types of products which should be delivered and highlighting the project management approach, including the management of risk, quality and legal issues. GEMINI is described in detail in Chapter 7. Reusability issues are also discussed when considering integration and configuration issues in Chapter 8.

1.5.3 Development life cycle

KBS have often been developed by using various ad hoc prototyping approaches which is something that has worried many individuals in commercial IT departments, both because of the difficulty in estimating and controlling the development process itself and also because of concern about the quality of software that can be obtained. The development of KBS methods has resulted in a wide range of different life cycles, of which some eschew prototyping completely while others embrace it with open arms. These very different approaches are causing some concern amongst potential KBS users about the 'correct' way to build KBS. These issues are discussed further in the next chapter where life cycles are looked at in more detail. Each of the individual chapters also looks at the life cycles used by each method.

Life cycles are also a major issue in conventional development. The traditional waterfall approach is starting to fall out of favour in many organisations. One of the approaches replacing it is a number of forms of rapid development in which systems are produced incrementally but with well defined control and management structures. A more detailed description of the use of rapid development methods can be found in Chapters 2 and 4.

1.5.4 Knowledge modelling

Data modelling through normalisation and the use of diagramming techniques such as Entity–Relationship diagrams are very widely accepted. There is no KBS equivalent of data modelling and some KBS workers doubt whether this can ever exist. A number of different approaches have been defined, some within development methods, some outside, but none are universally accepted. At one extreme there are simple extensions to data modelling as defined within methods derived from conventional methods such as Keller (Chapter 3). These approaches usually start on the basis that knowledge is not really very different from the data and processes modelled in conventional systems and thus no radically different approaches are required. At the other extreme, some methods have developed techniques for knowledge modelling which have very little in common with conventional software engineering. The most significant approach of this nature is KADS. The KADS knowledge engineering approach is described in Chapter 6.

1.5.5 User modelling

In conventional systems development, it is not particularly unusual to find members of IT departments who regard users as rather a nuisance. Users are viewed as people who are often not clear about their requirements for computer systems, do not really understand the documentation that the IT department produces which specifies the proposed system, and then to cap it all, when they receive the system that has been built for them, say that it is not quite what they wanted. Fortunately this view is slowly changing. Systems developers are starting to realise that users are human too and that they cannot be expected to enter the often mysterious world of software development – they simply want systems which will help them with their job.

It was realised fairly early on during the rise of KBS that users were very important people for a number of reasons. One is simply that the expert whose knowledge is elicited and put into the KBS is frequently not the final user of the system. If the KBS is designed to be suitable for the expert, and then given to users who have very little of the expert's knowledge, the result is usually a totally unusable system. KBS developers realised that it was necessary to distinguish between the expert and the user and to model the level of understanding for both parties. This then allows the interface to be designed so that the user can understand what is going on and use it in a work environment. A related problem is that KBS often do not interact with the user in the same way as conventional systems. A conventional computer system will usually have a series of (more or less) fixed menus – be they the conventional numbered lists often seen on mainframe systems or the more interactive pull-down menus seen on more recently developed systems. The user navigates around the system selecting options from menus and expects a fixed sequence of actions to occur depending on the options selected. With KBS this can change completely. The standard style of interaction which most people expect from KBS is a question and answer session with the questions being selected dynamically by the system as information is entered. This can leave the user somewhat confused if they are presented with a series of apparently random questions. Support which is sometimes provided includes permitting the user to ask why questions are being asked and how conclusions were reached by the system. Most systems do not provide anything more sophisticated. Approaches have now been defined which allow these dialogues to be more helpful by, for example, displaying the system's goals as they are generated, and allowing the user to see what is happening.

There is also a widespread misconception that all KBS have question and answer user interfaces. This could not be further from the truth. A large number of KBS have been built which are embedded in conventional systems with the user only seeing the conventional aspects. Other systems may be entirely batch and part of a larger run with no user interface at all.

Techniques for modelling users are very few and far between. Most methods do not build models of the user – they simply take the results of the analysis of the domain and then build a user interface based usually on what the designer has done before. One KBS method that has attempted to bring in some user modelling is KADS. However, this only looks at how the user interacts with the system being analysed; it does not look at the transfer of this to a design in any detail. The most frequent way of building a user interface is to prototype it with the user, thus going some way to ensuring that it is suitable.

1.5.6 Generic modelling

Finally in this section, we look at a topic which has probably caused more problems than any of the others for system developers when building the more complex knowledge based systems. When modelling systems for the implementation of conventional Information Systems, the level of abstraction required is generally low. For example, the step from understanding that one of the suppliers for an organisation is a company called F. Bloggs & Sons to the generic concept of Supplier is not large. However, in the modelling of knowledge for relatively complex KBS it is often necessary to take a step back from this generalisation, and, even more difficult, to generalise on the process and the knowledge that is required to solve problems in the selected domain.

An example of the additional level of modelling that is necessary can be taken from the typical KBS task of scheduling. It is relatively easy for people involved in the scheduling of printing to see that it is necessary to know the type of work that is to be carried out, deadlines, the capabilities of printers, and so on. However, when the knowledge modelling starts in detail and the knowledge engineer starts to think in terms of classifying tasks (print jobs) to determine the match between the task class and the set of resources (printers), it is not uncommon for the users to become completely confused and misunderstand the reason behind this level of abstraction. Users and experts can often believe that it is being done deliberately to show how difficult the KBS modelling is and how clever the developers are. At worst it can cause the downfall of the project; at best it may raise a barrier between the users and the developers. It is essential that the users understand what is going on so that they can contribute to the project, and preferably feel that it is their project being run specifically to help them in their work, which is after all the fundamental reason behind the development. In this way the users are much more likely to collaborate and the chances of success are considerably enhanced.

1.6 Summary

This chapter has provided a background for viewing knowledge based systems and methods from a commercial perspective and has introduced some of the important issues surrounding KBS development that have gone into shaping KBS methods.

Section 1.1 looked at the relationship between knowledge based systems and conventional IT. It suggested how KBS can be used to enhance the power of IT by fitting into the organisation and enhancing the functions carried out by conventional systems. The rise of KBS was then considered in Section 1.2, in particular the differences that can now be seen between the so-called first and second generation KBS, the former being easy to develop but limited in their scope, the latter being much more difficult and more expensive to develop but capable of achieving many more tasks. The claimed differences between KBS and conventional systems development were then examined in Section 1.3 and it was seen that in many cases the differences are more a matter of degree. The impact that these differences have on KBS methods will be seen in the chapters that follow. In Section 1.4, the impact of KBS on conventional systems development was surveyed and two ways in which KBS methods could be developed were examined. The first way was to take an existing conventional method and extend it to cover the problems outlined in the previous sections. The second was to build a new method from scratch. The final section, 1.5, looked at the major issues that face KBS developers in the consideration and selection of the methods themselves.

The next chapter takes a more detailed look at the relationship between software engineering and knowledge based systems, in particular at the ways methods are used, the development life cycles, and the evolution of KBS methods. Methods integration is examined and finally a model is presented which permits the integration of KBS and conventional SE approaches.

The central set of chapters – Chapters 3 to 7 – present detailed descriptions of KBS methods. Chapters 3 and 4 look at methods based firmly on current SE practices. Chapters 5 to 7 look at methods which have been developed largely independently of specific SE methods although often using general ideas of software development. Each method description covers a number of common topics. These include the history of the method, why the method was developed, who developed it, and how it fits into the overall picture; management issues are considered, including life cycles, quality, risk and so on; technical issues are described, including knowledge engineering, modelling and knowledge representation; and finally the future development of methods is considered.

2 Software Engineering and KBS

2.1 The rise of Software Engineering

2.1.1 Background

The term *Software Engineering* was coined at the first NATO conference in 1968 to describe the process of the development of software. The need for a rigorous approach similar to that used by engineering was perceived to be necessary. When determining the details of the construction of bridges, skyscrapers and so on, engineers tend to have approaches to design based on sound engineering principles allowing a much more rigorous approach to their design than those building software. If a bridge falls down, it is very public and can lead to significant loss of life. However, it seems to be believed that similar failures of software systems are not as important, even though there are examples where computer systems failure has, it is claimed, led directly to loss of life.

Very early software in the fifties was usually developed in an ad hoc fashion, all the development functions often being carried out by a small number of very technically oriented individuals. These people tended to have a considerable mystic aura surrounding them as this was the age of computers with flashing lights, huge arrays of switches and binary programming. At that time, there was little distinction between analyst and designer, between designer and programmer. The computer expert tended to be someone with programming skills who had to do the other jobs as required; the roles were not usually recognised as separate tasks.

Very early programming consisted of entering a program into the computer by setting switches connected directly to the processor. Programs were very short in today's terms and computers were a long way from commercial exploitation. The advent of assembler started to change the role of the computer. While it still needed very substantial technical expertise, it was gradually becoming less important to understand precisely how the computer worked. However, computers were still largely confined to universities and for military uses. From these early beginnings, languages such as FORTRAN and ALGOL appeared in the mid-1950s. These allowed the programmers to use mathematical expressions to develop programs. In the late 1950s, languages such as COBOL started to appear as well as updated versions of FORTRAN and ALGOL. It is interesting to note that LISP, now one of the foremost AI languages, also appeared at this time. The development of languages in the late 1950s meant that programming was no longer restricted to those individuals who had a deep understanding of the way the computer worked. It was possible for others to make successful attempts at programming to carry out straightforward tasks. At this time there was an increasing appreciation that computers were capable of playing a useful role in businesses and that the skills existed, or could be taught relatively easily, for business systems to be written. During the 1960s it was found necessary to set down more formal approaches to software construction. Early attempts were made in the area of program design through the initial attempts at structured programming approaches. One of the earliest descriptions of a software development life cycle came at the end of the decade with the appearance of the waterfall model. This indicated that software development should consist of a series of stages each following one after the other. This model has persisted for several decades and it is only now, more than twenty-five years later, that its pre-eminence is starting to be questioned.

Methods gradually became more sophisticated and started to spread from programming to the earlier stages in the life cycle, initially to design and then to analysis. During the late 1960s and early 1970s some of the early methods that were developed laid the foundations for current methods. The scope of these early methods was usually restricted to analysis and design with relatively little support for the stages after programming. A major reason for this was the understanding that the sooner mistakes were caught, the cheaper and easier they were to correct.

During most of the early years, the emphasis tended to be placed on the analysis of the processes to be automated. During the 1970s the role of data analysis increased dramatically and there was a considerable emphasis placed on the position of data in computer systems. At the same time, increasingly sophisticated methods of storing and retrieving data were developed and the early databases appeared on the market. The subsequent development and use of relational databases improved the usage of data and some databases now allow the storage of limited semantic information to describe relationships between data.

In the 1980s a more open approach started to appear. The proliferation of methods, each suited to its own particular environment and task, apparently meant that each organisation needed several to cover all eventualities. A more general approach appeared, including Multiview which claimed to be a generic method. The IFIP initiated a series of conferences aimed at methods modelling to identify the underlying concepts. A more detailed view of methods modelling is given later in this chapter.

The behavioural view of systems is relatively recent in commercial IT and is not yet well developed. It has mainly been seen in real-time methods where there is more emphasis on trying to model the timing and relationships of events, a topic of less significance to most conventional business systems. However, this is an aspect which has become increasingly important in KBS and is also found in Object Oriented methods.

Despite the term Software Engineering, the development of software has a long way to go before it can really be called engineering with the sense of a rigorous discipline.

2.1.2 Methods evolution

It has been said that most of the methods currently available in the UK can be traced back to three basic schools – BIS/Modus, Structured Analysis, and Information Engineering. The evolution of methods is shown in Figures 2.1, 2.2 and 2.3 adapted from Holloway (1991).

The root of the first school, BIS/Modus, made its initial appearance in the mid-1960s and was one of the first comprehensive attempts at a system development method (see Figure 2.1). It followed the standard waterfall approach. It led in the 1970s to the development of a method by another consultancy, LDBD from LBMS. This in turn provided the foundation for the CCTA's method SSADM. All three have evolved very considerably since their first appearance. In particular, BIS/Modus was one of the foundations for the Knowledge Based Systems Method (KBM) described further in Chapter 4. Just how far it has come in terms of sophistication and general approach to methods can be seen in that chapter.

The second school, Structured Analysis, is derived from the work of two people, Boehm and Jacopini (see Figure 2.2). They identified three basic structures which should make up all 'well structured' programs. These are sequence, selection and iteration, each confined to one entry and one exit point. Like many powerful and influential ideas, the basic concept is very simple and these structures have found their way into a very large number of different development methods, one of the highest profile methods being Jackson Structured Programming.

Figure 2.1
BIS/Modus methods school.
Source: Adapted from Holloway (1991)

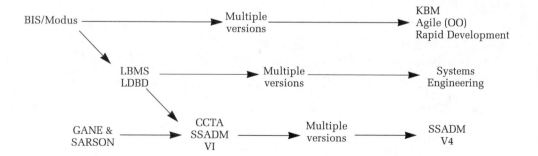

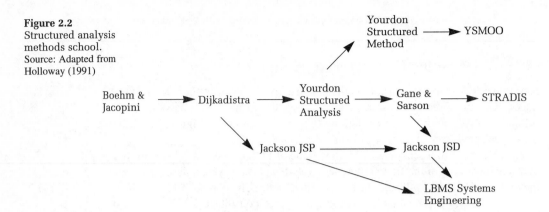

The last school, known as Information Engineering, has various foundations and is shown in Figure 2.3. The first of the two main sources is from CACI who developed a method known as Development of Data Sharing Systems, which tends to be known by the acronym D2S2. This was developed in the UK during the 1970s. The second primary source is from work at IBM by James Martin in the USA. Various company changes and personnel movements occurred during the beginning of the 1980s which eventually saw James Martin set up his own company and start to market a method known as Information Engineering. A number of other organisations also have variations on the original theme, often following the movement of personnel associated with the initial methods work. All of the methods cover the whole life cycle, and many organisations have started to computerise their methods through the use of CASE tools.

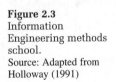

Figure 2.3
Information
Engineering methods
school.
Source: Adapted from
Holloway (1991)

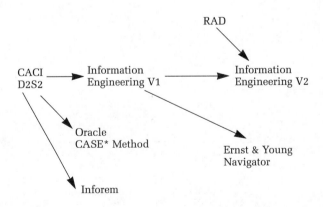

2.1.3 Cookbook methods

For much of the rise of software development methods, there has been a view prevailing that they should provide a 'cookbook' for the creation of software. The way in which methods were often laid out helped to contribute to this belief and indeed, many of the purveyors of methods themselves believed that if only people would follow them precisely, they would produce high quality systems. Some of the more enlightened software developers never believed that this was true and this belief is now gaining support. One of the reasons for this is that the appearance of development methods has apparently not significantly improved the delivery of software on time and to budget. One reason often put forward is that the complexity and size of systems is constantly increasing so a stasis in success rates can be regarded as success since one would expect more to fail the more complex they become. However, there have been some reports that methods have made the situation worse on projects. A number of reasons have been identified for the apparent lack of success of methods and these are examined in more detail below.

Techniques

There is a belief that structured methods not only provide a detailed set of tasks which will invariably generate a correct solution, but that the techniques they espouse are rigorous. Most of the techniques described are little more than drawing aids to assist the analyst sort through and structure large volumes of information. Data normalisation is on sounder ground but requires very significant expertise to carry out well. There is also the question of 'What is correct normalisation?'. Given a single organisation it is likely that different analysts would produce slightly different solutions. In this case can the technique be said to be rigorous?

Attempts have been made to develop formal methods which encode specifications in a provable way and these methods tend to be used more in real-time, process control and military applications. Formal methods tend to be based on a form of logic (predicate calculus) and, although they may be provably correct within themselves and provide a mechanism for generating code automatically, they do not provide a mechanism for going from a vague description of system requirements to a rigorous specification. The specification itself may be provably correct internally, but this does not mean that it reflects the requirements or the functions of the business. However, formal internal correctness is a significant improvement on the more informal approaches typically found in mainstream development methods.

Requirements

The real world is inherently uncertain and uncertainty is more difficult to manage than certainty. Development methods appear to offer rigorous ways of developing software by defining detailed sets of tasks to be executed in a strict order with the products being signed off by the individuals responsible for procuring the system. Unfortunately there are a number of major problems with this user/developer relationship. One difficulty is that the users of the proposed system often do not know what computer support they need.

Many systems have been built simply by automating current practice (and some still are) – even if that practice was inefficient. The inevitable result was even faster inefficient systems. Once this had been realised, analysts started to design systems they believed were more efficient than the manual system they were attempting to replace. However, this was usually done from the point of view of attempting to build a computer solution to a perceived departmental problem rather than developing a business solution to the problem and then attempting to produce a computer system to support the solution.

The process of signing-off a phase can cause immense problems. The documentation produced at the end of, for example, the analysis phase for a large system can run into many volumes. It will often contain detailed charts showing hundreds of processes and thousands of individual data items. The computer department then expect a user to agree that the specification meets their requirements. This assumes that the user has the free time to go through the documentation, has a good understanding of the terminology used by the computer department and is sufficiently thorough to check the entire document rigorously. The likelihood that all three will occur for every phase of every system is very low.

Rate of change

The rate of change of the world is increasing and organisations have to react quickly to those changes if they are to remain profitable. The use of a conventional waterfall life cycle on a large project can easily lead to projects of several years' duration. It is not unlikely that during this period changes will occur both within the business and externally that render all or part of the system invalid or even irrelevant. The monolithic projects generated by the use of waterfall models cannot respond to this type of change very easily – indeed in some cases it may prove necessary to throw away all the work done on the project and start again. This could prove a very expensive approach.

Rapid development methods

One of the changes that is now coming about in response to some of the problems described for a waterfall 'cookbook' mentality is the appearance of rapid development methods. These methods aim to procure software very rapidly by introducing iterative development and putting a strict time limit on each iteration, typically around three months. This may appear an impossible restriction on a project which would take several years using a waterfall method. The difference is that the rapid development method splits the full proposed system into a number of small chunks and implements each in turn. The 80/20 rule then comes into play – 80% of the essential functions can be programmed in 20% of the time. In many systems there are a small number of core functions which are essential to the successful performance of the organisation. These are identified through discussion and negotiation with the users and implemented first. Once developed and implemented it may be that the remaining functions are not as essential as first believed and that their implementation is not justifiable given the cost. Methods such as these are also able to respond to the changing needs of the organisation much more rapidly than the monolithic waterfall methods. This approach also ensures that the user department can see results of the work very quickly rather than having to wait many months for a weighty and possibly incomprehensible specification. The involvement of the user during the execution of a rapid development method is one of the keys to the success of this approach.

Another change is that many people are no longer viewing methods as the cookbook saviour for IT; they are realising that they have to be used intelligently and tailored to the requirements of individual projects. This means moving away from the prescriptive view. However, this view is very comfortable for many project managers because it means that they have a detailed framework with which to initiate and run projects. If this is replaced by a rapid development approach and accompanying guidelines, project management becomes much more demanding, but also more rewarding.

There is also an increased understanding that the purpose of documentation is to communicate. In a cookbook environment it is often regarded as a chore to be done at the end of a phase – whereas in reality the documentation should be generated 'as you go' during the phase and simply organised into a coherent whole at the end of the phase (or at an appropriate checkpoint/delivery time).

2.2 Software development life cycles

Software development life cycles address the issue of determining the order of the stages in a method and the transitions between stages. This is complementary to the method itself which describes the tasks, techniques and documents. Most methods have a life cycle closely associated with them and these days it is usually a waterfall model (or variant) or a Rapid Development (RD) approach. A number of other life cycles, or process models, as they are also known, are making an appearance. The highest profile process model, at least in connection with KBS development, is probably Boehm's spiral model.

Various models are introduced below and a selection of them are then described in greater detail.

2.2.1 Evolution of life cycles

At least five different shapes of life cycles can be identified and these have been called RUDE, waterfall, cascade, V-model and spiral. Most other life cycles are derivations of these.

Figure 2.4
RUDE life cycle

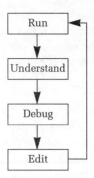

The simplest life cycle is **RUDE** which is an acronym of Run–Understand–Debug–Edit and forms the classic hackers' development method (Figure 2.4). This is also known as a code-and-fix model. It was the first 'method' to be developed and it is still widely used in some programming circles. It is extremely difficult to control and tends to result in systems that are never completed and rarely seem to meet the requirements. It has been adapted by merging it with more conventional life cycles to produce a number of different prototyping or rapid development methods.

Figure 2.5
Waterfall life cycle

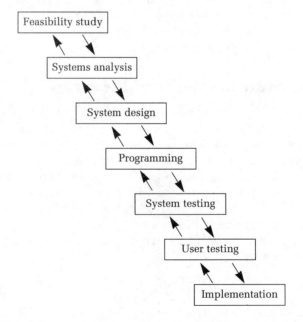

A more formal approach whose roots can be traced back as far as the mid-1950s (Bennington 1956) is the stagewise model which stated that software was developed in a series of stages: operational plan, operational specifications, coding specifications, coding, parameter testing, assembly testing, shakedown and system evaluation. It was over ten years before a refinement of this approach appeared which came to be known as the waterfall model. An example of this is given in Figure 2.5.

This was taken up very widely in IT and it is the model on which the vast majority of system development methods are based. The model has clear start and end points, usually beginning once a potential computer system has been identified and completing when the system has gone live. One of the biggest refinements over the stagewise approach was the recognition that there was interaction between the stages and this model permitted some feedback and iteration between successive stages.

The V-model is a refinement of the waterfall model and is similar in concept (see Figure 2.6). The main difference is that it shows that the development cycle does not have start and end points, but instead it forms a cycle. The waterfall model implies that each system built is stand-alone and that every project has clearly defined start and end points. It was recognised that this was not the case and that the initiation of a system development is part of the continuing process of automation within a business. At the end of a waterfall life cycle, once a

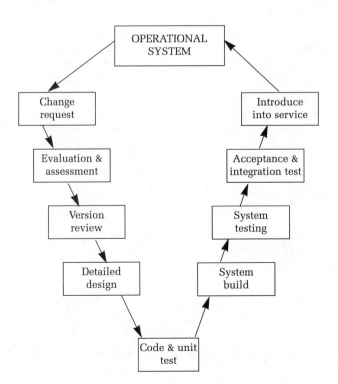

Figure 2.6
V Model life cycle

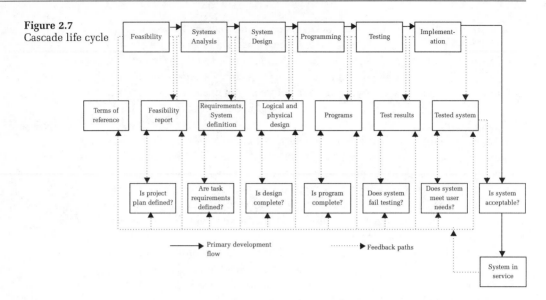

Figure 2.7
Cascade life cycle

system has been implemented, it does not disappear but needs to be maintained and extended and this is shown explicitly by the V-model approach. As this model is very similar to the waterfall model it will not be discussed further in connection with KBS development.

The cascade model is significantly different from both the life cycles just described (Figure 2.7). It consists of a discrete number of stages very similar to the waterfall model but it allows the project to go back to any of the previous stages. This destroys many of the benefits of the waterfall model by potentially reducing the control over the project. However, it reflects the degree of iteration that can exist in projects. This life cycle is not discussed further in this section. However, one of the methods in Chapter 4 (KEMRAS) uses this approach and it is discussed there.

The spiral model is different from all the above models in that it does not show explicitly a series of phases such as analysis, design, programming and so on. It views system development from a much higher level and subsumes other life cycles within it. It describes the life cycle in terms of four characteristic activities which are executed repeatedly in turn (see Figure 2.8):

- Determine objectives, alternatives, constraints
- Evaluate alternatives, identify and resolve risks
- Develop, verify next-level product
- Plan next phases

Each part of the project consists of these four in turn. By not making a series of tasks explicit it has the benefit that the develop quadrant can adopt many different life cycles including those given here.

A selection of the life cycle models introduced above are now discussed in more detail and their impact on KBS development is examined.

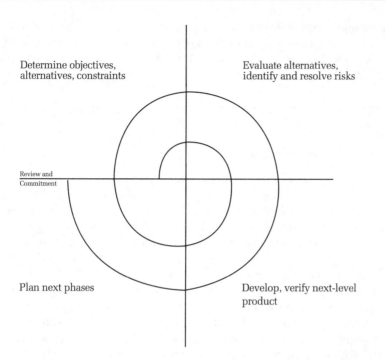

Figure 2.8
Spiral model.
Source: Adapted from
Boehm (1988)

Determine objectives,
alternatives, constraints

Evaluate alternatives,
identify and resolve risks

Review and
Commitment

Plan next phases

Develop, verify next-level
product

2.2.2 *Waterfall model*

The model contains a number of stages – typically feasibility, analysis, design, programming, testing and implementation – each of which has to be completed before the next is started. Some iteration is permitted between phases so that any errors traced back to the previous phase can be corrected. However, the predominant flow is forwards and very little can alter it. The project can become a monolithic giant which can take years to complete because of the need to ensure that each phase defines everything required as precisely as possible. The cost of correcting errors increases dramatically as the project proceeds because the later an error is discovered, the more work has to be carried out to correct it. The long duration of projects causes many other problems – it is not unusual for the business to have changed its requirements, making an application redundant even before it has been completed. Projects also usually generate large volumes of documentation which the user department is supposed to sign-off at strategic points during the project. This often causes problems since, not surprisingly, users are frequently not able to confirm that a 400 page system specification is correct down to the last full stop.

Many of the KBS methods that are based on software engineering methods have inherited a waterfall approach. One of the main problems with the waterfall model when applied to KBS is the requirement that each phase is complete before proceeding to the next. With KBS it is very difficult to build a complete knowledge model without a significant degree of iteration, typically between the analysis, design and programming phases. This is one reason why a prototyping approach has tended be to used in preference to the waterfall life cycle in many KBS developments. Some KBS methods are based on a waterfall approach but these generally provide a greater level of freedom than conventionally, and many either permit or actively encourage the use of prototyping as a technique within the analysis and design phases.

2.2.3 *Spiral model*

Boehm's spiral model (see figure 2.8) first appeared in 1986 and was updated two years later in a further paper (Boehm 1986, 1988). Its main features are the four quadrants delimited by a radial axis that shows the ever-increasing cost of software development through its life cycle. It should, however, be noted that the axis is not to any scale and is certainly not linear. The model shows that software projects pass through a sequence of steps repeatedly throughout the life cycle indicated by the four quadrants.

The first of the quadrants is 'Determine objectives, alternatives, constraints' and projects commence here. In this quadrant, the objectives of the project are identified and elaborated, the alternative ways in which this product can be developed are defined, and the constraints which need to be imposed on the alternatives are considered. The second quadrant is called 'Evaluate alternatives; identify and resolve risks'. During this step, the alternatives identified during the previous quadrant are evaluated and all areas of uncertainty and risk are identified. Ways in which this risk can be minimised and then managed are formulated. Typical risk resolution techniques identified by Boehm include prototyping, simulation, benchmarking and analytic modelling. If the risks are such that the continuation of the project is not justified without further investigation then this quadrant contains the development of a proving prototype. Once the problems causing the risk have been resolved, the project continues to the next quadrant. This is 'Develop, verify next-level product' which follows the more familiar waterfall life cycle which may be modified if appropriate to include an incremental approach. Once this quadrant has been completed, the last quadrant is initiated, which is 'Plan next phases'. During this, the remaining phases for the project are planned. If normal software development procedures are followed this will usually mean that the next phase is planned in detail and the outline plans for the remaining phases are updated in line with the results and experience of the last phase. Once this is complete, the project passes over the 'Review and commitment' line. At this point, all of the products developed during the previous circuit are reviewed, including the plans made in the last quadrant. All parties concerned then commit to continuing the project. This is the sign-off already discussed in the waterfall model context. It is also possible that this review process may result in the project being split into several developments which may be sequential, for example as may occur in an RD approach, or in parallel, for example where multiple teams develop different aspects of the system. If the project is subdivided then each part follows its own spiral model. It is also possible that aspects of the project may be dropped, either temporarily or permanently.

When applied to the standard commercial software development, the spiral is initiated when there is a belief that a particular business requirement may be met through the development of a software system. The first cycle is usually the determination of the feasibility of the potential system and involves the definition of objectives, determination of constraints and potential alternatives; identification and resolution of risks; and planning for the next phase. The Develop phase will normally consist of the authoring of a feasibility report, discussing the costs and benefits of the potential system and approaches for minimising and managing risk. Following this a commitment is made to either continue the project or abandon it. If the project is continued, the next iteration of the spiral will usually encompass the requirements definition, the following iteration the design of the product, and the final iteration the development from physical design through to implementation. If at any time it becomes apparent during the risk analysis that there are major issues which need to be resolved before continuing with the spiral, it is possible to initiate a subspiral to resolve these issues.

The spiral model has a number of benefits over the life cycle models already described. One is that it can subsume many of the life cycle options such as prototyping and the waterfall model. It therefore provides a high level framework for the configuration and use of existing life cycles; it explicitly imposes the very important commercial tasks of risk identification and management and the review/sign-off processes. It also permits the spinning-off of subprojects to carry out specific tasks identified during the main spiral. This provides an explicit method for tackling additional risks, such as those occurring on KBS projects, which cannot really be catered for within a strict definition of a waterfall model.

The spiral model developed by Boehm embodies a number of principles that already existed in many methods but have been made explicit in this model. Notable uses of forms of the spiral model are in KADS and GEMINI, although it has been adapted to some extent in these methods.

One point to note on the claim that the main distinguishing feature of the spiral model is that it creates a risk-driven rather than a specification-driven approach is that many commercial methods are risk-driven in as much as they provide multiple checkpoints which review the cost/benefit of the project throughout its life.

2.2.4 *Rapid development*

Rapid Development Methods (RDMs) are now appearing that allow projects to be split into small pieces, each of which is developed in a period of (usually) less than four months. This overcomes many of the problems of the waterfall model by providing software very rapidly. A key element of RDMs is that they usually demand the use of 4GLs to allow prototyping of on-line transactions in

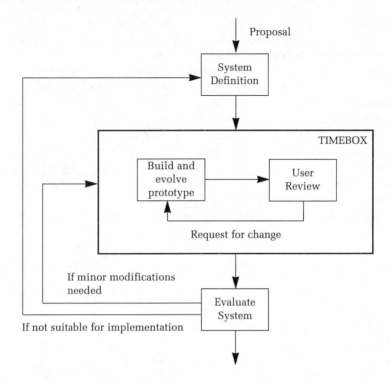

Figure 2.9
Rapid Development
life cycle.

conjunction with the user. The use of prototyping involves the users much more in the development process, thus increasing the likelihood that the system being developed is actually the one the user wants. This type of method also reduces the amount of paperwork the user is expected to read at any one time. The overall life cycle is shown in Figure 2.9.

This approach for system development, both for the analysis and design of the system and in the testing, means that the user is much closer to the system development. It therefore appears to be far more suited to KBS development as it stands than the waterfall approaches.

2.2.5 Prototyping

There is a belief among many KBS developers that prototyping is the only way to develop systems. There are two principal reasons cited for this. The first is that usually there is no clear definition of requirements; the users do not know precisely what they want because they have never had this type of support available before. The second reason given is that the elicitation and documentation of knowledge is extremely difficult to carry out on paper. Therefore the only way to develop a system under these circumstances is to prototype. Unfortunately, prototyping means many different things to many people and so it is impossible to say that prototyping in general is either good or bad Software Engineering. At its simplest, prototyping can be defined as a cyclic development activity producing code following something like the RUDE life cycle. For many in commercial IT management, this means that prototyping is regarded with horror as a totally uncontrolled hacking of code by individuals who do not have the discipline 'to do it properly'. At this extreme, from the software engineering point of view, it really can degenerate into uncontrolled hacking. Under these circumstances it is doubtful whether it can produce anything worthwhile that is commercially acceptable. However, as more control is placed on the activity, it becomes increasingly useful.

One, more controlled, view is that an analogy should be taken from engineering. It then appears that a prototype (for example a model of an aeroplane) is something which represents all or part of the final deliverable (a real aeroplane) that has been built to test some specific aspect of the final deliverable (for example its aerodynamics in a wind tunnel). This analogy is very helpful in defining what a useful prototype does – it is built to test or validate some aspect of the final system. It is not used as an approach to constructing the final deliverable itself. Looking at the development of KBS in general, it is apparent that there are a number of places in which this approach could be very useful, for example in testing whether a particular knowledge representation is sufficiently powerful to represent all of the domain knowledge. Another area is in the design of the user interface. It is very difficult for a potential user to determine whether a system is actually usable simply from screens drafted on paper, particularly now that so many systems are being developed with Graphical User Interfaces. Under these circumstances it is often far quicker and more effective to develop a prototype. A third area where prototypes can be used to great effect is in determining the availability of aspects of the proposed system, for example carrying out timing measurements to see if it will be possible to provide the response time necessary. These three views of prototyping mean that it is not used as a life cycle but as a technique within some other life cycle.

Yet another view is that prototyping should be used as the life cycle for systems development. The nearest that any method recognised by IT departments gets to a prototyping approach is rapid development which has already been outlined.

One of the dangers often quoted of prototyping is that it fixes the physical representation of the knowledge too early. The result of this is that subsequent knowledge may be forced into a representation that is not appropriate. Consequently, any prototyping carried out during the analysis and design of the system should be of the throwaway type so that once it has been used for its very specific purpose, the code is discarded and only the ideas, design, etc., that have been developed are kept. The selection of the wrong representation can force a project to be terminated prematurely and thus not deliver any system. The developer must always be very cautious about fixing the knowledge representation format too early and needs to have the courage (and the backing from higher levels of IT management) to throw away prototypes when necessary.

The use of prototyping as a life cycle has other problems that are concerned with the management and quality of the resulting project. It is very difficult to control unless it is carried out very rigorously, and this tends to mean that it is used either as a technique or as a form of Rapid Development. Prototyping also requires that the usual modes of quality assurance are dropped. This is not necessarily bad, but the existing QA practices need to be replaced by something appropriate otherwise the quality of the final system will suffer.

2.2.6 Beyond systems development

There have been considerable moves during the last ten years to expand the life cycle well beyond the process of development. This is perhaps most apparent at the top end in methods such as Information Engineering. In these approaches, data and information are regarded as corporate resources. Information Systems planning takes place initially at a very high level, attempting to ensure that the maximum use is made of Information Technology throughout the whole organisation.

Attempts have been made to specify methods which describe the phases beyond system implementation. However, these tend to be lumped together under the title of Maintenance. This is often very unpopular in IT departments, even though it is vital, with an estimated 80% of the total cost of a system being spent during this period.

2.3 The rise of KBS methods

The development of early KBS – those produced before 1980 – was almost exclusively confined to academic institutions and consequently the developers did not have the type of pressures on them that are felt by most commercial developers. One consequence of this is that most people did not start to think about KBS methods until the mid- to late 1980s. The history of KBS methods is therefore much shorter than that for conventional methods.

2.3.1 Early attempts

One of the earliest KBS methods to be described is in the book *Building Expert Systems* by Hayes-Roth, Waterman and Lenat (1983). All three of the authors come from an academic background and are acknowledged experts in the fields of Artificial Intelligence and Knowledge Based Systems. In this book they describe a five-stage method (summarised in Table 2.1) which has been widely quoted in the KBS literature. The stages are not clear-cut and claim only to be an approximation to the knowledge acquisition problem.

At a very high level, the mapping of this approach on to conventional software engineering phases is relatively straightforward. However, it should be noted that the Hayes-Roth method is not defined to any significant level of detail and that the resemblance, while relevant, is largely superficial. The mapping can be shown as follows:

Table 2.1 Stages in Haynes-Roth *et al.* life cycle

Phase	Objectives	Knowledge engineering tasks
Identification	Determines problem characteristics	Identification of problem area, scope and resource requirements. Sets goals
Conceptualisation	Finds concepts to represent knowledge	Identification of key concepts and relations, information flows, tasks and sub-tasks strategies, contraints
Formalisation	Designs structures to organise knowledge	Mapping key concepts and relations on to formal representation. Tool selection
Implementation	Formulated rules to embody knowledge	Implementation of a prototype
Testing	Validated rules that embody knowledge	Testing the prototype and revising it to meet the requirements

Source: Adapted from Hayes-Roth *et al.* (1983).

Identification	→	Feasibility
Conceptualisation	→	Analysis
Formalisation	→	Design (logical and physical)
Implementation	→	Programming
Testing	→	Testing

It is expected that a prototype will be built during the third phase (Formalisation) which provides a first-pass solution to the problem. Once this has been tested with the expert, the process then iterates. The system is gradually expanded through the definition of additional capabilities and new domain knowledge. It is recognised that this approach may well result in reassessing the structure of the system, requiring it to be completely rewritten.

Further work on methods for KBS was carried out at Amsterdam University during the early 1980s, work which eventually led to the KADS project (described in detail in Chapter 6). During this early work, four different approaches to the development of KBS were identified:

- Rapid prototyping
- Conventional analysis
- Expert as knowledge engineer
- Analysis from written material

Each of these is described in further detail below.

Rapid prototyping

This approach involves the construction of a system at a very early stage before extensive analysis has been carried out. At that time, prototyping tended to mean relatively little formal control. There was very little appreciation that prototyping could potentially be used as part of a conventional life cycle.

The claims made at that time for this approach include the continuing motivation for experts to contribute to the project as they see a system developing, and that the action of building a prototype helps clarify any initial vagueness in the problem. Both of these are still justifiably used as reasons for prototyping. Some systems developers stated that the most important thing in any KBS development was to build a prototype at the earliest possible opportunity. Others noted that although prototyping could provide a good start to systems development, there was also a considerable reluctance to throw away code in a commercial environment. This meant that any initial prototyping work almost invariably got carried forward into the final system.

Conventional analysis

It was suggested that conventional systems development approaches could be used with additional techniques for knowledge elicitation as necessary. This approach required that all of the knowledge was elicited from the expert before any coding was carried out. Experience of people who used this approach often indicated that a very long time could be spent during the initial knowledge engineering/analysis stages with relatively little progress being made. The major obstacle was that the knowledge engineer could not formalise the knowledge in a meaningful way that would allow it to be fed back to the expert for criticism.

The problems experienced with this approach still exist and the way many methods have got around it is by combining the prototyping and conventional development approaches.

Expert as knowledge engineer

This approach has been proposed by at least two very different parties. One is the KBS developers who have had some successes with providing an expert with a KBS shell, and leaving the expert to write the system. The other, somewhat inevitably, is the tool vendors. Many of the suppliers claimed that their products could be used by non-IT professionals to develop their own systems in much the same way that the vendors of spreadsheets and simple database packages made the same claims. This was found to be a successful approach in a number of cases, usually where the expert was technically minded, interested in KBS for their own sake, had time available, and the problem was fairly small. Once these circumstances were not met, the failure rate rose markedly. It is possible that these failures contributed to the fall in popularity of KBS during the late 1980s as users realised that perhaps developing KBS was not quite as simple as some of the media hype had suggested.

Analysis from written material

This approach attempts to overcome the problem often experienced with KBS development – the lack of availability of the expert. This is a very common problem in commercial developments because the expert is usually in high demand and therefore is less likely to be able to spare time for knowledge engineering. If used assiduously, this approach can be useful as long as there is sufficient relevant material available. This approach is still valid today.

2.3.2 The mid to late 1980s

A number of methods were developed in-house by consultancies and large organisations during the mid to late 1980s and these were almost invariably based on a conventional systems development approach. These are discussed further in Chapters 3 and 4. Most of the commercial methods now available have their roots in this period.

The 1980s also saw substantial work on the KADS project, a multi-partner consortium funded by the European Community to develop techniques for the analysis of knowledge. During its later stages it became more of a methods development project. This is one of the highest profile KBS methods development projects anywhere and it has had a significant impact on many KBS methods. Its academic work on the modelling of knowledge has been absorbed by several methods.

2.3.3 Takeup of KBS methods

The takeup of KBS methods has been relatively slow, even slower than the use of the technology itself. Many companies are more interested in internal development of projects and methods without the use of the organisations that normally develop and sell methods. One consequence of this is that KBS methods have been slower to develop than would perhaps have been the case in a more active market. A second problem with the takeup of KBS methods is that those with the highest profile have tended to be academic and most of the documentation, while public domain, has been very difficult to understand by those in commercial IT development with no significant background in KBS. Another difficulty has been scalability, particularly with the large methods such as KADS. Most organisations want to start developing KBS with relatively small projects, and many methods, conventional as well as KBS, do not lend themselves very easily to small systems developments without significant tailoring.

2.4   Methods modelling

Many apparently different conventional and KBS methods have been developed over the last 20 years. It would seem that it is not possible to develop some 'supermethod' which covers all of the aspects contained in current methods (and preferably cater for those which have yet to be developed) because of the wide variation in objectives of the different methods. One consequence of this is that the 1980s saw a significant rise in the number of attempts to produce models which attempt to provide a framework for all conventional methods. This work can be divided into a number of different categories. These are introduced below and then some of the projects carrying out this work are outlined to give a flavour of the work that has been undertaken.

Methods analysis. This approach is exemplified by the series of CRIS conferences and resulting publications. These are aimed as describing the contents of methods in great detail by developing a generic framework to illustrate the fundamental composition of methods.

High level methods models. A number of high level models have appeared, one of which has already been discussed – Boehm's spiral model. These attempt to model the software development process generically so that the principles can be applied to all methods. Another attempt is the modelling that has been carried out by Glasson.

Methods conversion. This is aimed at showing the formal equivalence of elements of different methods. Many methods have similar components so methods conversion tries to produce an approach to swapping between representations automatically. An example is the AMADEUS project.

Practical methods. A number of attempts have been made to develop a generic method which can be used to combine aspects of different approaches within a single method. One example of this is Multiview. An attempt by ACT to take this a step further into a methods repository is described in Chapter 8.

2.4.1 CRIS conferences

A working group was set up under the auspices of the IFIP who organised a conference in 1982 to discuss a comparative review of information system design methodologies (CRIS1). The aim of the conference was to compare a number of development methods by specifying a standard case. One design was produced according to each method and the results published. The exercise was useful but not as successful at identifying common features as had been hoped. A follow-up conference was held in 1983 which attempted to analyse the features of the methods. This second conference led to a greater appreciation of the differences and similarities between development methods. A third conference was held in 1986 and a fourth two years later. The latter turned to looking at computer-based support tools for systems development. A number of the workers on the CRIS project collaborated to produce a book which attempted to present systems development methods in a way that showed how they interact and how they could be integrated. This book contains a very detailed model of development methods.

2.4.2 Glasson's meta-model

Glasson (1989) describes a meta-model of system development which uses three main concepts – system evolution, system states and development deliverables. He takes the view that information systems are constantly evolving and uses system states to describe that evolutionary process. At any given time the system is in a particular state, for example *Identified problem* or *Specified requirements*. The evolution of a system is described in terms of a series of such states. The model provides a structure which allows sets of states to be organised into a system development sequence appropriate for a given project. The process of getting to a particular state is not described, therefore allowing total flexibility in the techniques used. For example, sets of techniques from many methods would allow a project to reach the state *Data analysis complete* even though there can only be one state where this is true. This makes the model very flexible. System states are comprised of, and defined by, a set of deliverables. Again the precise nature of the format of the document is not described in the meta-model. For example, a data dictionary is a deliverable but it can take many different forms.

The development process itself is defined as changing the system from one state with a given set of deliverables into another state with its set of deliverables. This type of approach thus focuses on the 'what' rather than the 'how'. One set of states and deliverables can be configured into a number of different life cycles depending on the requirements of the project.

2.4.3 *AMADEUS*

This project recognised the need for a multi-method approach although it did not particularly consider KBS/conventional methods (Loucopoulos *et al.* 1987). The AMADEUS project attempted to assist the integration process through the integration of methods at the semantic level (AMADEUS = A Multi-method Approach to DEveloping Unified Specifications). The aim of AMADEUS was to produce 'a unified conceptual model which is rich enough semantically to maintain system specifications derived from any of the leading contemporary development methods'. There can be considered to be two views of system development methods: *process control* which looks at the steps and transformations applied during analysis, and *model representation* which looks at the deliverables of the process. AMADEUS looked specifically at the model representation view and tried to develop a way of modelling the contents of methods such that they can be translated into the common model and then converted back into a different method. It was intended that this approach could be interfaced to tools so that users did not need an awareness of how AMADEUS operated. This approach would therefore support the use of multiple methods/tools on a single project.

AMADEUS is complementary to Glasson's work and Boehm's spiral model, both of which concentrate on the process aspects rather than the representation aspects.

2.5   Perspectives framework

An integrated view of computer systems in general can be developed which describes the different ways methods approach the systems development task. One element of this modelling approach which has been successful is based on describing the way the apparently disparate elements described during systems development are modelled by methods. The perspectives view of methods was developed during the 1980s and has been expanded during the early 1990s to cover KBS.

2.5.1 Perspectives components

For many years people have talked about the process and data approaches to systems development. The process approach was the first to appear formally, and methods which took this view modelled systems by describing (not surprisingly) their processes. Problems were discovered with this approach as more systems were built. It was realised that they often required access to the same data as the earlier systems but that the data were not formated appropriately for the new systems to use. This difficulty was often overcome by duplicating data across systems. A way intended to tackle this problem was the data approach which regarded the analysis of data as the most important aspect of systems development. This fitted well with the rise in use of databases because this software allowed data to be held in a way that made their subsequent reuse possible on new systems. These two views were termed the *process* and *data perspectives*.

In parallel with the rise of the data perspective, methods were produced which were more appropriate for the development of real-time systems. These emphasised the modelling of the ways systems responded to events and the states in which the systems could exist. This was subsequently dubbed the *behaviour perspective*. Some elements of behavioural modelling can also be found in conventional methods, for example in Entity Life Histories.

This view of behaviour needed to be expanded further with the advent of KBS as they do not fit entirely into the perspectives defined so far. In particular, the behaviour perspective also needed to define the expert behaviour of the system by describing how the tasks could be put together to solve problems and the details of the problem solving process itself.

To these three perspectives, a fourth perspective has been added – *knowledge*. This describes the objects that appear in the domain and the ways in which they are connected, in terms of both hierarchies, such as classification and

Figure 2.10
Perspectives model.

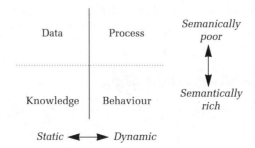

composition, and also the more complex relationships which can be modelled using techniques such as semantic nets.

The full complement of perspectives is therefore data, process, behaviour and knowledge. These can be used to show how different methods view the process of system development. This is illustrated in Figure 2.10.

Although Figure 2.10 shows the perspectives as four distinct entities, this is often not the case. The process and data perspectives can usually be divided quite clearly but the remaining perspectives tend to run into each other, in particular across the horizontal axis: data/knowledge and process/behaviour.

2.5.2 *Perspective relationships*

The model shown in Figure 2.10 can be split along the vertical line dividing the diagram into the static and dynamic aspects. The data and knowledge perspectives represent the more static view of systems which is ideally application independent. This is certainly the ideal to which relational databases aim, thus permitting many different applications to access the same data. It is also an ideal to which some KBS methods aspire but none have reached. There is a view amongst some KBS developers that this can never be achieved since the expression of knowledge always requires some content of how it will be used. If this view is correct it has important implications for KBS developers. It could mean that it is not possible to build a knowledge base which can be accessed by different systems in the way that databases can be used by multiple systems. This therefore implies that each knowledge base has to be built individually with probable overlaps in knowledge and all of the management and control problems that implies.

The static perspectives are used and manipulated by the dynamic perspectives, represented by process and behaviour. These record how the data are manipulated (largely by the process perspective) and the way in which the knowledge is used to solve problems (largely by the behaviour perspective). It is also important to note that the behaviour perspective can manipulate the tasks in the process perspective. It is not unusual to come across KBS where the main element of expertise is in knowing how to put tasks together to achieve a particular goal, each individual task being purely algorithmic. In this case the decision making process (behaviour perspective) sits on top of a collection of conventional tasks represented by the process perspective.

The vertical axis represents the semantic content of the perspectives, in particular the level of semantic content which can be accessed and manipulated by the system itself. Much of conventional data analysis is aimed at removing as much of the semantics from the data relationships as possible whereas in knowledge modelling, the objective is usually to capture the semantics meaningfully so that they can be encoded explicitly. A half-way house between the levels of semantics captured in conventional and KBS analysis currently gaining in popularity is object orientation. This was initially developed for the analysis and design of conventional systems but it captures more of the semantics than conventionally and can be extended relatively easily to support KBS development.

The distinction between knowledge and data is very fuzzy, probably because the distinction is historic rather than a genuine dichotomy. It would not be unreasonable to call the whole of the static side of the diagram 'information' since it generally represents that which is publicly known about a domain and only changes when new information becomes available or current information is shown to be wrong. However, some parts of the dynamic aspects of the model can differ between individuals, most notably the problem solving elements of the behaviour perspective. Different people may have different approaches to solving the same problem using a similar (not necessarily the same) set of information. This is one of the problems often encountered during knowledge elicitation with multiple experts.

The distinction between process and behaviour is a little less fuzzy although it is still debatable as to where exactly the line should be drawn (if it should be drawn at all). Processes are algorithmic and predetermined, task x always occurs before task y. There is no essential dependence on circumstances and events occurring externally to the system. This is generally more than adequate for the definition of conventional computer systems. However, this starts to become unacceptable when real-time systems are concerned. Processes may be triggered at different times depending on events, and different processes may be executed depending on external circumstances. Real-time methods are much more concerned with the behaviour of the world in which they exist. KBS bring in yet another element of behaviour depending not only upon events which have an impact on the problem solving process, but also on factors such as the availability of data and knowledge (therefore dealing with partial knowledge), the level of expertise of the user (and therefore the nature of the user/system interaction), the nature of the problem (and therefore the problem solving process itself), and many other factors.

The major components defined for each of the four perspectives are shown in Table 2.2.

Table 2.2 Major perspective components

Data perspective:	Process perspective:
data entities	task definitions
entity relationships	task decomposition
Knowledge perspective:	Behaviour perspective:
object definitions	event and state definitions
object relationships	strategies and tactics

One of the ways this model can be used is to show how different methods approach the task of systems analysis. For example a conventional method, such as Information Engineering, approaches its task very much from the data perspective, building a complete data model of an organisation. A method oriented towards real-time systems, such as Ward-Mellor, approaches the analysis much more from the behaviour perspective. KBS methods derived from conventional approaches tend to address their task from either the data or process perspective. KADS, however, takes the view that the analysis starts from a set of generic tasks that map on to the bottom of the diagram, therefore approaching the analysis from the behaviour and knowledge perspectives. By understanding how different methods approach the task of modelling systems, the process of methods integration can be made much easier.

2.5.3 Time element

The discussion so far on the perspectives model has concentrated on the elements involved during the analysis of a domain and therefore no mention has been made of classic knowledge representation methods such as rules and frames. The Perspectives model can be extended along the time axis so it shows the evolution of each of the perspective elements through the life of a project. This can best be illustrated through a simple example which takes the data and process perspectives :

1. The relevant part of the world is analysed and a description produced. For example, a form may be documented as an entity (data perspective), a clerk's job as a task (process perspective).
2. The analysis is used as a basis for producing a logical design for a computer system. The entity is translated into a data structure, the task into a function definition.
3. The logical design is translated into a physical design taking account of the physical environment and tools available. The data structure is converted into a database table definition, the function into a program specification.
4. The final transformation is the conversion of the physical design into an executable form. The table definition is used to generate a table in a database; the program specification is turned into code.

All of the elements defined in the perspectives model can be extended through time in this way, thus permitting each part of the analysis to be traced through to its final implemented state.

2.6   Methods comparison

The comparison of methods has been going on ever since there were enough methods to compare. One very major project involved in methods comparison and methods modelling was the series of CRIS conferences that have already been mentioned. These conferences looked at methods in very great detail. Since one of the objectives of this book is to enable the selection of KBS methods, it is appropriate to offer a comparison framework. However, this makes no attempt at the level of detail offered by the CRIS conferences, providing instead a set of pointers indicating the more important issues that need to be considered. As there are relatively few KBS methods currently available, this set will usually provide more than sufficient indicators to help reduce the potential set of methods down to just one or two.

This framework will be used for all of the methods descriptions in the following chapters and finally in Chapter 8 where the methods selection process is put into context. Whilst the tables can provide information to assist in the decision making process, they should not be taken as decision makers in themselves. The selection of a method is not a trivial task and the tables simply indicate the areas where further investigation is needed depending on the results of a detailed requirements analysis by the individual organisation.

The following paragraphs define the major issues of concern in the selection of a KBS method.

2.6.1 Selection criteria

Type of life cycle

Life cycles can be divided into three main groups:

- largely non-iterative, i.e. waterfall, V-model;
- highly iterative, i.e. RUDE, cascade;
- rapid development.

Each of these approaches can be integrated relatively easily into a conventional method which takes the same overall approach. Integration between different life cycle types is very difficult and although it can sometimes be achieved it is not recommended. The type of life cycle required for a KBS method can often raise questions about the life cycle currently being used for conventional systems development. There is a noticeable shift away from the more monolithic approaches and towards Rapid Development, particularly with the growth of Object Oriented methods which are particularly suited to Rapid Development. The take-on of a KBS method could therefore be the point at which the current method and life cycle are evaluated for their fit to business requirements.

The major decisions to be taken are whether the current conventional life cycle meets present and future requirements, and which life cycle should be adopted for KBS development.

Availability

The degree of availability of a method can have a significant impact on the choice. Methods which are freely available, such as KADS and GEMINI, have the advantage that the method, training, and subsequent support can be obtained from a number of different sources. It is, however, possible that the method definition or interpretation, particularly in the case of KADS, could differ slightly from one vendor to another, thus reducing the degree of compatibility. One needs to be aware of this particularly when selecting training courses.

Proprietary methods have the advantage that all the services required for the method can be obtained from a single organisation and so it should prove consistent. A 'one stop shop' approach is also much easier. The organisation is also likely to have significant interest in maintaining the method to a high standard. It does, however, tie all supply into one source which can cause problems if, for whatever reason, a change of supplier is required.

The major decision to be made is whether the advantages of a freely available method with the potential multiplicity of support sources are greater than the ability simply to use one organisation for everything but to be reliant upon it.

Depth of knowledge analysis

Most commercial KBS do not require a very deep level of knowledge analysis and so can be built with KBS methods that only provide an approach and notation to a relatively shallow level. However, if more complex systems are to be built then a greater depth of analysis may be necessary. This is particularly the case where a more generic system is to be built which can be used as a basis for developing a set of knowledge based systems for one particular type of application within the organisation; for example a system to be used for estimating many different types of development projects. A significant problem with some of the methods that provide a path for very deep analysis is that they can be very difficult to scale down to cater for the simpler systems. They are also much more difficult to learn.

These different levels of analysis are rarely all present in a single method and it is usually necessary either to use a set of different methods or to 'mix and match'. The major decision to be made is therefore to what depth will the analysis be generally required.

Scope of method

The scope of the method in terms of the phases it defines tends to be more restricted than for conventional methods. The majority of KBS methods look only at the problems of analysis and design, with some moving further back into feasibility. Very few address the earlier stages such as IT strategy, and even fewer attack the areas of implementation, verification and validation, and maintenance. There are a small number of, usually, proprietary methods, which make some attempt at providing support for the pre-analysis and post-design phases.

The major decision to be made is whether the importance of these phases can be balanced against the much more restricted choice of methods.

Project management

Some methods attack the problems of analysis and design with gusto but leave the project management, quality and so on, more or less untouched. These tend to provide much deeper knowledge modelling and a more complete view of how the knowledge can be elicited. These need to be supplemented with a detailed project management structure to become workable methods. At the opposite extreme are KBS methods which provide a very sound management structure but relatively little in the way of detailed knowledge modelling. While these methods are very useful at a higher level they need to be supplemented with the knowledge modelling aspects to become a complete method.

The major decision to be taken is whether several methods are to be mixed to provide comprehensive support at both the project management and knowledge modelling levels, or whether a compromise method is to be taken which provides support for both aspects but probably neither in great detail.

Links

In a commercial environment with the frequent demand for the development of hybrid systems, KBS methods often cannot be used completely stand-alone but need integrating into conventional methods. Even where hybrid systems are not required, the use of two completely separate development methods within a single IT department is not to be recommended. Some of the methods described in the following chapters make explicit links to other methods, most notably those which are proprietary and form part of a family of methods/standards support for IT. This often encompasses conventional development methods, project management, use of packages, IT strategies and so on.

The major decisions to be taken are how important are these interconnections and will they provide support in linking the chosen method into the current environment? In particular, if a proprietary method is already used, should the KBS method (if offered) be used from the same organisation even if it does not provide all the facilities required?

Perspectives

The coverage of the four perspectives is a very good indicator of a method's technical scope. Conventional methods tend to cover just the data and process perspectives with some impinging on the behaviour perspective. The nature of the systems to be built can be mapped on to the perspectives model and compared with the method proposed. If there is a good match then clearly the method has the appropriate coverage; if not then there may be significant elements which cannot be modelled with the proposed method.

2.6.2 Mix and match?

When considering all of the above aspects it is also necessary to assess whether a 'mix and match' approach should be taken. This will involve obtaining the details of all aspects of the relevant methods and integrating them to provide a single KBS method. This will then cover all of the aspects to a significant depth. While this approach may eventually yield the most comprehensive method, methods integration of this type is an expert task. It is an approach which is hard work, demands significant knowledge of all of the methods being integrated, and has the major danger that if it is carried out with insufficient knowledge and expertise the result will omit one or more important aspects.

Part II KBS methods

3 Conventional methods adapted for KBS

The first two chapters have set the scene for the more detailed discussions of conventional and KBS methods that follow. In this chapter, we start our detailed look at methods for KBS by seeing how conventional methods have been used for the development of KBS. A number of approaches to KBS development which are not formally based on any conventional method but nevertheless take a fairly conventional view of development are also considered. Some of the major issues with using conventional methods for KBS are described and problems and benefits are discussed.

3.1 Use of conventional approaches

Many of the differences between KBS and conventional methods were outlined in the first chapter. This section sets out to describe some of the approaches that have been taken to extend conventional methods to cater for KBS.

3.1.1 Life cycle

The major elements of KBS development which need to be kept in mind when considering the selection and use of a life cycle are:

- KBS are difficult to specify fully in advance of design;
- the final user of the system and the expert providing the knowledge are frequently two very different sets of individuals with different levels of knowledge and expertise;
- users often do not know what they want because they may have never had to tackle the task before;
- the expert may have the expertise in the selected area but may well not understand what it is that the business actually needs to make it more efficient;
- as well as building data and process models, the KBS development needs to analyse knowledge and behaviour in some way.

Given these differences, should a conventional waterfall model be used for KBS or does it need to be changed? Most conventional development methods make use of a waterfall approach with each major phase having to be completed and signed-off before the following phase commences. While this may be considered appropriate for conventional development, although even this is now disputed, it is not often appropriate for KBS development, one of the main reasons being the difficulty of specification.

One approach has been to adapt the waterfall approach so that instead of limiting iterations to within a phase, and at worst between two consecutive phases, iterations are permitted throughout the life cycle. This can give rise to the cascade life cycle that was introduced in Chapter 2.

The management of a life cycle of this type, in particular the estimation of timescales and costs, is very difficult. One of the benefits claimed for the waterfall model is that as iteration is tightly controlled, it is relatively easy to manage and estimate. This is probably true if each stage of the life cycle is carried out with 100% accuracy and there is never any need to go back and correct errors. However, many years of experience have shown that this is very rarely, if ever, the case. Estimation of cost and effort on waterfall-based projects is notoriously inaccurate, with overruns of 100% not exceptional.

Other problems which can, and frequently do, occur with both the waterfall and cascade models for all developments are:

- the rate of change of the business, meaning that systems which take years to deliver will be substantially out of date by the time they are delivered;
- the creeping functionality of systems which tends to occur when users know they will not see a system for a year or more and so continually add functions to the specification.

These problems are starting to be addressed by the rapid development (RD) approach already defined where the time to deliver a system usually falls to around four months. This approach has much in common with the approach proposed and used by KBS developers for many years. However, RD has the added benefit that it has been developed by businesses to meet the needs of the businesses. It is being taken up with increasing frequency as an important way of building systems and in some organisations it is supplanting the waterfall approach. RD is much easier to integrate with the requirements of KBS development.

Other life cycles have been used which bear more than a passing resemblance to the waterfall approach. These can usually be found in papers and books which talk about KBS development but very rarely provide sufficient detail to be worthy of being considered as complete commercial methods.

3.1.2 Knowledge modelling

The second major issue is that of knowledge modelling. Conventional development methods are very good at producing detailed definitions of the data used and the processing carried out on those data. Some methods also include the modelling of events and states but these tend to be at a relatively high level. No conventional method, by definition, contains a model of the knowledge of the domain.

Knowledge modelling can be divided into three parts:

- the elicitation of the knowledge from the experts and/or documentary evidence;
- the analysis of the knowledge gathered;
- the formal recording of that knowledge either on paper or directly in software.

The first is usually dealt with in conventional methods in much the same way as within KBS-based methods, that is by the inclusion of a number of interviewing techniques and approaches to the analysis of documentation. These vary enormously in depth, with some methods simply adding a few sections on how to interview, others recording dozens of specific techniques, with KBS methods tending to be far more detailed in this area. This is one area that is very well documented in the many books on how to elicit knowledge for KBS. It is also important to remember that interviewing is not restricted to the development of KBS. There are many other areas that have developed very powerful interviewing techniques including psychology, personnel management and even sales. All of these are potentially rich sources of information on interviewing. These techniques tell the reader about the actual process of interviewing but will not often provide specific guidance on the type of information and knowledge that needs to be elicited. This tends to be recorded more in the KBS-specific methods which are covered in later chapters.

Many of the conventionally based KBS methods ground their analysis techniques on the use of interview transcripts. In general this does not go much beyond working through the transcript and annotating it to indicate where knowledge is used. Many of these techniques are also used in Object Oriented analysis which is discussed later in this chapter.

The third part of knowledge modelling – the documentation of the knowledge – is much less well defined by conventional-based methods. They tend to take existing documentation methods, such as data flow diagrams, and extend them to take account of the knowledge aspects. This appears to be a very good approach in that it allows systems developers familiar with conventional techniques to adapt very rapidly to the approaches used for KBS. However, it has the drawback that unless a conventional diagram can be found to cover all the needs of the knowledge engineer, it is necessary to develop new documentation techniques. This effectively places the methods developer almost back at square one – having to develop a knowledge modelling approach. KBS-based methods start from the premise that a knowledge model is needed and then develop one, unconstrained by conventional analysis techniques although perhaps taking ideas from standard analysis as appropriate. It has been said that KBS documentation techniques must be based on conventional techniques otherwise the developers from a background will not understand them. This begs the question of how systems developers learned the techniques in the first place. It is also not very complementary about the learning skills of analysts.

3.1.3 Post-implementation issues

Testing is a major area of contention in conventional systems as well as in KBS. It has been said that the former can be fully tested but that the latter cannot so all KBS must be unreliable. This is based on a severe misunderstanding of testing of conventional systems. There are probably no systems in existence that have been fully tested – the combinatorial explosion of potential paths through even a conventional system means that this is not possible. It is only ever possible to test a subset of all paths. The difference between KBS and conventional testing is one of scale – there are usually substantially more potential paths through a KBS of comparable size. This is not an area which has been solved by conventional software development – if it had there would be no bugs in any released systems. The difficulties with KBS testing add to the problems, particularly when some form of uncertainty management is used and the KBS produces answers together with degrees of uncertainty. This issue of testing KBS has been much talked about but few solutions offered. Relatively few conventional methods address testing in any detail and this is reflected in the sparse nature of the testing phase definitions of KBS methods based on conventional development. Very few KBS methods offer any support at all for this vital issue.

Once a system has been tested and accepted by the users, the thorny issue of maintenance arises. With conventional systems this is often carried out by a team of people who are separate from the original developers. In theory, the maintenance is carried out by examining the documentation from the development, identifying what needs to be done to the system, changing the documentation and then changing the code. However, in practice maintenance is usually carried out at code level so the documentation gradually becomes more and more out of step with the system until it is not only useless but dangerous to use. KBS maintenance is also usually carried out at code level and there is frequently even less adequate documentation from the development phase then conventionally. As with testing, very little support is offered for maintenance that is specific for KBS.

3.1.4 Method definitions

The rest of the chapter describes a number of different approaches adapted for KBS. This shows how the problem of adapting conventional methods has been tackled through the use of a number of different techniques. This also acts to set the scene for the following chapter which describes one SE-based method in considerable detail.

3.2   Keller/Yourdon

One of the earliest conventional methods adapted for KBS that is publicly available is that developed by Keller, which is based on the Yourdon structured method (Keller 1987). It was developed during the mid-1980s and at the time of writing, the book describing it was no longer easily available. However, it is worth looking at briefly, partly for its historical context and also so that the approach can be considered in the light of other SE-based methods.

It is not defined in the level of detail of many of the commercially available methods – there are no detailed task lists and product definitions, for example. The basic phases in the life cycle are shown in Table 3.1. The Implementation phase is not described here since the hardware technology has changed considerably. Technology change has also had an impact on earlier phases, which is discussed in the context of the individual phases.

Table 3.1 Keller's KBS life cycle

Survey

Structured analysis
  Current system
    Current physical systems
    Current functional systems
  New system
    New functional systems
    New physical systems

Design
Implementation

3.2.1 Survey

The phase which initiates the method looks at the corporate strategy for KBS and the selection of suitable applications. It is a combination of what some methods regard as high level planning/determining corporate strategy, and a feasibility study. Individuals in the organisation are interviewed and problems identified which are suitable for the application of KBS techniques. There are two main outputs generated by the Survey – a report into the potential deployment of KBS within the organisation, and a more detailed discussion of promising applications.

The first report details the recommended steps for integrating KBS technology into the organisation for both the short and long term. Individual potential applications are also identified and descriptions of these may be developed which include cost/benefit analysis and a definition of how the potential application(s) fit into the current structure of the organisation.

The second report provides a more detailed analysis of those areas showing the greatest promise for KBS development. These are considered in some depth by carrying out a more detailed analysis of the costs of implementing the system and the benefits to be gained. The system is defined by considering its context within the organisation, the data requirements and its functionality. This is in effect a very high level pass at the Structured analysis phase which follows. Initial knowledge engineering is carried out and an attempt made to develop some rules based on the expertise elicited. Initial prototyping may also be undertaken although it is recognised that this is a very early prototype which may well be thrown away during the later stages of the project.

3.2.2 *Structured analysis*

The Structured analysis phase looks at the application selected and outlined by the Survey. The main outputs of this phase are a structured specification of the system and a prototype. Both are regarded as essential. The Structural analysis phase is split into two major components – the definition of the current system, and the definition of the new system.

One of the main techniques of the analysis phase is function decomposition. Another is the generation of a data dictionary and the associated Data Flow Diagrams.

The main steps in defining the current system are:

- To carry out knowledge engineering to define how the expert currently executes the task and to document this. The output document from this stage is the definition of the 'Current physical system'.
- This documentation is then used to produce a logical definition of how the expert carries out the task. This is called the 'Current functional system'.

The main steps in defining the new system are :

- Defining any additional functions to be added to the proposed system that are required because of the business environment. This is still at a logical level – no consideration is given to the way in which the system will be physically implemented. The output is a definition of the 'New functional system'.
- Specifying the physical details of the system including considerations such as the hardware technology that will be used to implement the system. This is documented as the 'New physical system'.

3.2.3 *Design*

The purpose of a conventional design phase is to take the output from the analysis which describes the way tasks are currently carried out and transform these descriptions into a physical design for a computer system. This documentation splits the system into the appropriate modules and defines precisely what algorithms should be used. However, a difficulty is perceived here in that the conventional languages such as COBOL are not seen as appropriate for KBS development and languages such as Prolog and LISP are not as readily available as they need to be for commercial success. This view is significantly coloured by the date of publication of the method (1987). The method outlines a number of different ways in which the problem can be tackled. These are outlined below but it is important to note that since this method first appeared in

1987, the hardware and software technology has moved on significantly and has affected many of the points originally made. This is another indication of the speed at which KBS methods have to move to keep up with developments. The alternatives proposed are as follows:

- Using KBS shells and environments. While these offer much of the required functionality for KBS already built into the software, they can also be very restrictive in the way in which systems are implemented. Caution is therefore required when selecting these tools.
- If the tools available are not appropriate for the whole system, it is suggested that KBS can be designed and implemented using conventional languages. If necessary some KBS components can be built using KBS tools which interface with the conventional languages. The method points out that this approach may not go far. During the first few years of the 1990s, an increasing number of KBS tools have appeared which make this a much more realistic possibility and a significant number of systems have now been implemented in this way.
- The use of specialised hardware such as AI workstations or LISP machines. These have been designed and built specially to cater for the demands of the more sophisticated KBS/AI tools. This is regarded as potentially a very expensive option. The speed of change of hardware technology has changed the situation. While specialised workstations still have advantages to offer, development of PC hardware is rapidly causing a convergence in performance and the cost of workstations is dropping significantly.
- Buying in AI. This approach buys in the necessary expertise, treating it as something separate from IT. It is then integrated with the conventional systems, if necessary, once it has been completed. This approach is not recommended by Keller as the organisation involved will learn nothing about the development of KBS.

The principal recommendation made is to start as soon as possible. The technology is moving rapidly, there are significant benefits to be gained, and if organisations do not get on to the bandwagon soon they may miss it completely. The main approach recommended if significant expertise is not available within the organisation is to buy in the necessary expertise through the use of consultants but ensuring that knowledge transfer takes place.

3.2.4 *Knowledge acquisition*

Knowledge acquisition is viewed simply as a part of analysis rather than as a separate task. The difference is not so much one of its purpose – both model what happens in a business – but one of emphasis. Structured analysis examines the functional components of systems whereas knowledge elicitation examines the logical content of an expert's domain.

3.2.5 Staffing

The method definition describes some of the resource issues which tend to crop up in KBS development. Keller notes that the term 'knowledge engineer' has replaced the more usual term 'systems analyst' despite the fact that they are apparently doing the same job – talking to the people who carry out a task so that it can be automated. The distinction made between the two is one of quantity rather than quality. Both the knowledge engineer and the systems analyst are expected to gather information about tasks that is accurate and reliable. However, the knowledge engineer is expected to gather rather more information. They need to elicit information (or knowledge) on the deeper reasoning that goes into solving problems rather than the higher level descriptions of activities that is adequate for most of systems analysis. It is essential for the success of KBS in commerce that systems analysts can be trained to extend their skill in analysis to the skills required for knowledge engineering. If specialists are required for knowledge engineering then the technology is unlikely to succeed in any substantial way.

3.3 Object Oriented methods

Including Object Orientation in this chapter is something of a fraud since there are no OO methods that also claim to be KBS methods. However, OO has much that the KBS community can learn from, particularly in the area of diagramming notation. This section also includes an introduction to an OO method which has been deliberately extended to include some elements of KBS.

The principal benefits usually claimed by the Object Oriented enthusiasts are reusability and extensibility. Reusability refers to the ability to assemble systems from existing components with relatively little effort. This is currently more of an ideal than a practicality for the majority of business applications. While the development of, for example, Graphical User Interfaces (GUI) is considerably enhanced by the increasing availability of libraries of GUI objects, there are as yet no corresponding libraries of the high level functions which businesses typically require. There are, however, many libraries of the lower level functions that can be used to support the development of business functions. The term extensibility refers to extending the system created with reusable components without the need to change any of those components.

Object Orientation differs from conventional systems development in the way that it views the world. Conventional analysis is concerned primarily with analysing the data that are relevant to the application being built and with describing the set of processes which make use of those data. Object Oriented analysis views the world as a set of objects, each of which is described by a set of attributes and has a set of methods associated with it. Thus a conventional system for the banking industry may have a table in a database called Account Details. A number of different programs will create, update and delete the data. In Object Oriented analysis an object called Account will be created. This will have attributes, just as a database table, such as account number, account name, and balance. However, the Account object will also have procedures (or methods, in OO-speak) which will create and delete accounts, update the balance, calculate and add charges, and so on. Therefore all of the processes that can be carried out on an account are held in one place, with the definition of account. This approach is characterised by two terms – abstraction and inheritance.

3.3.1 Abstraction

The definition of abstraction given in Graham's book is 'Representing the essential features of something without including background or unessential detail' (Graham 1993). This is achieved through the definition of a set of attributes and a set of procedures or methods. A set of attributes for an Account object could be Account No., Account Name, and Balance. Methods which create and delete instances of the object, i.e. open new account and delete existing account, are not usually explicitly defined within the set of methods but always exist. An additional method which carries out operations on the account data itself could be Calculate Charges. An example of a typical notation for an object is given in Figure 3.1.

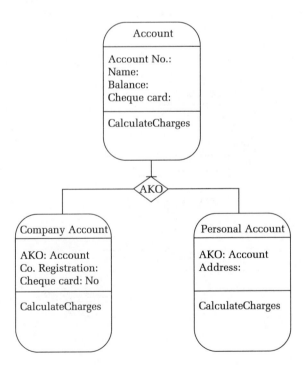

Figure 3.1
Object Oriented classification structure.

This defines the class of Account and it applies to all of the accounts held by the bank. This can then be subdivided, or specialised, into two further objects – Company Account and Personal Account. Each of the classes can be subdivided into a complete hierarchy of classes providing whatever level of detail is required. The diagramming convention for the individual objects is that the top part gives the name of the object, the second section gives a list of the attributes, and the bottom part lists the methods associated with the object. The type of decomposition shown in the diagram is indicated by the letters in the diamond, in this case AKO or A Kind Of, also known as classification hierarchies. The bar at the top of the diamond shows which way the AKO relationship applies and is shown at the end of the diamond corresponding to the higher level of classification. This is so that in large complex diagrams the parent class can always be identified even where the parent is not at the top of the page. In this way the definitions of the objects with which the bank deals are abstracted to different levels. Once the classification of objects has been completed, individual instances may be defined. For example, an instance of the Company Account class may be The Acme Insurance Company. An instance of the Personal Account class may be John Smith.

The second form of abstraction is the creation of composition (A Part Of, or APO) hierarchies. These are represented in exactly the same way but with the annotation in the diamond changed from AKO to APO. These deal with the physical decomposition of objects. An example referring to cars is given in Figure 3.2.

Figure 3.2
Object Oriented composition structure.

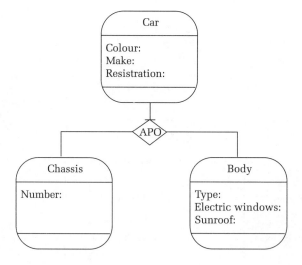

Abstraction is a concept widely used in KBS development and the definitions of AKO and APO structures in OO methods have direct counterparts in most KBS development methods. It is possible to use many of the OO techniques of object identification and the hierarchies unchanged in KBS methods.

3.3.2 Inheritance

The ideas of inheritance have their origins in AI where techniques such as semantic nets and frames represent stereotypical concepts and objects. The example in Figure 3.1 shows that the Account object has a number of attributes. These are inherited by the objects belonging to the Account class – Company Account and Personal Account. Thus these also have the account number and account name attributes even though they are not shown explicitly on the individual objects. Note that by defining an attribute again in an object but by giving it a value, the Company Account object overrides the value of the Cheque Card attribute defined at the higher level.

The individual objects are allowed to inherit the values of the attributes and the methods from the class object. Thus it is necessary to define these once only, in the class object, for all instances to inherit them. This ensures that procedures are defined only once in a system. It is not uncommon to find that procedures are defined several times in a conventionally designed system or that similar procedures are defined in several different places, therefore making the maintenance difficult. For example, in the case of the Add Charges method, this may consist of Add Private Account Charges, and Add Company Account Charges. Conventional systems may well split these over two (or more) programs, for example dealing with private and company accounts respectively. The OO approach encapsulates both within the Account object, thereby making changes to processes that refer to accounts much neater and cleaner.

Usually, inheritance occurs from only one parent in OO methods but it is possible that a class (or instance) may belong to more than one class and inherit different values for the same attribute from several classes. Under these circumstances it is necessary to define procedures to resolve any conflict between different inherited values.

3.3.3 Object Oriented methods and KBS

KBS methods tend to deal with the use and manipulation of things in a way that is very similar to OO techniques. At least half a dozen OO methods are described in detail in books and papers. However, very few of these take the step of moving towards KBS even though the initial steps are very small. While there are no OO methods yet available which can truly also be called KBS methods, at least one definition has moved very substantially towards KBS. This is SOMA which is defined in the book by Graham and is outlined here briefly.

SOMA extends OO notation principally by adding a fourth component to the object definition – rules. Figure 3.3 shows how the simple classification structure from Figure 3.1 can be extended in this way.

Figure 3.3
Object with rules.

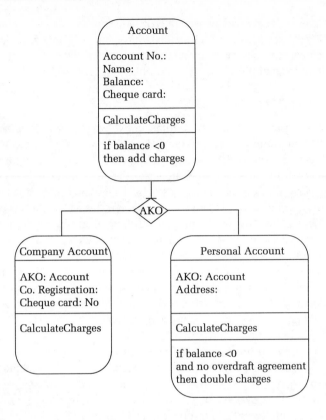

This notation enables all the rules associated with an object to be documented explicitly as part of that object. This ensures that rules are kept with the appropriate objects and helps significantly to structure the rules. They may be inherited down the hierarchy in the same way as attributes and methods. This notation also allows conflict resolution rules for inheritance to be expressed in a high level object where they are generic and at lower levels where they become more specific. Thus this approach to documentation now happily deals with:

- classification hierarchies (a-kind-of or AKO);
- composition hierarchies (a-part-of or APO);
- rules embedded in objects;
- abstraction;
- inheritance, including conflict resolution in multiple inheritance.

While OO does not provide a complete KBS method, it does provide some useful documentation approaches which assist in the integration of KBS and OO methods which is now being carried out increasingly in commercial IT departments.

3.4 Consultancy methods

A number of the major consultancies in the UK have developed KBS methods based on their own conventional development methods and some of these are outlined here. Unfortunately, the consultancies tend to be reluctant to divulge much information on their proprietary methods for commercial reasons. One of the consequences of this is that it restricts the further development of methods since a whole area of experience is not available. In a way this is similar to the situation with many proprietary conventional methods which are also only available from consultancies and methods organisations. Relatively few conventional methods are in the public domain. This contrasts significantly with OO methods, most of which have been well documented in books. However, a number of methods are outlined in this section to give a flavour of what has been done by basing KBS methods on a conventional approach.

3.4.1 Model/1

The Model/1 method was developed by Anderson Consulting and is part of their Foundation set of development methods and support tools. The full range of methods available include their conventional method known as Method/1, an Object Oriented method and a Project management method.

Model/1 is integrated with the family of methods to which it belongs. The early phases of systems development, including identification and feasibility study, are covered by the conventional methods. Little attention is paid to the KBS-specific elements such as the increased difficulty of assessing technical viability and cost/benefit analysis for KBS. The main support is provided by the analysis and design phases. These contain extensions to the notations defined in the conventional method and have been supplemented by KADS for the more complex knowledge aspects not covered by the conventional method extensions.

3.4.2 Summit-Dk

The Summit-Dk method has been developed by Coopers & Lybrand. As with the Model/1 method, it forms part of a family of methods (known as Summit) which include conventional development. It is fully integrated with their conventional method Summit-D and shares many of its tasks. It has additions as appropriate for the more KBS-oriented elements. Summit-Dk advocates a process based more on prototyping than the conventional waterfall model. The use of interactive development is strongly encouraged with the initial stage of a prototype covering the core functions. This is then gradually expanded until the whole system has been developed. This process is managed through the use of a set of milestones and deliverables defined for all stages of the project. It also advocates the use of throw-away prototypes where necessary. The notation used by the method is a mixture of conventional and KBS-specific and has a similarity to KADS in that it provides an initial starting point for some types of tasks based on generic models.

3.4.3 STAGES

STAGES has been developed by Ernst & Young since the mid-1980s. As with the methods already outlined, STAGES has been designed to be an integral part of the conventional software engineering methods produced by Ernst & Young – the Navigator family – and wherever possible it uses extensions of this conventional method.

The life cycle it proposes contains four main phases – investigation, analysis, development and delivery. The first phase, investigation, follows conventional systems development in as much as it defines the scope and objectives of the proposed system. The domain of interest is explored at a relatively high level of detail and an assessment is made of the feasibility of the system. The second phase is analysis which covers the analysis and design of the proposed system. During this phase, STAGES makes extensive use of a number of techniques, some of which are direct extensions of conventional systems development techniques. These include Modified Data Flow Diagrams, Modified Logical Data Structures, and Knowledge Base Maps. The development phase follows and this consists of the physical design of the system and the coding. The phase is completed by testing of the system. This feeds into the final phase – delivery – in which the system is installed and training is provided for the users.

3.5 Summary and Conclusions

Five approaches to using conventional methods for the construction of KBS have been described:

- Keller/Yourdon
- Object Orientation
- Model/1
- Summit-Dk
- STAGES

The Keller/Yourdon method is in the public domain in as much as a book describing the approach has been published. This is a relatively old approach in KBS terms, having been published in 1987, and any work based on this approach must be tempered with that in mind. It does not provide a great depth in knowledge modelling but does give an overall project structure.

The use of Object Oriented methods as a basis for KBS methods is not one which has yet taken off – partly because OO is itself still in its infancy. However, OO shows much greater signs of becoming a major technology in the 1990s than does KBS, probably because it is applicable to all commercial developments. The use of OO techniques in a Rapid Development environment has the potential to speed up development very significantly and is already doing so for some farsighted organisations. OO and KBS, in particular the frames aspects of KBS, have much in common and a significant part of KBS modelling overlaps with OO. As such, OO and KBS methods have great potential for integration, particularly as OO allows different technologies to be mixed easily.

The remaining three methods are proprietary and so very little information is available about them. All have grown out of conventional methods and the use of KADS to supplement them in the deeper knowledge modelling is significant.

Table 3.2 lists the criteria given in Chapter 2 to support the assessment of methods and rates each of the methods described in this chapter against them.

Table 3.2 Conventional methods assessment criteria

Criterion	Keller	OO	Model/1	Summit-DK	STAGES
Type of life cycle	Waterfall	RAD/OO	Waterfall	Waterfall+ prototyping	Waterfall
Availability	Freely available	Freely available	Proprietary	Proprietary	Proprietary
Depth of knowlege analysis	Shallow	Shallow	Shallow+ KADS	Fair	Shallow+ KADS
Scope of method	Survey to Implementation	Analysis to Programming	Mainly Analysis and Design	Mainly Analysis and Design	Investigation to Delivery
Project Management	Fair	Generally poor	Good	Good	Good
Links	None	None explicitly	Project mgt etc. in Method/1 family	Project mgt etc. in Summit family	Project mgt etc. in Navigator family
Perspectives:					
Data	Good	Good	Good	Good	Good
Process	Good	Good	Good	Good	Good
Behaviour	Poor	Fair	Fair	Fair	Fair
Knowledge	Poor	Fair	Fair	Fair	Fair

A number of the methods in the table make use of KADS to provide the deep knowledge analysis; the entries in the table correspond to the proprietary part of the method and therefore exclude the additional elements which are explicitly from another method such as KADS.

4 KBM – The ACT KBS method

This chapter looks in detail at one of the earliest commercial KBS methods to be developed. It examines the contents of the original KBS method which was based on the approach used by the company in the mid-1980s for conventional systems. The reasons why it developed to the KBS form in the way that it did are discussed. The life cycles it uses, in particular the way in which it incorporates prototyping, are looked at and compared with both conventional systems development and other approaches to KBS development. The issue of the way in which knowledge is modelled is then considered. However, this does not look purely at knowledge modelling; the ACT approach integrates both conventional and KBS elements and thus the system model is an integrated view of both aspects of systems development. Its latest stage of evolution is examined including the incorporation of the Perspectives model as a way of modelling both conventional and KBS aspects of systems. Finally, the way in which the method is now presented is discussed – as a methods repository.

4.1 History

KBM had its origins in the early to mid-1980s when work first started within the company to develop KBS commercially. It was during this period that companies started to develop KBS, partly to see what the technology could do, and for the more adventurous to tackle real problems which existed in their organisations. This early development was usually carried out by one or two individuals, often with little or no experience of the accepted processes of developing commercial software, and was frequently *ad hoc*. A number of organisations and research departments in universities had identified the need to impose some form of rigour on the commercial exploitation of KBS and the approach often identified was to use a conventional development method. However, it rapidly became apparent to ACT that this approach was not adequate and work started within the company on the definition of methods specifically for KBS development. The initial work carried out was on identifying the additions that were necessary to the in-house conventional method, Modus, to make it more appropriate for KBS development. Recruitment at that time brought additional skills into the organisation which included both conventional and KBS methods use and development. This led to a significant acceleration in the methods programme.

Throughout the early period of development, the emerging method was used on in-house projects and in an informal way to assist other companies to build KBS. The definition gradually became more detailed and its first detailed exposure to the world occurred in 1988 with a number of methods installation projects and training programmes. The method continued to develop over the following years as a result of in-house research and experience of building systems. This was given a major boost by the initiation, in 1990, of a major research and development project part-funded by the UK government in which BIS, Expert Systems Ltd and Aston University investigated the problems associated with integrating KBS methods with mainstream IT methods. Substantial work was carried out during the early 1990s which resulted in the development of a KBS Methods Repository. This was supported by the use of a number of abstract methods models, one of which was the Perspectives model that has already been introduced. The Repository approach permitted integration of KBS development approaches into a wide variety of conventional methods in a much more rapid, consistent and accurate way than had been possible in the past.

The basic starting material for KBM was derived from Modus. This was an evolution of the original method developed by BIS which was widely taken up in the IT community through its various derivations as outlined in Chapter 2. This method followed a conventional waterfall model life cycle and covered the phases from initial Opportunities Evaluation through the development phases to post-Implementation review and maintenance. It also covered the use of software packages, the development of small systems, various other sets of technical documentation, and a comprehensive approach to project management. The basic method definition for the main part of the development life cycle was found in three volumes -- Documents, Procedures and Techniques – but these were backed up by a set of training courses and considerable supplementary material, making it a very complete definition. Of the basic material, the Documents record the output generated by the system development process and include phase reports and detailed technical documentation. The Procedures describe the tasks which are carried out during the development process and that produce the documents. The Techniques give details of how many of the tasks are carried out, providing additional support to the development process. This documentation forms the core of the method definition.

There has long been a belief within the BIS/ACT methods group that methods were not there simply to be sold and left. Consequently there has always been a substantial support service to tailor methods, not only Modus but the full range of commercially available methods, to clients' individual requirements and to encourage further tailoring of the method as appropriate for each individual project. This continued into KBM which was always tailored to clients' requirements.

This was the background for the development of KBM. The initial sources for KBS elements added to Modus included the expertise of the KBS group, publications on knowledge engineering (which were voluminous in the mid-1980s), and the very early deliverables from a European project which was subsequently to evolve into KADS. The method was gradually added to as the experience of the

KBS team developed and as more information and papers were published about the way in which others had gone about KBS development. However, one characteristic of many of the more commercially oriented articles was they presented a high level life cycle of building KBS but rarely went into any detail. It was even rarer to find descriptions of disastrous developments. Since one of the most effective ways of learning how to carry out a task is to hear of what can go wrong if carried out badly, this avenue was unfortunately closed to methods developers; we all had to make our own mistakes. The details of KBS development had to be gathered from practical experience of building KBS and academic papers which concentrated on very specific areas of development. Unfortunately the papers usually only described the effects of a particular approach on research projects which were not usually constrained by the commercial measures of success. This usually meant that it was necessary to test the ideas cautiously in a safe commercial environment before considering how they could best be incorporated into the method.

Throughout its life, KBM has been used very flexibly. It has never been used as a cookbook for KBS development, at least in part because of the relative newness of the area, but mostly because the developers did not believe in this approach. The individual techniques have been tried out not only on KBS projects but in projects using other technologies. In particular many of the interviewing techniques have been fed directly into work on object orientation. The modelling approaches used, which have built on existing data and process modelling, have been used successfully at a higher level allowing the modelling of the use of expertise through an organisation.

One major change in the use of KBM has been the move away from a waterfall approach (even though it incorporated prototyping), to the use of a Rapid Development approach. The latter is now used almost exclusively on KBS projects. The original waterfall approach is discussed at some length in the next three sections because it provides many of the basic concepts that have been carried forward to an RD approach and to provide the context for the development of the methods repository. The use of Rapid Development is described in Section 4.6.

Although considerable original work has been and remains necessary in an area like KBS methods development, it is also very important to recognise the contribution that has been made by existing software engineering practices. People have been building commercial computer systems to support business for over 30 years; it would be foolish to throw away all of that expertise.

4.2   Main phases

The initial approach of KBM was very similar to that of conventional methods. A set of phases were defined that followed the usual pattern of assessing the feasibility, analysing the business, designing the system, coding, testing and finally rolling the system out to the users for live running. A number of relatively minor changes were made to the Modus life cycle during the early development of the KBM. These involved the introduction of an explicit Link testing phase whose purpose was to test the links between the conventional and KBS components, and a slightly different approach to the validation of the system which consisted of a period where the system was used live but in a very controlled environment followed by a formal Review phase to assess the success of the system before rolling it out to all of the users. The overall life cycle created is shown in Figure 4.1. While this appears to be a conventional waterfall life cycle, there were a number of major differences; the biggest was probably in the introduction of prototyping as a technique to support various of the more difficult aspects of KBS development such as requirements analysis and knowledge engineering. The use of prototyping is pursued in more detail in Section 4.3.

Each of the phases in the life cycle is discussed in more detail in the following sections.

Figure 4.1
KBM waterfall life cycle.

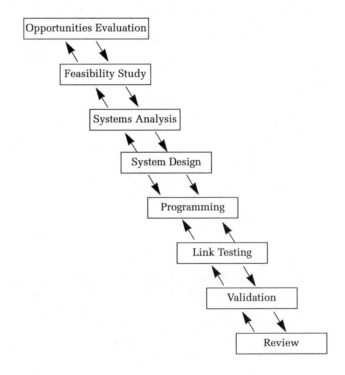

4.2.1 *Opportunities evaluation*

There has been a shift in emphasis in this phase over the last few years because its main focus depends on the current state of activity of KBS in the organisation where the method is being applied. In organisations where the technology is new, the Opportunities Evaluation tends to examine the business in the way that a conventional IT strategy does and identify areas where KBS technology can be usefully employed to solve or ease some of the organisation's existing problems. This can often result in revisiting problems that had been identified in the past but rejected because no solution was deemed possible given the state of technology at that time. There is always a danger that this approach can turn into 'technology looking for a solution' and it has to be managed carefully. It must be reiterated that there is little point in building a KBS simply for the exercise; there should always be a valid cost justification.

Once KBS are well established in the organisation, the Opportunities Evaluation tends to become a very high level feasibility study, the main aim being the rapid examination of the business problem identified to see if any type of computer solution is possible – KBS and conventional solutions are considered as well as any other technology that is deemed appropriate, for example neural nets, multi-media, document image management/processing, EDI, and so on. The days when the only IT solution was a batch system written in COBOL disappeared many years ago. This phase then becomes a natural progression from the IT strategy which is company-wide and sets the approach for IT for the coming years.

4.2.2 Feasibility study

As with conventional systems, the purpose of this phase is to determine whether the proposed project is feasible. This is approached in much the same way as for conventional systems development. This is inevitable as at this stage it is not usually possible to know absolutely whether the business problem can best be solved through the use of conventional technology, KBS or any one of the other IT-related approaches. Both the users and the experts need to be consulted at some length during this phase.

Business feasibility

KBS tend to address problems that are more difficult than those tackled by conventional systems and this difference usually starts to appear during the feasibility study. Typical characteristics are:

- difficulty in defining the benefits exactly because they are intangible or difficult to quantify, for example 'improved customer service';
- the need to ensure that the organisation can accommodate the proposed KBS and that any working practices that will change as a result of the implementation of the system are workable;
- difficulties in estimating development time, and therefore costs.

Technical feasibility

The technical feasibility of potential KBS can also be difficult to assess because of a wide range of factors. These include:

- lack of expertise in the area of KBS development;

- uncertainty about whether the system is possible given the current state of the technology and tools;
- uncertainty over whether the required knowledge can be elicited and coded.

It is not unusual to build a small prototype at this stage to identify the boundaries of the system more clearly and to ensure that the knowledge engineer has understood the problem correctly. This is almost invariably a throw-away prototype.

It is essential that the feasibility of the system is constantly kept under review throughout the project. Both the business feasibility and the technical feasibility may be altered by changes in the business environment and technical advances.

4.2.3 Systems analysis

The analysis stage is concerned with the elicitation of the detailed knowledge from the experts and the development of a model of the expertise. This stage will usually commence with more detailed interviews with the experts than were carried out during the feasibility study. It continues with the analysis of the results aimed at producing a comprehensive system model which includes the conventional aspects of data and process as well as the details of the knowledge that needs to be captured in the system. It is in the knowledge modelling that conventional and KBS systems development are most different. This process is described in more detail in Section 4.5 where the form of the KBS system model is described.

4.2.4 System design

The design of KBS is still something of a black art as there are very few methods which tackle this area as comprehensively as conventional development methods. As KBM is designed to cater for both conventional systems and KBS, it has absorbed many of the good design practices of conventional systems development. The primary requirement is to maintain the separation of domain knowledge from the processing which is carried out upon it, thus maintaining the split that was initially developed during the analysis phase. This ensures that the mapping of the knowledge model on to the design, and subsequently the code, follows as simply as possible. This not only helps the design process but makes the task of maintenance much easier.

4.2.5 Programming

KBM gives relatively little support for the programming phase apart from a discussion of the general principles. The tools and languages for KBS development show a much greater divergence than do conventional languages and it has not proved sensible to develop a set of generic programming methods which can be applied to any KBS/AI development tool. However, the basic principles of programming such as well documented source code, structuring and modularity are as valid for KBS as for conventional languages. Documentation developed to support this phase has focused on the individual languages and tools used to build KBS and provide guidelines on the structuring and coding of programs.

4.2.6 *Link testing*

The testing of a system with both conventional and KBS elements can often be more complex than for conventional systems alone. The reasons for this include:

- The use of both technologies can easily result in a mixture of development languages being used which need interfacing.
- The requirements for the KBS elements may not be as well defined as the conventional elements. This is one area where there needs to be constant feedback between the developers and the users throughout the whole project.
- It may be more difficult to provide comprehensive test data for the KBS elements than for the conventional elements because of problems of combinatorial explosion.
- If the KBS element has to deal with uncertainty this will compound the problems of combinatorial explosion and make the determination of the acceptability of the system even more difficult.
- It may be necessary to accept KBS results on the basis of adequacy rather than on absolute values.

4.2.7 *Validation*

The Validation stage is concerned primarily with ensuring that the system meets the requirements of the users. It is possible that the requirements will have changed during the life of the project and it is essential that the system reflects the needs of the user now rather than at some point in the past. Throughout the programming and testing phases, the bugs in the code should have been found and removed and very few should come to light at this point. During the Validation phase, the users run the system in a live environment to ensure that it meets the required levels of performance and that it is usable in a normal work environment. This validation is normally carried out with a restricted number of users so that progress can be monitored closely for input to the next phase.

4.2.8 *Review*

Once the system has been running live for some time, usually several months, a formal review is carried out. The purpose of this is to check the success of the system against the set of success factors developed during the early stages of the project and to determine what, if any, reworking is required before the system is rolled out to all of the users. Formal maintenance procedures are also set up in preparation for the live running.

4.2.9 *Maintenance*

After the system has been reviewed and has gone live, the long task of maintenance starts. This covers all of the tasks normally expected during maintenance, but for KBS also includes additional elements. Knowledge and expertise tend to change over time and these changes need to be reflected in the

KBS. The structure of KBS – the separation of the domain knowledge and the problem solving knowledge – means that they are often targeted in areas where the domain changes more rapidly than for conventional systems, for example in technical areas where expertise is constantly added to, legal areas where new laws are passed and existing laws are changed. These place additional demands on the maintenance of the system.

4.3 Prototyping

Within KBM, prototyping is used largely as a technique to supplement the process of developing a KBS. Two different stages are identified at which prototyping can be employed. The first use tends to be relatively short and occurs during the early stages of requirements definition. This is described as the Primary Prototype. This helps in the definition of the scope and objectives of the system. The second stage is described by Prototype Refinement which may then be used to support the analysis and design phases.

4.3.1 Primary Prototype

The purpose of the Primary Prototype phase is to set up the conditions required for full prototyping. It covers such topics as the selection of the tool required for the prototyping, defining the outline system in sufficient detail for the initial small prototype, development of the prototype and then, if appropriate, the planning for a full prototype development phase. The scope of the initial prototype depends on the purpose for which prototyping is to be carried out. Typical reasons include:

- User interface development. In this case the Primary Prototype simply covers the development of an initial set of screens to the point where they can be reviewed with the user.
- Feasibility assessment. The Primary Prototype consists of a first pass at the problem with no particular attempt at solving anything significant. However, it should demonstrate that the principal requirements are achievable.

Under no circumstances does the Primary Prototype phase take more than 10 days' elapsed time, a time period which is now possible given the very sophisticated tools which are available.

Once completed, the principal output from this stage is the prototype itself. It may be appropriate to document some aspects of the prototype, for example the solution to technical problems, but there is little point in documenting for the sake of documentation. A prototype provides a far better and more accurate demonstration of the appearance of a user interface than a set of hand-drawn screen layouts could ever do. If it is necessary to document the layout of screens, then screen images captured and described in a word-processed document are a simple, rapid and efficient means of doing this.

4.3.2 *Prototype Refinement*

Prototype Refinement is an iterative phase which builds on the Primary Prototype. It starts with a review of its scope, continues with the required analysis and knowledge engineering, logical and physical design, prototype construction and validation. This is not a rapid development approach since it is entirely subsumed by the Analysis phase and never takes more than four elapsed weeks for each iteration. It is unlikely that any detailed intermediate documentation will be produced. As with the Primary Prototype phase, the main output of each iteration is the software, though there are some aspects which need separate documentation. These include records of:

- the objectives of the prototype iteration;
- expert interviews, usually in the form of interview tapes or preferably transcripts;
- user interviews, again in transcript form;
- the user comments on the prototype;
- the major technical decisions taken during the design and coding;
- 'work-arounds' necessary to make the chosen tool carry out the required functions.

This provides a documentary trail of the work carried out so that it can be referred to at later stages during the project and also act as guides/reminders to the developers of solutions that have been tried during the prototypes. The latter can be very valuable in ensuring that problems are not solved more than once as can often be the case, particularly when getting to grips with a sophisticated development tool.

Prototyping is permitted extensively within KBM under very controlled circumstances but it is used largely as a technique rather than a life cycle in its own right. It can be attached to both the waterfall and Rapid Development life cycles. It is a very efficient method of validating user interfaces, determining feasibility of technical aspects, eliciting and validating expert knowledge.

Initial broad and shallow

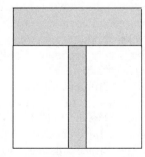
Narrow and deep refinement

Figure 4.2
Divide and conquer.

4.4 Divide and conquer

The particular version of the divide and conquer concept described here is very important for both the waterfall and rapid development life cycle used with KBS. It has two main stages (see Figure 4.2).

Initially the top of the domain is skimmed at a relatively high level producing a 'broad and shallow' view of the potential system. This assists in the scoping of the domain. It is often supported by the use of prototyping, in particular by the development of a prototype user interface which can be validated by the users, thus ensuring that they can feed back impressions on the scope of the system at a very early stage. This usually occurs either during a Feasibility Study or very early in the Analysis and corresponds to the Primary Prototype phase already discussed. In a Rapid Development approach it corresponds to the initial Requirements Analysis.

Once the scope of the system has been validated, one area is selected for investigation in detail. This is then driven down to the level of detail that is required to build a functional system thus providing a 'narrow and deep' protoype. The area selected will usually be one of sufficient complexity to demonstrate that the system is feasible and also one that is of use to the business. In this way the feasibility is demonstrated and the business gets a prototype which can be used in a sensible way to support a subset of the original functions. The functionality of the system is then expanded, either by developing outwards from the core system, or by driving down different aspects of the system identified during the scoping exercise. This aspect of systems development may correspond to successive timeboxes if a Rapid Development approach is being used, or to a series of prototypes developed during the analysis and design phases of a more conventional waterfall approach.

Project standards are defined during the first detailed work and carried forward to subsequent work to ensure that the whole system is built uniformly.

4.5 Waterfall approach

The major phases in KBM have been described in Sections 4.2 and 4.3. This section looks at how the individual phases are put together to define a waterfall life cycle for a project. It is important to note that KBM explicitly recognises the difference between the life cycle model (LCM) and the method itself. The LCM describes the general approach to the project; the method itself describes the individual tasks, products and techniques which make up the method. This differentiation is very important as will be seen when the methods repository is examined in Chapter 8.

The principal difference between the KBS waterfall model and more conventional methods is that it allows prototyping as a technique to be used at a number of points. The location of prototyping depends on its function.

Prototyping is defined through two phases – Primary Prototype and Prototype Refinement. The former is the initiation stage and its depth depends on the size of the prototype. One of its main functions is the selection of an appropriate prototyping tool. If prototyping is purely to develop the user interface then almost any tool which allows screen painting in the appropriate environment can be used. However, if the prototyping is to go further and model the domain knowledge then the prototype selection needs further consideration. The use of these two phases is described in further detail below and a number of different circumstances in which they may be used are given.

Prototyping may take place during the Feasibility Study to assist in determining the feasibility of the proposed system. There may also be doubt about the performance of the system on the required hardware/software platform and the construction of a small prototype is required to explore response times. An example of this is the use of scheduling and configuration systems on PCs where the response time is important. A prototype will help give an indication of the order of magnitude of the response time. Although this can be very useful it is important that both the developers and potential users realise that this is only a prototype and that the response is only an approximation. This type of prototyping requires careful tool selection since this will affect the timings considerably. If possible, the tool that will be used to implement the final system should be used. This may not be a problem in organisations which have a limited set of software for system development but is likely to present more of a problem where there are no restrictions.

The administrative aspects of the two prototyping phases, primarily planning and review, are likely to be reduced to the smallest possible so that the majority of the time can be spent attempting to solve the technical problems which are being addressed. However, it is important to document the results carefully and the route by which they were achieved.

Another use of prototyping at an early stage is to define the boundaries of the required system. The boundaries can have a very significant impact on the cost/benefit justification of a system. A simple prototype that is a mock-up of the functions to be implemented will indicate the functional boundaries of the proposed system. However, it will not indicate the boundaries of the knowledge that is required to carry out those functions. That can only be determined reliably during detailed knowledge engineering.

The use of prototyping is more common during the analysis stage (Figure 4.3). When used at this point, the Primary Prototype phase usually spends more time on the tool selection as there is a greater possibility that it will eventually become the software in which the final system is developed. Once an appropriate tool has been selected, the bulk of the prototyping is carried out by iteration within the Prototype Refinement phase. One of the most common uses of prototyping during the analysis phase is to model the knowledge that is being gained from the expert interviews. This allows its completeness and consistency to be verified and also permits the results to be shown to the expert in a dynamic form. This allows the expert to criticise the knowledge model much more easily than if it were only on paper. However, this must be carried out very carefully as it is possible for the developers to become trapped into the use of a particular tool. Where prototyping is used for knowledge elicitation and validation, it is very important that the

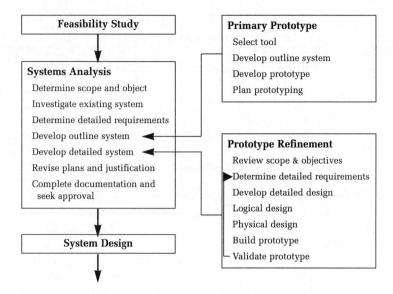

Figure 4.3
Prototyping during analysis.

knowledge is reengineered and documented in a form that is independent of the tool. This will allow the system to be designed as a whole once the knowledge has been elicited so that the knowledge representation is uniform and consistent. Recoding is often necessary in environments where performance is an important issue; software that provides good prototyping facilities can sometimes perform very poorly in production. A significant number of KBS developed using sophisticated tools have been recoded subsequently in a very efficient language such as C. Even if the system is not recoded in a different language, it can eventually prove necessary to recode it because repeated changes to the knowledge have caused the original structure to have been largely destroyed. Subsequent development and maintenance is often only practical if the system is reengineered.

A third way in which prototyping can be used is to develop the KBS aspects of a hybrid system while the conventional aspects are developed using conventional sequential analysis, design and programming phases (see Figure 4.4).

This can often be a very efficient way of developing a system which requires the use of substantial elements of both conventional and KBS technology. This life cycle is now approaching a hybrid of waterfall and Rapid Development approaches. The conventional analysis is carried out as usual and the initial knowledge modelling is executed at a relatively high level, possibly supported by initial prototypes. The analysis phase defines all of the interfaces between the conventional and KBS elements that are required, thus providing a firm foundation for the system development. The planning activities at the end of the analysis phase determine the prototyping requirements for the knowledge engineering which is to be carried out in parallel to the rest of the design. The Prototype Refinement phase is then carried out iteratively in parallel with the System Design and Programming phases. At intervals during the Programming phase, link testing is performed to ensure that the two streams are still working to the original plans

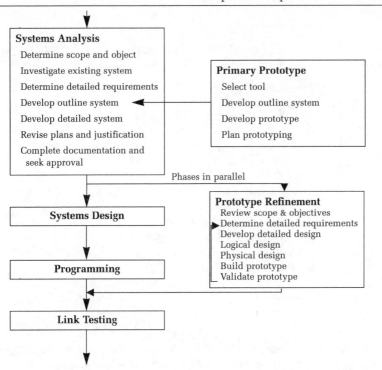

Figure 4.4
Evolutionary prototyping

and that the planned linkages can be achieved. If there is any doubt about the linkages then the feasibility of this should be established during the early stages of the project, possibly as a Feasibility Study prototype. At the end of programming, the two parallel streams combine and enter a Link Testing phase whose purpose is to validate the links between the conventional and KBS elements.

4.6 Rapid Development

Rapid Development (see Figure 4.5) provides an alternative life cycle to the waterfall approach and is particularly appropriate for KBS where the development risks are often higher than with conventional systems and where requirements are often less well defined.

The initial phases are very similar to a Feasibility Study and high level Systems Analysis for conventional development. The purpose of the Feasibility study is as conventionally – to determine that the cost/benefits justify the risks of developing the system. This is followed by a Requirements Definition stage which carries out high level interviewing of users and experts to determine the requirements of the system and to build a high level knowledge model. At this point Rapid Development starts to diverge from the waterfall life cycle. A number of 'timeboxes' are identified. These are mini-projects, each of a duration of no more than 3–4 months elapsed time (not person-months). Each provides a well defined set of related functions that have been identified during

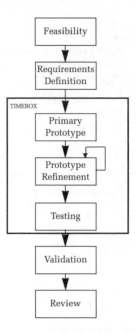

Figure 4.5
KBM Rapid
Development.

Requirements Definition. The timeboxes are then ordered according to the benefits that each will provide for the business, the first giving the main core of benefits with subsequent timeboxes providing additional functionality. The reasoning behind this is that often 80% of the users' problems are answered by 20% of the system; the timebox approach helps to ensure that the important 20% is identified and is the first to be built and rolled out to the users. With KBS it has sometimes been found that this provides sufficient benefit for the project to be terminated at that point. When ordering the timeboxes there can be circumstances where it would prove beneficial to deviate from a totally requirements driven ordering because of technical constraints and feasibility issues. This can be because the development of the system requires deep knowledge to be modelled in some of the later timeboxes which may not be required for the early functions. Under these conditions it may be better to tackle the more difficult timeboxes initially to lay the groundwork for subsequent iterations. This overcomes the potential problem that if the simplest timeboxes are developed first these may result in structures incompatible with the more complex structures which may prove necessary during later stages. If this occurs it can cause significant rewriting of the early timeboxes. Once the requirements have been identified and the timeboxes ordered, detailed planning of the scope, contents and schedules for the timeboxes is carried out. Each timebox development is a mini-project in itself covering analysis, design, coding, testing and implementation. Once each timebox has been implemented it is reviewed as for any system implementation.

The RD approach to KBS development is increasing in use and most developments now follow this approach.

4.7 Initial system modelling

A problem that has been identified on a number of occasions is that of making the conventional systems analysis and KBS analysis compatible. The approach taken by KBM is not to take two different views of systems development – a conventional view and a KBS view – but to regard KBS as simply an extension of IT in much the same way as relational databases have been regarded over the last ten years. In this way a single coherent view of systems development can be obtained.

The early work on the development of KBM gave rise to a three-part model, known rather uninspiringly as the Knowledge Model. This was a rather unfortunate name as the model covered the conventional data and process aspects as well as the KBS elements. A diagram of the model is given in Figure 4.6. It consists of three main elements – the Task model, the Strategy model and the Conceptual model.

4.7.1 Task model

The Task model is a process and data picture of the domain as it is built up during conventional systems analysis. It presents a view of the tasks carried out in order to solve the problem, and the data required by the processes. The Task model

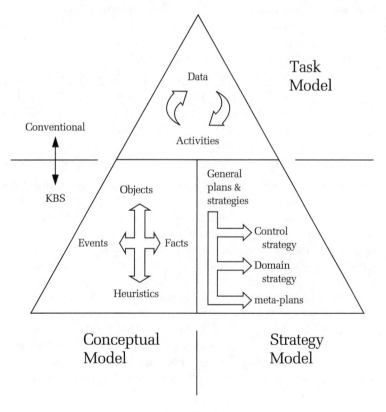

Figure 4.6
KBM knowledge model.

therefore describes *all* the tasks carried out whether they require conventional algorithmic support and file accessing or a KBS approach. The Task model is common to both the conventional and KBS aspects of a system. The main categories of information held in this model are described below.

Data

Data analysis proceeds as for a conventional system. The input to and output from the domain are established and any additional data required within the processes are gathered. The more esoteric information requirements which are KBS-oriented rather than conventionally oriented are not captured yet although markers are laid down for future reference. The data that have been captured are documented. If a primarily conventional analysis approach is being followed, the data are normalised and a standard data model is developed, typically using diagramming techniques such as Entity-Relationship models.

Activities

Top-down analysis of the activities is carried out with the aim of splitting the problem down into a hierarchy of discrete activities. An activity can be defined as a task that is carried out with a specific objective in mind and is usually triggered by the presence of a particular piece of information. For example, part of an insurance application system could involve the following activities (not necessarily carried out in the order presented):

Task 1: determine whether the medical condition of someone applying for insurance allows acceptance and whether it requires endorsements on the policy;

Task 2: calculate the premium of the policy depending on the endorsements identified and send a letter with the details;

Task 3: send a letter explaining why the application has been refused.

As analysis on these activities proceeds, the first activity might result in a series of heuristics which would be implemented as a KBS activity, while the second and third activities might emerge as conventional activities.

A potential problem when trying to identify activities is becoming too involved with identifying the sequence in which tasks are carried out. In the example given, task 1 clearly identifies that either task 2 or task 3 is carried out, but not both. This is not relevant for the description of the individual processes. In this case the relationship is noted as part of the strategy model and is dealt with there. The aim of the task model is simply to describe each activity independently.

All the activities the expert carries out are identified and described at a functional level – that is they describe the steps required and not any algorithms, reasoning or additional knowledge that is required. The activities are also cross-referenced to the data that are required as would be done for a conventional IT system.

Documentation and techniques

Documentation methods used in the task model typically consist of techniques such as:

- activity diagrams/data flow diagrams;
- functional decomposition diagrams;
- normalised data models;
- data cross-reference sheets;
- entity relationship diagrams.

Since the true nature of a system is not known until some analysis has been carried out, it is very important that standard IT documentation is employed. In this way, the initial analysis can proceed without any emphasis being placed on the nature of the technology that will eventually be used to solve the problem. Consequently, all the benefits of following a standard methodology can be gained during the early stages, ensuring that the Task model processes and data are complete and consistent. This also ensures that the most appropriate technology can be used for each part of the system.

Object oriented analysis has been suggested as a complete method for systems analysis and it can be used as an alternative to more conventional techniques for analysing and documenting the task model. This can be advantageous as object oriented analysis can be extended and used very successfully for the Conceptual model.

4.7.2 Conceptual model

This model contains background knowledge and data about the domain and the knowledge that is necessary in order to operate in the domain. It is declarative in form and primarily describes facts, objects, and events, and defines their relationships. It effectively describes the behaviour of the domain (*not* the expert) and will usually include domain knowledge heuristics which the expert uses in order to manipulate the domain information.

Objects

In the Conceptual model, object analysis is carried out in considerable detail. Note that although there are similarities to OO techniques, it was not originally planned as an OO approach. However, this has been successfully modified to use standard OO techniques for more recent projects.

The object analysis will usually be based on the data analysis initiated during the construction of the high level task model. A good starting point for object analysis can be the generation of a glossary of domain specific terms. By employing rigorous object analysis techniques that make use of pre-defined object forms, a considerable amount of relevant information can be obtained which would not necessarily be captured for a conventional system but is very important for a complete definition of a knowledge based system. Formal techniques such as Kelly grids and card sorts can be performed on the objects to help identify underlying relationships and to identify and complete object attributes.

Much of the information gathered at this stage and documented as part of the objects can also be used to construct detailed explanatory help text concerned with the domain (as opposed to the problem solving techniques being employed by the system). This is particularly important if the system is to be used for training.

Events

Events are described in a similar way to objects. The circumstances that are necessary to make it possible for events to occur, and the triggers that make them actually occur, and the events or changes that are caused when they do occur are all described. Time relationships between events are also described.

Diagramming techniques such as Petri Nets, State Transition Diagrams and Entity Life Histories can be used to model the behaviour of systems.

Relationships

This describes compound relationships relating all the above information:

- between object and object;
- between event and event;
- relationships between events and objects, the changes in objects that cause events and vice versa (i.e. causal relationships).

Object analysis will identify the basic relationships between objects such as APO (A Part Of, or composition) and AKO (A Kind Of, or classification) relationships. The conceptual model also describes the more complex relationships. For example, the medical diagnosis system PIP uses frames (i.e. objects) to represent each illness, and each frame holds heuristic relationship knowledge such as *caused-by*, *complicated-by* and *associated-with*. These types of relationships between objects can be shown using diagramming techniques such as classification and composition hierarchies, semantic nets and causal nets.

The inclusion of this type of information in the Conceptual model ties together the elements described so far and produces a coherent model of the domain. Indeed the term 'Intelligent model-based system' has been coined for systems which are based on models in preference to the more commonly used knowledge based system. Detailed domain models often permit the system to reason from first principles. The benefits of this approach can include more comprehensive explanations – since a model-based system will contain more deep knowledge – and the ability of the system to cope with new problems more efficiently. They also become much less sensitive to problems at the boundaries of the domain since they have the capability and the knowledge to reason from first principles.

The Conceptual model also describes feedback where it is part of the domain, for example when one object in a domain changes, it causes others to change, which in turn causes the initial object to change again. A simple example of this is a thermostat which turns on a heater when the temperature exceeds a threshold. This causes the temperature to rise thus causing the thermostat to switch off the heater.

The use of feedback to control problem solving is recorded as part of the strategy model.

Documentation and techniques

Techniques and documentation methods that can be used profitably for the acquisition and analysis of the Conceptual model include:

- object analysis;
- classification and composition hierarchies;
- semantic nets;
- state transition diagrams;
- Petri nets;
- causal nets.

4.7.3 Strategy model

This model shows how the expert uses the tasks described in the Task model to solve a problem. It brings together the relationship information described in the Conceptual model and relates it to the tasks.

Control strategy

This describes the high level problem solving strategy that is employed by the expert under normal circumstances. It also shows how this overall strategy is altered for more unusual problems where the normal strategy is inadequate. It therefore also contains exception procedures and heuristics relating strategies to circumstances. This is all at a high level and the control techniques are the general techniques that may be applied to any KBS. Taking the insurance application described in the Task model section the strategy would become:

> Carry out Task 1
> if this succeeds
>   carry out Task 2
> else
>   carry out Task 3

Where this becomes larger one approach is to represent it graphically by using a decision tree. An example of a more complex strategy that is also more generic is one used in many diagnostic systems:

1. Gather initial information about the problem.
2. Form a series of hypotheses.
3. Investigate each hypothesis asking low cost questions first.
4. Review hypotheses in light of answers given to questions.

Methods such as this can sometimes be documented through the use of conventional flow charts or structure diagrams. If the strategy involves multiple iterations and feedback then state transition diagrams can be used. It may then be possible to map the strategy identified on to a very simple physical strategy such as 'forward chain to generate a set of hypotheses then backward chain on each in turn'; however, it may require more complex planning techniques requiring further detailed analysis. Where multiple strategies are employed by the expert, these can be described individually and then related to the appropriate domain knowledge and recorded by using documentation techniques such as decision trees or structured English.

Novices in a domain generally do not have an appreciation of the appropriate problem solving strategies that an expert has. This results in the familiar cry of 'I'm stuck, what should I do next?'. The novice understands something of the domain (the Conceptual model) and the tasks (the Task model) that can be performed but does not have the practical experience which has led the expert to formulate a series of problem solving strategies (the Strategy model). Much of the information in the Task and Conceptual models can be found from paper-based documentation, but strategy information often cannot. Experts often succeed where others fail because they know of different ways of approaching the problem and what to do when encountering difficulties. They will also have a deeper understanding of the domain and have developed Conceptual model heuristics which may cause a response from the novice of 'I didn't realise these things were related in that way'. Relationships such as these should emerge as a result of the analysis of the Conceptual model.

Domain strategy

The domain strategy describes in detail each of the bottom level tasks outlined by the Task model and gives the strategies that are pursued within each task. The Conceptual knowledge is related to the domain strategy by identifying the objects used in the strategy and the role each plays. For example, in a medical system spots can be regarded both as a symptom indicating an illness (such as measles) and as a medical condition itself (for example acne). The individual tasks whose strategies are described are highly dependent on the knowledge in the domain and thus contain detailed domain specific heuristics, plans, meta-plans and meta-knowledge.

Areas where conflicts may occur are identified and described and conflict resolution strategies are defined. When domain knowledge is described (within the Conceptual model) it will often have hierarchies of objects in which inheritance can occur. Conflict can occur if an object inherits different values for the same item. In this case the domain strategy describes how this is resolved for the particular problem in hand. It is important to note that this conflict resolution will depend on the way the knowledge is being used and so can alter depending on the current problem.

The domain strategy expands on general strategies such as 'explore least cost alternatives first' by making the order of tasks explicit. For example, in an electronic troubleshooting system, cost-related heuristics could start with 'check that the fuse has not blown' and gradually increase in cost up to a point where extensive testing and component replacement is carried out. This strategy would give an overall approach to the testing but would be modifiable in the light of test results – some testing tasks would become irrelevant as results from other tasks become available.

Once the problem solving strategies have been described it may be necessary to tailor them so that the system can be used by operators with different levels of experience. A very detailed step-by-step strategy may be required when the system is consulted by a relative novice so that it will lead the user through the problem solving process. On the other hand, such a strategy would rapidly become tedious for an expert in the domain who simply wished to use the system as a decision support tool. The identification and description of such strategies at this stage mean that the system can be coded with these alternative uses well defined beforehand.

Explanations

The flow through the system is controlled by the Strategy model and so this model must control the display of explanations of the problem solving. Explanations for most rule-based systems tend to be simply displays of the trace of the rules executed. If the user does not understand the strategy being used by the system then such displays can be very confusing. By making use of the concepts of topics and landmarks the quality of explanations can be considerably improved (Southwick 1988).

The concept of a topic is very similar to that of an activity as defined in the Task model. A topic can be defined as a logical and conceptual entity in the knowledge base. The landmark for a topic (or activity) is the topmost node of that part of the hierarchy. The landmark identifies an intuitional point in the knowledge base. Conventional rule-based systems often ask a long series of questions which may at times seem unrelated and rambling. However, displaying landmarks when they are encountered helps to show the way the system is solving the problem and can help make the dialogue seem more focused. Taking the insurance example given in the Task model description, the point where it becomes necessary to consider medical conditions could be regarded as a landmark. When the dialogue reaches this point it would display to the user 'Now checking the applicant's medical condition in order to determine whether any endorsements are necessary'.

Splitting the analysis of the problem into Task and Strategy models automatically creates activities (or topics) and their associated landmarks as part of the Task model and provides an explicit strategy in the Strategy model. Explanations of the domain itself can be provided by the rules and text associated with the relevant sections of the Conceptual model.

Documentation and techniques

Approaches that can be used to analyse and document the Strategy model include:

- flow charts;
- structure charts;
- state transition diagrams;
- decision tables;
- decision trees;
- structured English.

4.8 System model and the methods repository

The initial knowledge model defined in the previous section was in use for some time and proved to be very successful at integrating the conventional and KBS aspects. This was subsequently developed further, both as part of the IED project which has already been mentioned and as part of the ongoing initiative in KBS methods. Other ideas were drawn into the model including some from KADS which by then had completed its first major development phase (KADS-I). The development of the Perspectives model, which was carried out independently of the methods development work, resulted in the splitting of the Task model into two in parallel with the structure of the Perspectives model. The Task model therefore became the Data model and the Process model. The Conceptual and Strategy models were also re-examined and a more precise definition of these was developed, the two models eventually becoming the Knowledge and Behaviour models. The revised model therefore maps closely on to the Perspectives. The major documentation components of the four elements of the revised System model are shown in Table 4.1.

Table 4.1 Perspectives components

Data model	Process model
Data definitions	Activity definitions
Entity Relationship diagrams	Activity diagrams
Data Flow Diagrams (*)	Task decomposition hierarchies
	Straegy diagrams (*)
Knowledge model	Behaviour model
Object definitions (*)	Entity Life Histories (*)
Classification Hierarchies	Event Definitions
Composition Hierarchies	State Transition Diagrams
Sibling Relationships	Conversation Structures (*)

Note: * Elements reflecting relationships between different elements of the model.

It is important to note that some of the elements of the System model reflect the relationships between different elements of the model and these are indicated in the table by the use of an asterisk.

The second major change is that the method definition has become a method repository. In a way this is more relevant for consultancies who are likely to be installing KBS methods on a wide range of client sites. However, the approach is also valid for individual organisations since it provides additional power to the method by explicitly showing the relationships between the parts of the method. It can also be used to ensure that the method is tailored accurately and consistently for individual projects. The repository helps to move methods away from an apparent cookbook definition and place a structure on the use of a much more flexible approach. The concepts behind a repository are explored in greater detail in Chapter 8. A repository is simply a comprehensive set of methods components, including tasks, techniques and products, that are documented in such a way as to support the adaptation of the method to the requirements of different projects to ensure maximum compatibility between the system to be built and the way in which it is built.

At first sight this change to a repository may appear to be little more than cosmetic. Although the actual KBS technical content is largely unchanged, the shift of emphasis from a complete method which tries to define all aspects of KBS development to a comprehensive set of discrete components is very significant. All of the individual components which are KBS-related are now documented as individual elements. This means that only KBS components and how they fit into standard system modelling need to be defined. For example the KBM System model shows that events can usefully be included on Activity Diagrams and provides an approach for their inclusion. However, most organisations will already use some form of modelling the relationships between data and processes, so the repository approach permits the additional KBS-related components, in this case events, to be added to the already existing documentary technique.

Another major advantage of this approach is that it allows KBM to absorb valuable techniques from elsewhere. This has included a number from KADS including the inference model library and conversation structures. These provide a greater level of abstraction for more complex systems. Many ideas from Object Oriented techniques have also been used. These include the standard classification and composition techniques and notations and event modelling. This then provides an immediate link into Object Orientation so projects which require both OO and KBS techniques can also make use of the methods repository very easily and rapidly.

The methods repository approach has been used on a significant number of projects to date and has been found to operate very effectively and to provide many advantages over the more conventional methods approach.

4.9 Summary and conclusions

The method described in this chapter was based on conventional systems development but has grown considerably since its origin in the mid 1980s – helped on its way by the major R&D project between 1990 and 1993. Although originally based on a waterfall life cycle, it has been adapted to use Rapid Development and it has moved to a repository-based approach. It has also been successfully integrated with an Object Oriented method. The knowledge modelling is intended to cover the depth of analysis required for the majority of commercial KBS but it can easily be supplemented by the very deep modelling provided by methods such as KADS if necessary.

Table 4.2 lists the criteria given in Chapter 2 to support the assessment of methods and rates KBM against them.

Table 4.2 KBM assessment criteria

Crierion	KBM
Type of life cycle	Waterfall and Rapid Development
Availability	Proprietary
Depth of knowledge analysis	Moderate, can be easily extended as required
Scope of method	Survey to Implementation
Project Management	Fair, can be easily extended
Links	Project mgt etc. in ACT methods family, can be integrated with other methods
Perspectives: Data Process Behaviour Knowledge	 Good Good Good Good

5   KBS Methods

A significant number of methods have been developed for KBS which are not overtly based on any pre-existing conventional development method and a selection of these are outlined in this chapter. These methods are from a variety of origins but most have a significant academic component. The major differences in approach between these methods and those based on conventional development methods are described. The two methods given separate chapters, KADS and GEMINI, are introduced and their relationship to other methods is outlined.

5.1 Introduction

A major characteristic of most of the methods described in this chapter is that they were developed from within academic institutions, often as a result of UK government or European funding. This has resulted in approaches which sometimes differ markedly in detail from conventional methods but nevertheless have many similarities. The trend found in conventional methods of a concentration on the analysis and design can also be found across all of the KBS methods; very few make any attempt at the very early stages of a project. It is also very unusual to find any KBS method which goes beyond the logical design phase; even fewer consider these aspects than do the methods developed from an SE approach. This is partly because the analysis and design stages are seen as particularly important – the earlier that errors are made the more expensive they are to correct – but also because most workers tend to find the problems of analysis and design more interesting. A difficulty also occurs with the dependence of the physical design on the tools selected to implement the KBS. There is considerably more variation between KBS tools than is seen in the more conventional languages. The issues of testing and maintaining KBS have also not received nearly as much attention in research as the earlier phases. The result is that even if methods developers wanted to extend KBS methods into the later phases there would be very little source material upon which to draw.

There is a strong belief among many of the KBS-specific methods developers that conventional methods are simply inadequate for KBS. The track record of conventional methods, which is far from ideal, is also taken as an indicator that a total break from conventional software engineering is required. Even so, the basic principles of analysing the current domain, generating a system design which is independent of the implementation environment (the logical design), and then converting the logical design into a design which can be physically implemented are visible in all of the methods examined. However, the terminology tends to differ, sometimes considerably even for more or less the same things, and the analyses of process and data that are found in conventional systems are either not found at all or found only in a much modified way.

The life cycles vary considerably in KBS-specific methods, from a purely prototyping approach to an apparently rigorous waterfall approach. At one extreme, in particular in the early days of both academic and commercial KBS development, the way of developing KBS was often to sit one or more 'KBS whiz-kids' in a corner with a KBS tool and let them get on with it. Perhaps surprisingly, this totally different approach from conventional software development did work in a small number of cases. However, the process was not visible to anyone other than the developers themselves and so for commercial organisations it was very difficult to manage and the problems of controlling cost and timescales were not acceptable. Both academia and business then attempted to address the problem by defining methods for KBS. Commercial organisations tended to address this by taking existing methods and adapting them for KBS development, academic institutions address it by starting from scratch.

5.2 KADS overview

The KBS-specific method with the highest profile is undoubtably KADS. The original KADS project started in 1983 and has been running ever since in a series of reincarnations. Its origins were in work carried out by the University of Amsterdam and since its inception it has involved over ten partners from various European countries. It has been funded by the European Community and has the intention of producing a KBS method that will become the European standard for KBS development.

The first major KADS project (which ended in 1988, the output being known as KADS-I) produced many deliverables but no complete KBS method. A follow-up project was initiated in 1990. The latter had the intention of producing a definition called 'Common KADS' to encompass all of the work carried out on KADS-II and deliver a definition of a KBS method.

A major problem with KADS-I was the volume and comprehensibility of the deliverables for commercial IT departments. There was also a degree of inconsistency between deliverables as ideas developed. This is quite understandable from the point of view of a large multi-partner research project which broke much new ground but is not very helpful to commercial KBS developers. One consequence of this is that a number of KADS-based methods have appeared, largely but by no means exclusively from the members of the KADS consortium, that have attempted to make the output from the project useful commercially. In addition to these KADS derivatives, some of the ideas have been taken up by other methods, including some of the SE-based methods described in previous chapters, and also in GEMINI which is introduced in the next section. The two main concepts used by other methods are the four layer knowledge model and the use of an interpretation model library. Both of these are described further in Chapter 6.

The follow-up project, KADS-II, puts considerably more flesh on the skeleton of KADS-I and introduces many of the aspects of project management that are missing. The work that has been carried out on KADS-II promises to be a major advance on KADS-I.

5.3 GEMINI overview

GEMINI is a guidance for KBS development that has been produced by a consortium commissioned by the CCTA. The CCTA is the government organisation that is responsible for, among other things, the methods and standards recommended for use in IT development throughout all government departments. The highest profile method to have been backed by the CCTA is SSADM which is their conventional development method. Not only is SSADM widely used in government departments but it has also been taken up extensively by commercial organisations. This is partly because the method is easily available from HMSO bookshops at a nominal price, but training is also widely supplied by many organisations. In this sense, GEMINI can be said to have a very good pedigree. The original GEMINI concept was first mooted in 1988 and it was to be a short rapid development of some guidelines for KBS development. This grew somewhat over the following years into a major project to define a KBS development method that would be part of the same IT library as the conventional development method SSADM.

Given that GEMINI has had very commercial origins, it may seem odd to place it in the category of 'KBS methods' rather than 'Software Engineering based methods'. This placing has been chosen because GEMINI has not evolved from a specific software engineering method but was developed from scratch by a consortium.

The approach to developing GEMINI was, as with KADS, through a consortium although with GEMINI all the members were commercial organisations. They were all actively involved in commercial KBS development so the approach is essentially practical. It draws heavily on the experiences of the consortium members and their own in-house KBS methods. The main external influence has been KADS, partly because it was the highest profile KBS method with freely available documentation, and partly because of an overlap between the GEMINI and KADS consortia. It has also made extensive use of Boehm's spiral model within the management aspects of its definition.

GEMINI is no longer called a method but is referred to as a guidance. It provides support for the control and management of KBS projects in a way that conforms to the CCTA's project management method PRINCE. Its technical support is limited to definitions of the deliverables that should be produced on a KBS project and some support on how they should be produced. It does not go nearly to the level of detail that, for example, SSADM does.

GEMINI is the first generally available commercial approach to KBS development. It is described in much more detail in Chapter 7.

5.4 Keats

The Keats methodology was developed at the Open University's Human Cognition Research Laboratory, with the primary funding coming from British Telecom. The project took on two phases, with the later (Keats-2) building on the successes and failures of the earlier (Keats-1). Much that follows is based on the second phase of the project.

There are many interesting similarities between Keats and KADS, some of which will be noted in the following descriptions. Perhaps the most important difference is the relationship between the method and its tool support. Keats takes the view that the methodology and tool are closely related, and it is impossible to use one without the other. KADS also has tool support, called Shelley, but unlike Keats the method is essentially paper-based. An outline of the support that is provided by the Keatstools is also included in this section.

Keats, like KADS, takes the view that KBS development is best understood as a process of model refinement, transforming an unknown representation in the expert's mind into a formal, machine resident representation, with each stage producing a qualitatively different model. None of the models defined in Keats is tied to any particular knowledge representation formalism, and none demands any particular knowledge elicitation technique. The tools provided exist primarily to support knowledge analysis – the transformation from one model to another.

Although Keats contains a phase called Feasibility, it is rather different from a conventional Feasibility Study since it does not explicitly contain many of the assessment and planning activities normally associated with feasibility, such as cost/benefit analysis. It is aimed primarily at generating a 'first pass' analysis of the domain as a basis for further work and to assist in the assessment of the technical feasibility of the system. At the back end of the system development process, Keats has something to say on verification, validation and maintenance, although this is rather thin (at least in the published versions of Keats).

Keats does not address the issue of the integration between KBS and conventional systems, unlike GEMINI for example. The heavy reliance between the system and its software environment also raises the issue of its suitability to hybrid KBS/conventional systems.

5.4.1 Life-cycle activities

At a coarse-grained level, the KBS development process is viewed by Keats as consisting of the following three activities:

- Problem Conceptualisation
- Knowledge Encoding
- Debugging

The first two occur sequentially. The Debugging activity forms a parallel stream alongside the first two, employing various techniques to correct faults with the models at all stages.

Problem Conceptualisation

The Problem Conceptualisation stage can be further decomposed into a number of sub-tasks:

- Feasibility Study (bottom-up knowledge acquisition):
  - Knowledge Elicitation
  - Data Analysis
  - Data Conceptualisation
- Skeletal Model Instantiation (top-down knowledge acquisition).

This is shown in Figure 5.1. The Knowledge Elicitation activity consists of interviewing and collecting background material. The output is the Raw Data, the results of research into the domain with no attempt to analyse them.

The Raw Data are then input to the Data Analysis activity. This aims to get rid of unwanted data; and to group the remaining knowledge into chunks, or generic concepts. These aims are supported by the Acquist module of the software

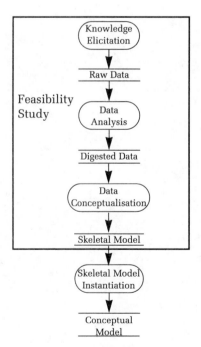

Figure 5.1
Keats Problem
Conceptualisation.
Source: Adapted from
Motta *et al.* (1989)

environment, which provides hypertext facilities for the manipulation of transcripts and background text. The result is a set of Digested Data, not yet a model of the problem.

The Digested Data form the starting point for Data Conceptualisation, the last stage of the bottom-up approach to knowledge acquisition. This is an attempt to impose a global structure on the data collected so far. The data are organised into appropriate structures: taxonomic hierarchies, causal networks, tables, flow diagrams, and so on. The aim is to produce a model of the structure of the task and the expert's problem solving behaviour. The result is the Skeletal Model, a generic problem-solving model.

The Skeletal Model Instantiation activity uses the Skeletal Model to drive the remaining knowledge elicitation in a top-down fashion. The construction of the Skeletal Model will make the developers aware of gaps in their knowledge of the domain, and interviews can be instigated to fill these. The resultant refinement is the Conceptual Model.

Knowledge Encoding

Once the Conceptual Model is complete, work proceeds to the Knowledge Encoding phase. This too has various sub-tasks:

- Knowledge Formalisation;
- Knowledge Representation;
- Implementation.

This is shown in Figure 5.2.

Figure 5.2
Keats Knowledge
Encoding.
Source: Adapted from
Motta *et al.* (1989)

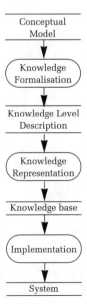

Knowledge Formalisation aims to build a representation and machine-independent description of a knowledge base. Abstract data types, inference types, and generic control structures will be defined. This activity is the nearest Keats equivalent to a logical design phase. The resultant model is the Knowledge Level Description and unfortunately Keats provides little guidance on how to transform the Conceptual Model into the Knowledge Level Description.

The Knowledge Level Description is used as input to the Knowledge Representation stage. This takes the abstract descriptions from the previous activity, and finds concrete knowledge representation formalisms (i.e. frames, rules, etc.) and inference strategies (i.e. forward, backward chaining, etc.) for them. The Keats software environment supports a variety of formalisms and strategies. The output of this stage is the knowledge base itself.

The final stage of Keats's KBS development is Implementation. Unfortunately like many other methodologies, Keats provides little guidance on how implementation is to be achieved. The final output of this stage is the completed system.

Debugging

The Debugging phase is a stream parallel to the two other main development activities. It is carried out on each model produced. It has two aims: to validate and to verify. Validation is concerned with the accuracy of the mapping between a model and what it is supposed to represent; verification checks the consistency and completeness of the model itself.

Validation can be split into two types – representational and functional. Representational validation assesses the accuracy of the mapping between the expert's knowledge and the Conceptual Model. This is a difficult task, and much of the validation is aimed at ensuring the adequacy of the Conceptual Model, rather than its accuracy. Functional validation checks the mapping between the Conceptual Model and the implemented system. This focuses on the similarity of the structures in the Conceptual Model and the eventual implementation.

Verification investigates the consistency and completeness of the knowledge base. Hence it is only relevant at the Knowledge Encoding level. Verification will be helped by using representations which are both semantically sound (the truth/falsity of a statement is formally provable) and syntactically simple (to minimise the chances of mistakes), for example by using first-order predicate calculus.

5.4.2 *Tools and techniques*

Keats takes the view that the methodology and the tool support for it are inseparably linked. Consequently, there will be no attempt here to discuss tools and techniques separately. Inevitably there are some general knowledge engineering techniques (such as the various interviewing methods) that are not supported by Keats, but they are not prescribed by the methodology either.

The full set of tools in the Keats environment is:

- Acquist: a hypertext transcript analysis tool. This is used primarily in support of bottom-up knowledge acquisition.
- FLIK: Frame Language In Keats, a frame-based representation language. Used to build the knowledge base.
- ERI: Essential Rule Interpreter, a forward/backward chaining rule interpreter. Used for knowledge base design.
- GIS: Graphical Interface System, a semantic network, sketch-pad. Used during implementation.
- TRI: Transparent Rule Interpreter, a graphical debugger for rule-based systems. Used primarily in the programming/debugging stages.
- TMS: Truth Maintenance System, integrated with the rule interpreter. Used for knowledge base design and debugging.
- TMV: Truth Maintenance Viewer, a graphical interface for TMS.
- Tables: an intelligent spreadsheet interface used as a programming aid.
- CS: a constraint based language.
- Coding Sheets: this has the aim of supporting top-down knowledge acquisition, by providing a hypertext tool which allows the definition of a template for the problem solving task.

5.4.3 Additional techniques

Keats also provides additional techniques that are not part of the toolset. The first provides support for instantiating the Skeletal Model. This technique assumes that top-down knowledge acquisition will always follow bottom-up – and indeed this is usually the case. A Skeletal Model is a generic model of the task, domain structure and problem-solving behaviour of the expert which indicates the form the final system will take. It also allows further, model-driven knowledge acquisition. Keats is not too clear about the form the Skeletal Model will take. It would appear to consist of hierarchies of domain concepts identified by Acquist, together with some control knowledge. Skeletal Models are created as one-offs by the knowledge engineer, and there seems little provision for their reuse. It is worth noting that, although at first appearing similar, the Keats Skeletal Model does not perform quite the same function as the KADS Interpretation Model. First, Keats does not aim to provide a library of such models as KADS does; and second, the KADS model is less flexible as it prescribes a form (the Four Layers) and some notation for the model. Keats does not, considering such decisions are better left to the design stages. Indeed, in many ways it is true to say that the KADS Four Layer Model more closely resembles the Knowledge Level Description of the Conceptual Model in eats, in which case it is an interesting methodological difference that Keats prefers strict knowledge-typing to be left to the design stages of a development, whereas in KADS it must be done during analysis.

The second major technique not supported by the toolset is for the Knowledge Level Description. This is an abstract, machine-independent description of the knowledge base. It defines the important difference between the Knowledge Level Description and the Conceptual Model itself: the Conceptual Model describes the external world (the expert's problem solving behaviour, etc.) whereas the Knowledge Level is a description of the system being developed. It has already been noted that Keats opposes the KADS view that the Conceptual Model should be itself formally described; however, Keats provides little guidance on how this model should be defined. The transformation of Conceptual Model to Knowledge Level Description is left to the experience of the knowledge engineer; and the representation is also left to his/her discretion, with the proviso that it will be more formal than the Conceptual Model. It would seem to be possible to 'plug-in' other KBS modelling techniques (for example predicate calculus) at this stage.

5.5   KEMRAS

5.5.1 Background

The KEMRAS methodology for KBS development was created by Alvey project IKBS:098. It was a collaboration between a number of academic and industrial partners – BHRA (The Fluid Engineering Centre); ERA Technology Ltd; The Building Services Research & Information Association; The Research Association for the Paper & Board, Printing & Packaging Industries; The Welding Institute; The University of Liverpool; Loughborough University of Technology; and University College London.

The project produced a manual aimed at Research Associations in the belief that KBS developments in academic research departments and industrial R&D departments are sufficiently similar to allow a single set of guidelines to be produced. The Alvey project was completed in 1989. The project produced a manual (in two parts) which provides a complete KBS lifecycle, and directions for the execution of each stage within it.

KEMRAS takes the commonly held view that knowledge elicitation should aim to synthesise a Knowledge Model of the task the KBS is to carry out and prototyping should only be used when the model reaches certain points. Hence, the production of the Knowledge Model is decomposable into stages, which according to the methodology require different types and levels of knowledge. It does not define its own forms or knowledge representation, preferring to suggest established techniques, and believes that this will increase the availability of the knowledge so captured. KEMRAS does not have its own software support, again believing that the recommendation of generic tools will facilitate acceptance.

This method has been included as an example of another way of viewing the KBS software development through the use of the cascade life cycle. The process it describes is essentially iterative; it is possible for any one activity to send the development back to any previous activity. While this provides a suitable mechanism for escaping from the strictures of the waterfall method, its controllability is open to question. The very open nature of the life cycle presents the type of management problems seen in pure prototyping. While this approach does explicitly recognise the occasional need to go back to previous phases, there is some justification for saying that it leaves this too open without providing enough controls to ensure that any iteration is managed sufficiently tightly.

KEMRAS is mainly concerned with the classifying and structuring of knowledge elicitation techniques: hence feasibility, requirements engineering, analysis and design are all discussed in terms of which elicitation technique should be used; there is very little discussion of representation and tool support activities. KEMRAS does not explicitly address the question of hybrid KBS/conventional systems. Finally, a result of the KEMRAS iterative structure is that certain decisions may not be made until what other, more structured, methodologies would consider a very late stage. For instance, requirements may still be altered at the Implementation stage.

5.5.2 *Life cycle*

KEMRAS differs notably from the other methods in that it does not use a waterfall (early KADS and possibly Keats) or spiral (later KADS and GEMINI) life cycle model. Instead, it views the knowledge elicitation process as fundamentally iterative: any activity can cause an iteration of any previous activity. A diagram showing these dependencies is given in Figure 5.3. Iteration becomes more likely as the elicitation process progresses and becomes more complex.

Figure 5.3
KEMRAS life cycle.
Source: Adapted from
BHRA (1989)

The seven distinct stages of knowledge engineering identified in the life cycle are:

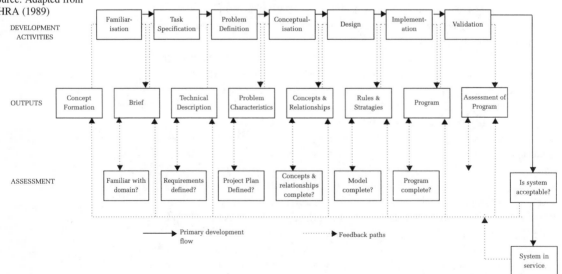

- Familiarisation with Problem Domain;
- Task Specification;
- Problem Definition;
- Knowledge Conceptualisation;
- Detailed Design;
- Implementation;
- Validation.

In addition to the development flow, there are associated assessment activities. These provide a means of deciding when development should go back to a previous activity, and also an in-built means of risk assessment and management.

Familiarisation with Problem Domain

The first activity in the KBS development process aims to provide the knowledge engineer with broad knowledge of the domain. No decision should be made at this stage as to the form any KBS solution might eventually take. The activity will proceed by informal elicitation interviews and background reading (which should be referenced for use by the rest of the project).

Task Specification

The knowledge engineer then attempts to compile a detailed (possibly contractual) specification of the task which the KBS should perform. A distinction is made between required and desired functionality. The result should be a clear picture of the requirements, together with the criteria to be used to assess whether the end system meets the requirements – these are known as the Technical Description. The activity proceeds by systems analysis interviews supplemented by questionnaires and checklists.

Problem Definition

This stage considers the resources that are available for carrying out the KBS development. The term 'resources' covers domain expertise, knowledge engineering experience, tools and techniques available, etc. It aims to put a clear boundary on the domain knowledge that will be elicited, by distinguishing what the system should know, what the user will be expected to provide, and what may be common to them both (this approach is an echo of the KADS Modality Analysis whereby task decomposition and ingredient ownership are defined as a preliminary to detailed elicitation).

The output from this activity is two documents. One defines the characteristics of the domain problem, the other describes the management issues for the rest of the development. Both of these will need more structured interviewing techniques than the previous stage.

Conceptualisation

The Conceptualisation stage represents the knowledge modelling. It identifies the key concepts in the domain, together with their attributes and relationships, and the expert's problem solving strategy. A distinction is made between *what* (declarative) knowledge and *how* (procedural) knowledge. The product of this activity is a Knowledge Model of the domain problem and ways of solving it. Unlike some other methods, KEMRAS does not prescribe any way of representing the Knowledge Model. It prefers that the representation chosen should be one sympathetic to the problem domain – probably supplemented with rules, strategies, and so on. The elicitation techniques include focused and structured interviews, introspection, protocol analysis, repertory grids, and various other standard approaches. Prototypes may be built as part of the assessment of the Knowledge Model.

Detailed Design

This activity takes the Conceptual Model from the Conceptualisation stage and refines and completes it. The result will be a functional specification; it will be complete in functional aspects, but independent of any specific programs or tools to be used. However, at this time the tools and programming languages to be used in implementation will need to be considered by the development team. The output will consist of detailed domain concepts, attributes and relations, reasoning strategies and their control, and interface requirements. The activity uses further knowledge elicitation and analysis; prototyping may also be used to assess the validity of the Conceptual Model.

Implementation

Implementation takes the Conceptual Model of the structure and processes of the problem solving task and realises it in a computer program. The method of achieving this will vary depending on whether rapid prototyping has been employed as part of the development, in which case it may be possible to fill-in an earlier prototype with the detailed knowledge from the Conceptual Model. Otherwise, the system will be built from the complete Conceptual Model.

At this stage a definite decision will be reached as to the tool to be used for programming. The implementation process should ideally be a mapping of the Conceptual Model to the representation of the chosen software. KEMRAS suggests that deficiencies in the tool chosen may mean that the functionality of the entire KBS has to be reviewed, leading the development process back several steps.

Validation

The Validation activity is concerned with the validation of the *functionality* of the system – it is assumed that individual stages, such as the mapping of the Conceptual Model to the tool, will have been validated by the appropriate assessment stage. The original definition of requirements was produced by the Task Definition stage. If a deficiency in the functionality is found, the team must identify where in the development the mistake occurred, and attempt to rectify it by going back to the appropriate activity. This process is repeated until the system is accepted by the client's organisation.

5.6 Other KBS Methods

There are a variety of other methods that are seen in the press from time to time. These are listed briefly here and their provenance is indicated.

- The KnAcq. This is a tool for constructing backward-chaining rule-bases built upon an implementation of Popper's falsificationism. This is effectively a KBS tool rather than a methodology as defined in this book, although it is often mentioned as a method.
- SKE (Structured Knowledge Engineering). This is a European KADS-derivative from the Netherlands. It is particularly notable because it is probably the oldest commercial use of KADS.
- KOD. This is another European KADS-derivative.
- VITAL. This derives from an Esprit project which is producing a 'methodology-based workbench'. It uses some KADS ideas but does not follow it slavishly. It takes ideas from Keats and ACKnowledge.
- ACKnowledge. Another Esprit project which aimed to build a tool to support knowledge acquisition in a structured manner.
- EDESIRL. Salford University *et al*. The method is stated to be 'client centred'. It does not appear to have been influenced by KADS; indeed it often takes a reverse approach – the client should be empowered, by the appropriate tools and techniques, to construct the KBS by themselves.

5.7 Summary and conclusions

This chapter has discussed the KBS methods that have been developed independently, often with academic origins, rather than derived directly from a pre-existing conventional development method. Two methods which have their own chapters, KADS and GEMINI, were outlined initially to place them in context. KADS in particular has had a very major influence over most, if not all, current KBS methods and its influence is now so pervasive that it is becoming difficult to track explicitly. This was followed by descriptions of a number of KBS methods that have had origins in academic institutions. Keats was developed jointly by the Open University and British Telecom and is inseparable from the toolset that has been developed to support it. KEMRAS on the other hand has produced a manual rather than a toolset and is aimed more at research institutions than at the commercial world. It uses a very iterative life cycle but does not offer very detailed advice on the project management aspects of how this is controlled. This was followed by a very brief look at some of the other methods whose names are occasionally identified in the press and journals.

Table 5.1 lists the criteria given in Chapter 2 to support the assessment of methods and assess the main methods described in this chapter against them. Note that the two methods which have their own chapters, KADS and GEMINI, are not included below and so the table only shows the two main methods described – Keats and KEMRAS.

Table 5.1 KBM methods assessment criteria

Criterion	Keats	KEMRAS
Type of life cycle	Waterfall	Cascade
Availability	Partially available	Available
Depth of knowledge analysis	Moderate	Shallow
Scope of method	Analysis to Programming	Feasibility to Validation
Project Management	Some	Some
Links	None	None
Perspectives:		
Data	Poor	Poor
Process	Poor	Poor
Behaviour	Good	Fair
Knowledge	Good	Fair

6 KADS

This chapter introduces the KADS method. It has been the subject of much discussion since the work originally began in 1983, probably more so than any other KBS method, and it has received plentiful brickbats and bouquets. The history of the KADS series of projects is discussed and its major achievements are described. The ways in which these relate to more conventional methods are considered and the ways in which the KADS ideas can be applied to KBS development are discussed. Given that some of the KADS ideas are used extensively in other methods, the principal KADS models are examined in some detail. Finally, the future development of KADS through the KADS-II project is considered.

6.1 Introduction

6.1.1 Background

The KADS project came into being in mid-1983 when a pilot project was launched that was partly funded by the EC under the ESPRIT programme. In that project, a joint Anglo-Dutch team from the Polytechnic of the South Bank and Amsterdam University set out to define a development method for knowledge based systems that was based on sound software engineering principles and supported by tools. While this pilot project (P12) did not achieve that goal, it laid the groundwork for a series of follow-on projects. The major components to come out of P12 were an early attempt at a systematic analysis of the many knowledge elicitation techniques that had been documented in papers and books, and perhaps more significantly an attempt at modelling expertise at 'the knowledge level'. This was based on earlier academic work in AI and was aimed at producing a framework for the definition of knowledge that was more formal than anything that had been developed to date. It was intended to provide guidance for the knowledge engineer through the knowledge elicitation and knowledge documentation processes. Although not explicitly defined, the basis was there for the subsequent development of the four layer knowledge model and the interpretation models that form the foundation for the later versions of KADS.

Following the completion of this project, a number of more commercially oriented organisations expressed an interest in the aims of the research. Among these were Scicon and STC from the UK, SCS GmbH from Germany and Cap

Gemini Sogeti from France. A short project (P314) was initiated to explore the results of P12 and as a result a very large project, which was really the first major KADS project, was set up. This was also funded by ESPRIT, as project P1098, with a total planned effort of 80 person-years. In addition to the companies already involved, a further German company joined the consortium – NTE NeuTech. The project was divided into three main areas of work, the development of the knowledge modelling theory initiated in the earlier projects, the production of one or more tools to support the method that would emerge from the theory stream, and the testing of the method by the more commercially oriented members of the consortium. It is the results of this project that are now known as KADS or KADS-I and these are the principal results that are reported in this chapter. A number of the organisations taking part in the consortium underwent name changes during the course of the project. The group at the South Bank Polytechnic formed the Knowledge Based Systems Centre, this then became an independent consultancy which was subsequently taken over by Touche Ross. STC was also part of the takeovers and mergers of the 1980s and is now known as BNR.

When the KADS project ended in 1989, it was recognised that it was not complete and that it had not achieved some of its original goals. The problems included the lack of a core set of documentation that could reasonably be called 'The KADS Method' and an overly academic bias in many of the documents delivered. In short, the results were not easily exploitable by commercial organisations and substantial additional work to shape the results was necessary. However, many of the ideas developed by the project have now found their way into other methods and have been redocumented in a more commercial fashion. There are also organisations marketing their own versions of KADS; the main ones in the UK are all members of one of the two main consortia of KADS-I or KADS-II – Touche Ross, Lloyds Register, and BNR.

Not surprisingly, a follow-up project to P1098 was defined and started work in 1990, known as KADS-II. This project was of a similar size to KADS-I (about 80 person-years). It has very similar goals in that it wants to deliver a commercial KBS method and aspires to become the European standard for KBS development. One of the objectives of the project is to develop a 'CommonKADS' which will define the basic components of a KADS method. The work on this is reported at the end of this chapter.

As has already been noted, the descriptions in this chapter are based largely on KADS-I rather than KADS-II. This is for a number of reasons. Most of the results of KADS-I are now in the public domain and easily obtainable. A number of books have also been published which present views on the KADS project. Although KADS-II has published some results, very little concrete information has been made publicly available. There are also moves from part of the KADS-II consortium to keep some of the results confidential for commercial exploitation at the end of the project. There is therefore some doubt as to whether the results of KADS-II will be as freely available as KADS-I. The second major reason is that the KADS-I deliverables are now final; there is no chance of them changing, even if subsequent work decides that they were incorrect. The third major reason is that KADS-I has, to some degree, been tested. It is also commercially available both in the UK and in Europe and training is available. It will be some years before the KADS-II project can match this.

There are some moves within KADS-II to change some of the earlier terminology; where this is likely to cause confusion when comparing the definitions of KADS-I in this chapter with KADS-II documents, the relationship between them is described.

All references in the rest of this chapter to KADS are specifically to the output of the KADS-I project. The results of the KADS-II project are explicitly labelled as such.

6.1.2 Main principles

KADS is based on two key principles, the use of *models* and *knowledge-level modelling*. The use of models has already been described in looking at a number of other methods and the KADS use of the term is the same. A number of models are defined in various project documents but the main set to have emerged are:

- Organisational Model;
- Application Model;
- Task Model;
- Model of Cooperation;
- Model of Expertise;
- Conceptual Model;
- Design Model.

Together they represent the entire output from a KADS project. These are discussed further as each of the phases are considered in the next section.

The second major principle is the knowledge level modelling. This is based on major research on the structure of knowledge (epistemology) initially carried out during the late 1970s and early 1980s. In this, a number of fundamentally different types of knowledge were identified. The KADS project took these and developed the definitions of the different levels of knowledge further. It also changed the emphasis. The original intention behind the knowledge level hypothesis was that it would enable people to develop cognitive models of tasks. KADS has developed this with the specific purpose of use in the construction of KBS. The development of the knowledge level concepts was originally, at least in part, a response to the difficulties experienced with first generation systems (described in Chapter 1). The identification and definition of the knowledge layers provided a major contribution to the possibility of building second generation systems by making the different kinds of knowledge more explicit. The four layer model of expertise developed by the KADS project is a key element of the model of expertise.

KADS uses a level of modelling of knowledge which goes beyond that of which many people have common experience. The modelling of data and processes is well understood by the IT community, and indeed by many people outside IT who are involved in organisation and business modelling. The level of abstraction used in these activities is relatively low. The development of KBS tends to introduce additional modelling concepts because of the need to extend the modelling of data and processes to knowledge. As has been seen in the methods based on conventional systems development, this additional level of modelling can often be successfully achieved, at least for the more straightforward KBS, simply by extending existing methods. However, there are times when this level of modelling is not adequate. This tends to occur when attempts are made to build systems that can be used to support a number of different functions, such as decision support and training, or when a system is being built to support a more generic task, such as the design of all databases. In the latter case, it is not sufficient to model how database x operates and then try to transfer that expertise to database y. It is necessary to model how all databases operate at a generic level. This level of abstraction can be very complex and cause many problems during the development, particularly amongst less experienced developers. KADS attempts to bring structure to this type of knowledge through the techniques that have been developed. This level of modelling is essential in the more complex systems but doubts have been cast on its usability for simpler run-of-the-mill KBS that are often produced in a commercial environment. However, there is much that can be learnt from KADS and applied to all commercial developments and at least one attempt has been made to develop a version of KADS which is appropriate for small systems development. This is described further in Section 6.5.

6.1.3 KADS and conventional modelling

On the face of it, KADS looks like a very different approach to systems development when compared with conventional systems. Conventional systems talk about the analysis of data and processes, KADS talks about modelling expertise, the four layer model, system–user cooperation, and so on. In fact a parallel can be drawn between the various elements of KADS and the more conventional approach although this analogy should not be taken too far.

The analysis of the knowledge contained in the target domain can be regarded as an extension of the data analysis. Its purpose is to look at the static information used by an expert in solving a problem. This may consist of simple data just as would be found in a conventional database; it may also consist of more complex relationships between the various pieces of information that are not captured in a database. For example in a diagnostic system, the relationships between the observed symptoms and the possible causes will be classified as knowledge whereas the separate measurements carried out on the individual components could easily be analysed through conventional data analysis techniques. The Domain layer of the four layer model captures this type of static domain knowledge. Looking now at the process side of conventional analysis, the objective of this is to identify the processes carried out on the data. Similarly, the Model of Cooperation in KADS is aimed at identifying the tasks carried out and relating them to the knowledge that is used.

6.1.4 Task breakdown

The tasks in KADS can be placed into a task breakdown structure as shown in Table 6.1. This indicates that the overall structure of KADS is very similar to most development methods, at least in outline. The major differences occur at the more detailed level where the analysis considers expertise and modality analysis rather than data and process analysis. These stages are described in detail in Sections 6.2 to 6.4.

Table 6.1 KADS task breakdown structure

Scoping
   Pre-project scoping
   Project scoping
Analysis
   Requirements analysis
      Analyse present situation
      Analyse objectives and constraints
      Determine functional requirements
   Expertise analysis
     Analyse static knowledge
     Analyse problem solving tasks/select interpretation models
     Construct model of expertise
      Construct inference layer
      Construct task layer
      Construct strategy layer
   Modality analysis
     Achieve global task model
     Achieve negotiation space
     Construct model of cooperation
      Identify ingredients and ownership
      Assign initiatives
Design
   Functional design
   Behavioural design
   Physical design

6.1.5 Terminology

KADS can often appear to live in a world of its own with a complex and esoteric terminology. One possible reason for this is that it was developed by a consortium whose members were a mixture of individuals from academia and business spread across Europe. Given the size and spread of the consortium it is impressive that it achieved as much as it did. However, we are left with the resulting terminology which can be complex. If any of the KADS-I deliverables are to be read and understood, it is necessary to understand the terminology. This has been explained within the body of the chapter at the point where the term is introduced. Where possible, an accepted IT equivalent is given although this is not always a direct translation. In some cases the term has a very specific meaning in KADS and then it is used as it stands.

6.2 Initial stages

The initial stages of KADS are not defined in any detail. The scoping, assessment of feasibility, generation of a cost/benefit case, and so on, are not defined and no techniques are provided. It is assumed that the normal processes in an IT department will provide the necessary support for these areas. The only pre-Analysis phase defined in KADS is Scoping. This is divided into two parts – Pre-project Scoping and Determine Project Scope. Both of these are largely planning activities and do not address the issues of feasibility in any depth. It is left to the organisation using KADS to supply the necessary tasks and techniques.

Pre-project Scoping

The Pre-project Scoping is defined as those activities which refer to a project before it is fully defined. The output from this activity is the Scoping Report which is effectively a Terms of Reference for the project. This requires agreement from the clients and is signed-off.

Determine Project Scope

This is the first task once contracts have been signed. The output consists of a set of documents:

- Background and pre-requisites
- Project terms and directives
- Project life cycle model
- Project plans
- Project organisation

These can be largely equated with the more conventional methods documents of similar names.

6.3 Analysis

There has been significantly more work done on KADS Analysis than on any other part of the life cycle. Analysis is split into three streams of activities which may be carried out in parallel although this is not a pre-requisite. If there is some degree of parallelism, then the activities do not need to start or end together. The tasks are (see Figure 6.1):

- *External.* This defines the external nature of the information obtained – it is external to the system to be built.

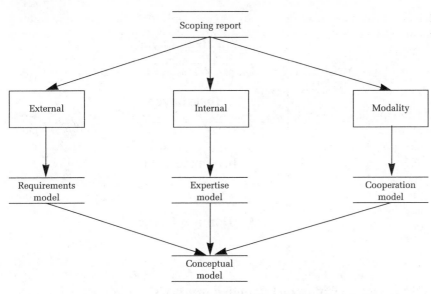

Figure 6.1
Analysis activities.

- *Internal*. The internal analysis refers to the internal nature of the activities carried out – that is the detailed analysis of the expertise required to carry out the task.
- *Modality*. The modality analysis addresses the usability issues – the interactions between the system and user.

6.3.1 External/Requirements analysis

These tasks are similar to conventional systems analysis requirements activities in that a detailed description of the problem, a specification of the solution, and constraints on its development are defined. A Requirements model is produced which describes the KBS-specific aspects in more detail than the more standard elements.

Of the three streams in analysis, this is the least well defined. This is partly because KADS recognises the potentially fluid nature of requirements and that they will almost inevitably change during the life of a project. It also allows elements of conventional requirements analysis to be brought in to ensure they are covered as well as the KBS elements. KADS defines a set of Requirements Analysis documentation that includes:

- models of the business activity, descriptions of the problem and the chosen solution;
- demands on the system, expressed as objectives and constraints;
- solution details and consequences;
- requirements for the rest of development.

KADS does not offer any specific techniques for requirements analysis.

Figure 6.2
Four layer model.

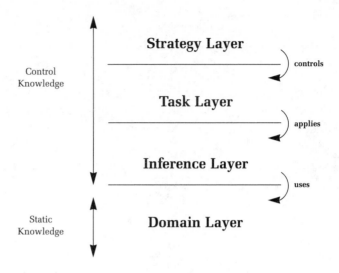

6.3.2 *Internal/Expertise analysis*

This is the heart of KADS, containing the four layer Model of Expertise described in detail later in this section. The KADS notion of reuse through the selection and modification of Interpretation Models is also described. This model is unique to KADS and KBS although a number of similarities between this model and conventional systems analysis will be noted as it is described.

The analysis of expertise in KADS is based on the four layer model. The layers are *Domain*, *Inference*, *Task* and *Strategy*. These can be divided into static knowledge – the Domain Layer, and control knowledge – the remaining three. These are shown in Figure 6.2.

Domain Layer

The Domain Layer contains all of the static knowledge of the domain in question and is said to provide a *domain theory* of the application area. This is a significant difference between KADS and many of the methods already examined. Most simply record the domain knowledge that appears to be relevant to building the system; KADS, however, constructs a domain theory as part of the knowledge model. One consequence of this is that the domain model is *task neutral* and can, in theory at least, be reused for different problems in the same domain.

The Domain Layer knowledge is modelled by using a set of five *primitives*, which are the things that are modelled. The first two primitives, concept and property/value, define the basic objects that are found in the domain, and correspond very closely to conventional data analysis.

Concept. These are objects of importance in the domain and correspond to entities.

Property/value. These are the properties of the concept and can be equated to the attributes of an entity (concept).

If an Object Oriented approach is taken to identifying these, such as has been described in Chapter 3, then an element of reusability starts to appear. Just as objects defined in OO analysis can be reused in subsequent systems, so KADS concepts can be reused in the same way. Indeed, if the concepts of OO analysis are carried further during the Domain Layer analysis, it is possible to start to build a reusable OO model as part of this layer. This not only makes the integration of KBS and conventional systems easier, it significantly increases the reusability of the analysis carried out.

Having defined the concepts in the domain, the next three primitives define the relationships between the first two.

Relation between concepts. In addition to the conventional data modelling relationship definitions (such as the cardinality expressed on an Entity–Relationship diagram), there are also the two additional major types of relationships mentioned in earlier chapters – classification and composition. There may also be additional variants on these.

Relation between property expressions. This defines the relationships between the properties that are defined for a concept. This is more unusual when compared with conventional analysis and often expresses causal relationships. For example, the changes to the balance (a property) on a customer's account (the concept) may cause charges to be added to the balance. This relationship also appears in OO analysis although often less explicitly.

Structure. A structure represents a complex object, for example where a number of sub-components (each defined as concepts) combine to make a large object (also defined as a concept).

While the first two primitives can be said to have equivalents in conventional analysis, the remaining three are starting to diverge, although they have much in common with OO analysis. In OO analysis the two principal object relationships identified are classification and composition, both of which are used extensively in KBS. Causal relationships are partly modelled through the use of methods within an object that respond to events.

Figure 6.3 shows part of the analysis of a credit card domain using many of the ideas introduced above and combines the Object Oriented notation introduced in Chapter 3, conventional E–R diagramming, and added information about the relationships between objects/concepts. The description below shows how the diagram can be read and indicates where the above primitives are used:

> A customer (concept) has one or more (relation between concepts) accounts; each account is owned by one customer. An account has attributes of Type, Name and Balance (property/value). If the account goes overdrawn then a procedure which adds charges is invoked (relation between property expressions). Part of each customer definition is a customer profile (structure – company set of generic profiles) and the sales department sends sales information to the customer depending on the customer profile.

Traditional data modelling approaches are very efficient at modelling data. However, they are not adequate when dealing with the much more complex

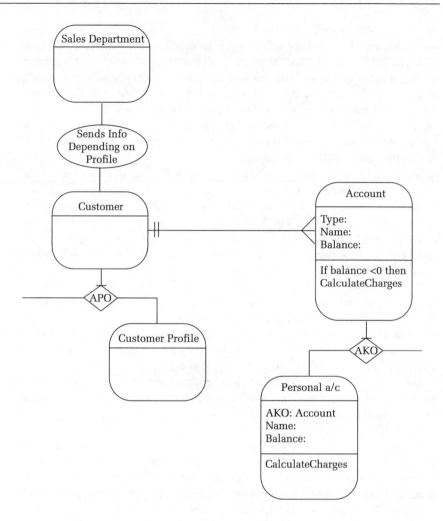

domain of knowledge. In this area it is necessary to model not only entities and their straightforward relationships but also classification, composition and causal relationships, rule relationships between data items and so on. To a large extent this can be overcome by adding Object Oriented notation to conventional notation as shown in Figure 6.3. However, when KADS was originally developed, these OO notations were not in commercial use so a Domain Definition Language (DDL) was developed. This makes use of many of the standard data modelling concepts, takes a chunk of concepts from set theory, and develops some new ideas. The result is a language which is highly structured and is defined very precisely, but at the same time allows a relatively informal description of the knowledge. DDL is not another knowledge representation approach in the sense of rules, frames and so on, but is generic to the construction of all KBS and so provides an implementation-independent definition of the domain knowledge. Ideally it would be possible to map the DDL directly on to the formalism used in a tool so that the executable knowledge could be tracked directly back to the analysis of the knowledge. A full definition and discussion of DDL is well beyond this text but interested readers are pointed to the Bibliography where references to these definitions can be found.

Inference Layer

Immediately above the Domain Layer is the Inference Layer – the first of the three control layers. The Inference Layer uses the contents of the Domain Layer. Two primitives are defined for this layer, knowledge sources and meta-classes.

Knowledge sources. A knowledge source is a form of activity. It is the simplest possible generic activity that can be performed on a component defined in the Domain Layer. Typical knowledge sources are decompose, select and compare. The input and output of a knowledge source are meta-classes.

Meta-classes. A meta-class is a basic piece of information from the Domain Layer. However, it is important to understand that it is not simply a datastore (or its KBS equivalent) but defines instead either the role that a set of domain knowledge items can play or the type of information that is used by the knowledge source. Typical meta-classes are complaint, observable and hypothesis.

Knowledge sources and meta-classes are combined to give an inference structure and a simple example is given in Figure 6.4. This diagram is read simply:

> The parameter values and the variable values are input to a compare process which generates an output of the differences between them.

In this example, the parameter and variable values correspond directly to a set of values defined in the Domain Layer. For example the variable values could be a set of variables which define the customer profile, the parameter values a set of fixed parameters used to describe a new set of sales material to be used for a

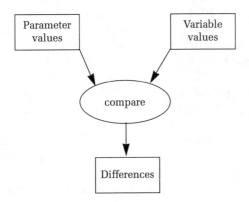

Figure 6.4
Example Inference
Structure.

mailshot. The Inference Structure therefore shows that these two sets of values are compared and the differences between them found. This could then be analysed further to determine whether the intended sales material should be sent to the targeted customer.

One way of viewing an Inference Structure is as the KBS equivalent of a Data Flow Diagram (DFD) although this analogy should not be taken too far. A DFD shows the data and the activities that can be performed and the data that are referenced, whereas an Inference Structure shows the roles that concepts in the domain can play and the ways in which these are used by processes. It is, however, very important to note that an Inference Structure shows what is possible rather than what is actually carried out, that it is more abstract than a DFD (and therefore potentially more generic), and that the arrows indicate the relationships, not sequence.

Task Layer

The Task Layer is the third layer of the four layer model and the second of the three control layers. It defines how the elementary inferences defined in the Inference Layer are assembled to produce tasks which achieve a certain goal. In KADS this is carried out at a relatively high level of abstraction with the task definitions referring only to the inferences and not directly to the domain knowledge. This higher level of abstraction can be difficult to understand initially since it is more abstract than that generally used by IT developers. However, it does mean that the issue of reuse is again tackled head-on as the task definitions for particular sets of typical knowledge based tasks, such as diagnose, analyse, etc., can be reused in many KBS developments. A task definition contains five main elements – the goal, input, output, control terms, and the task structure. Each of these is examined in turn.

The *goal* is the primary objective of a task – it defines why the task is being carried out. It is possible to have more than one task with the same goal; in this case there will be a 'super task' which determines which task is most appropriate for reaching the goal under a particular set of circumstances.

The *input* is largely self explanatory. It defines the input required for the task to execute. At the task definition level, this may be more complex than a simple piece of data; it can represent something like a 'complaint' or a 'system model'.

The *output* from the task is defined in the same way as the input.

The *control terms* are specific to KADS. This is simply a label for a set of members of a meta-class as defined in the previous layer. A typical meta-class is 'hypothesis' and represents a possible diagnosis from a diagnostic system. The control term used to describe a set of hypotheses is 'differential'. While this may seem an unnecessary complication, the use of the term 'differential' is relatively common in diagnostic tasks. For example, when making a medical diagnosis an approach known as differential diagnosis will often be used (and is known as such by the medical profession). During this process the doctor will initially consider a number of hypotheses that are consistent with the observed symptoms (i.e. a set). As the diagnosis continues and the doctor gathers further information, the symptoms will be further analysed, the hypotheses will be refined and reduced in number, and the doctor will eventually come to a 'differential diagnosis' which indicates the most likely cause of the symptoms.

The final element of the task definition is the *Task Structure*. This defines how the task is carried out by defining any sub-tasks that are executed and the control structures needed to carry out the task. To assist in the definition of a task structure, three types of tasks are defined:

1. Primitive problem solving tasks.
2. Composite problem solving tasks.
3. Transfer tasks.

Primitive problem solving tasks correspond directly to inferences which have been specified at the Inference Layer, for example select, specify and compare.

Composite problem solving tasks are tasks specified elsewhere as a task structure. While this is often simply a sub-task, thus allowing a task hierarchy to be built up, it may also be a recursive call to itself. The latter is an extension to the more conventional approach of defining task decomposition in conventional systems.

Transfer tasks move something between the system and the outside world. Note that in this context, the word system is used in its generic sense to mean a collection of functions which achieve a specific end rather than in the much more restrictive IT sense of a software system. At this point no decision has been made about the boundaries of what will be automated. The outside world, which is known as the external agent, may be a human or another system of some description. There are two obvious types of transfer tasks – into and out of the domain. However, each of these can also be split into two depending on how the transfer was initiated. This brings in another term that has a specific meaning in KADS – initiative. The four types of transfer, named from the point of view of the system, are Obtain, Present, Receive and Provide. The detailed definitions of these and the way in which they are used is considered further as part of the Model of Cooperation.

The final part of a Task Structure is control. This is the same as in conventional process analysis where the three options are sequence, selection and iteration.

When defining Task Structures it is very easy to fall into the trap of simply writing pseudo-code using the names of the variables that are found in the target domain. While this may be a valid exercise at some point during the analysis and design of a system, it is not the purpose of a Task Structure. The Task Structure is a generic definition of the way in which the interpretation model is used dynamically and as such it should only contain references to the meta-classes and knowledge sources that are used within the interpretation model.

Strategy Layer

The fourth and last component, the third of the three control layers, is the Strategy Layer, and it is the least well defined and understood. Its objective is to determine which goals are relevant when attempting to solve a particular problem; it therefore primarily manipulates the goals that have been defined as part of each task definition at the previous layer. It will also come into play when individual tasks fail to find a solution and the Strategy Layer then plans a way of configuring different tasks to get around the impasse. Much commercial KBS development has not had any call for this level of knowledge to date since commercial KBS tend to be relatively straightforward. However, this is not to say that the Strategy Layer does not have value in larger, more complex systems.

Reuse of knowledge sources

Work in KADS has identified that the number of different knowledge sources is limited and so a set of knowledge sources has been defined. The set makes no attempt to be definitive; indeed the developers clearly state that the inclusion of elements has been somewhat arbitrary. Part of the set that has been defined in Schreiber *et al.* (1993) is shown in Table 6.2.

Table 6.2 Table of knowledge sources

Operation type	Knowledge source	Arguments
General concept/instance	instantiate	concept → instance
	classify	instance → concept
	generalise	set of instances → concept
	abstract	concept → concept
	specify	concept → concept
	select	set → concept
Differentiating values/structures	compare	value + value → value
	match	structure + structure → structure

Source: Adapted from Schreiber *et al.* (1993).

The table can be read more simply than its appearance implies. The first column shows the operations carried out on concepts. For example, the first could correspond to the creation of a new customer or a new sales pack in the example introduced in the last section. The set of knowledge sources which correspond to this are listed in the second column with the arguments in the third column. Continuing the example, the concept of customer can be *instantiate*d to the instance J. Public. The third column indicates that the input to the operation is the concept, i.e. customer, and the output is the instance J. Public. Taking a second example, the sales pack 'Loans for exotic holidays' is *select*ed from the set of sales packs, the input being the set of all sales packs, and the output is the concept of a specific sales pack.

As the set of knowledge sources is used within an organisation, it is likely that a slightly different set will emerge that is useful for the particular industrial or commercial sector in which the organisation is positioned. This increases the value of the reuse significantly. It is, however, very important that the general nature of the knowledge sources is maintained so that they do not simply become a set of common tasks in the organisation.

Reuse of Interpretation Models

One of the benefits of a model of knowledge as presented in the four layer model is that as it is generic, it can be reused across different applications. To this end a number of major components have been developed to support the reuse of knowledge models. These correspond primarily to the second and third layers of the model – the inference and task layers. A set of Inference Structures have been defined in KADS which describe expert tasks such as diagnosis, planning and monitoring. Each of these Inference Structures is then supported by Task Structures, the pair being known as an Interpretation Model. One of the major benefits of this reuse capability is that it provides guidance for the knowledge engineer when faced with a new problem. The knowledge engineer can investigate the domain in outline to determine the most likely type of tasks involved and then select one or more of the standard models from the Interpretation Model library. These are used as a basis for guiding the knowledge engineering. It is inevitable that the models will not give the precise results required and so the knowledge engineer is encouraged to change the models as knowledge accumulates. It is likely that once a number of the different models have been built for a particular business sector, it will become possible to construct variants of the standard library of models that are specific to individual organisations. This will significantly increase the reuse possible.

A KADS deliverable (A1) defines the Interpretation Models in detail and provides a library of standard models. A taxonomy of all the potential models has also been created and the set of models available include diagnosis, assessment, classification, prediction, design, configuration, planning and scheduling.

6.3.3 *Modality analysis*

The analysis of the way in which the system and the user (or other systems, data feeds etc.) interact is a major element of KADS and the method identifies a number of different tasks in modelling system–user cooperation. These are described in the following paragraphs.

Task decomposition

Task decomposition in KADS corresponds directly to conventional task decomposition. The purpose is to use a divide and conquer principle to decompose the domain in a set of individual tasks. KADS notes that this will often be an iterative process with each of the next two tasks – Identification of interdependencies and Distribution over agents. Conventional techniques may be used for the decomposition. It may, however, be appropriate to annotate the task decomposition to indicate where tasks are iterated, where they are optional, and where there are alternative ways of achieving the same end result. This is something of a departure from conventional task decompositions. The control structures that determine which of the tasks are to be carried out also need to supplement the more conventional task definitions.

Identification of interdependencies

Dependencies between tasks refers principally to product dependencies and KADS recommends the use of conventional data flow diagrams to show the data and tasks.

Distribution over agents

The distribution of tasks over agents defines who (or what) carries out each of the tasks. The three typical agents are the target system, the human user of the system, and other computer systems with which the target system has to communicate. This distribution is also carried out conventionally between the target system (and therefore is an algorithmic task) and the user (all other tasks) although it tends not to be called distribution and is often implicit. With KBS the objective is exactly the same but the additional power of computer systems when KBS are included must be taken into account. It is often found that tasks which would conventionally have been carried out by the user are now carried out either entirely by the system or by the user and the system working together. The precise nature of the technology to be used to implement any of the tasks is not relevant at this point, only the distribution between the proposed system and other agents.

Each bottom-level task should be carried out by one, and only one, agent. If a task needs the cooperation of more than one agent, then it should be decomposed until only one agent executes each sub-task.

The allocation of tasks between a computer system and a human user will depend on the level of expertise of the user. For example, if the system is to provide support for the expert, it will need to carry out a different distribution of tasks than one aimed at a relative novice who is using the system to actually make the decisions for him/her. It may therefore be necessary to construct several distributions where the system is to be used by multiple users under various circumstances. This makes the differences explicit and helps ensure that the system is designed and developed so that it is of use to all potential users. It is therefore essential that all agents are clearly identified. An example list of agents for a credit assessment application could be:

- credit rating system (target system);
- credit rating expert (domain expert);
- credit card application clerks (users);
- accounting system (system for interfacing).

Producing the Model of Cooperation

The Model of Cooperation specifies the cooperation between the agents that have been defined in the previous step. This defines who initiates processes, who is in control, when they are in control, and when control is transferred between the agents. In conventional systems this is often not a serious issue since the computer is in almost permanent control once a process has been triggered – the user has to do what the system wants. With the advent of event driven systems, the user has much more flexibility. The model of cooperation helps to define and document this additional type of interaction.

The model shows which agent is in control during the execution of each task, and the information that has to flow between the agents. To define this, three new terms are defined – Initiative, Ownership and Ingredient.

The *Initiative* defines which of the agents is responsible for starting a communication. For example, if the user initiates a process by clicking on an icon, then the user has the initiative.

The *Ownership* defines who owns whatever it is that is passed between the agents. For example if the system provides a list of accounts that are overdrawn from its database, the system owns that information.

The *Ingredient* is that which is passed between the agents. In the above example this would be the list of accounts.

Given that the flow of information (i.e. the flow of ingredients) can be in either direction between the agents participating in a conversation, and that either can have control, there are four possible combinations of initiative and ingredient. These are shown in Figure 6.5 and described below.

Receive. The system is provided with a piece of information from the user that the system did not ask for. For example, in an event driven system, the user clicks on an icon to tell the system to perform a particular action.

Obtain. The system requests information from the external agent. The system is therefore said to have the initiative since it is in control. A typical IT

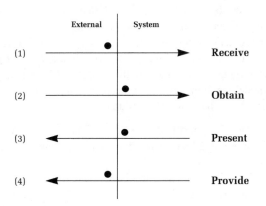

Figure 6.5
Conversation structure conventions.

example would be when a system prompts the user for a particular piece of information and the user is required to enter it before the system will proceed.

Present. The system presents of piece of information to the external agent. The system has determined what should be presented and when it is given. The system is said to have the initiative. A typical example occurs when the system presents the results of an operation to the user.

Provide. The system provides the external agent with some information at the request of the external agent. A typical example would be when a system displays a set of data requested by the user.

These four types of transfer are used explicitly in the task structures and are the only types of transfer tasks that are permitted in these definitions.

KADS distinguishes between three different types of ingredients – information, knowledge and skill. The information corresponds to that which is normally transferred between agents in a conventional system, such as simple data. The knowledge which may be transferred is that used for explanations and teaching. The system has therefore to be designed specifically with this type of transfer in mind if it is to be comprehensible to the user. The third type of ingredient – skill – refers to instructions which may be passed that tell the other agent how to perform a particular task. An example of the user helping a system might be when the system has reached an impasse and cannot continue with the problem solving process, in which case the user suggests ways in which the system may proceed. An example of the system helping the user is in the domain of Computer Assisted Learning. The system has recognised a problem with the way in which the user is working and so tries to take the user step-by-step through the correct problem solving process.

6.4 Design

The Design stage is less well defined than the Analysis. One possible way identified by KADS of removing the design process completely is to use the four layer model as a executable specification. Unfortunately this is a very long way from being practical and in the foreseeable future it will be necessary to carry out a design stage. As with conventional analysis, the intention of the design is to carry out a one-to-one mapping of the elements of the Conceptual Model on to the elements of some implementation language. One major problem with this at present is that there are no implementation tools powerful enough to cater for the elements in the conceptual model. Indeed most of the simple KBS shells available are totally incapable of modelling at the level of sophistication provided by KADS.

Design consists of three main parts which are carried out in sequence:

- Functional Design. The Requirements and the Conceptual Model are transformed into Functional Blocks. Standard AI paradigms guide this process.
- Behavioural Design. This describes how the Functional Blocks are realised. Appropriate AI methods are selected.

- Physical Design. The Physical Design addresses the physical structure in terms of the system's modules and interactions; it helps choose a representation, formalises issues of interaction with conventional systems, encapsulation and so on.

6.4.1 Functional Design

The main elements of Functional Design have corresponding approaches in conventional systems design. The two major parts are functional decomposition, and a definition of the dependencies between the functions. The functional decomposition is shown through the use of a consists-of hierarchy, which is the same as a standard functional decomposition diagram. The definition of dependencies has several elements – the dependency of functions on other functions, for example time relationships, and dependencies based on data or information. Again these are both represented in conventional analysis through techniques such as data flow diagrams.

KADS also bring architectural issues into the Functional Design in a way that is not seen in conventional systems development. One of the guiding rules of early KBS development was that the inference mechanisms, usually simply forward and backward chaining built into simple expert systems shells, should be separated from the domain knowledge, which was usually coded in the form of rules. The two should not be mixed. For simple KBS this was not a problem since the inferencing was built into the shell and therefore not coded by the user. However, it did not require a particularly complex system for the developer to have to start entering control rules into the knowledge base. At this point the separation of the inferencing and control mechanisms becomes very important. By employing a sophisticated structure in the knowledge base it is possible to separate out all four layers of the model of expertise. This requires not only an understanding of the functions of the system being built from the users' point of view, but also an understanding of what role each function plays in the model of expertise. This approach reduces the differences between the logical definition of the knowledge in the model of expertise and the physical implementation of the expertise.

6.4.2 Behavioural Design

The Behavioural Model does not have a corresponding set of tasks in conventional systems development. Its purpose is to define how each of the functions (defined in the Functional design) are to be implemented in terms of AI methods, including approaches such as Hierarchical classification, the A* algorithm, and the Production system. This immediately assumes that all of the functional blocks defined in the previous step are knowledge based. Although not explicitly stated by KADS, the only functions which it is relevant to pass into the Behavioural Design are those which are to be implemented using KBS/AI approaches; the other functions are presumably split off, designed and implemented separately. KADS also assumes that the functional decomposition can be continued to a point where each bottom-level function can be tackled by the application of some AI/KBS method. Each method requires a set of corresponding design elements and some of these have been defined in KADS. A table giving two of these methods together with the corresponding design element is shown in Table 6.3.

Table 6.3 Methods and design elements

Method	Design element
A* algorithm	Search procedure
	State operators
	Heuristic estimates
	State description
	Start state
	Goal state
Production system	Rule interpreter
	Production rules

Source: Adapted from Hesketh and Barrett (1990).

The selection of appropriate methods is straightforward in many cases. This is particularly the case in commercial organisations where there is often only experience of rule-based systems. In this case the choice is the Production system (another name for rules) simply because there is no experience of anything else. However, KADS does provide support for the selection of alternative methods which are more common in AI than in KBS and these are relevant where there is a problem which is not amenable to the more usual rule-based approach. For example, many configuration or scheduling tasks can be carried out more effectively using techniques found more often in AI than in KBS.

A second major element of Behavioural Design is the consideration to be given to the user interface. The analysis stage has already defined four types of transfer tasks where information is passed between the system and an external agent. Where the interaction is between the system and a user, these specify the information that flows between the two and which has the initiative. This helps in the definition of the user interface but KADS does not go significantly further than this in offering interface design support.

6.4.3 Physical Design

The Physical Design is also known as the Structural Viewpoint since it represents the mapping of the logical design produced in the two previous steps on to the structure of the selected tool. Tables similar to Table 6.3 can be drawn up to represent the methods and design elements that can be found in the tools to be examined. For example, Table 6.4 shows Prolog.

Table 6.4 Prolog design elements

Method	Design elements
Depth-first backward chaining	Rule interpreter
	Single world database
	Horn clause logic
	Database procedures

Source: Adapted from Hesketh and Barrett (1990).

One of the problems of design is that the methods and design elements provided by a development tool will almost certainly not correspond directly to the methods and design elements that have been identified as part of the Behavioural Design. If this occurs it is necessary to start compromising the logical design to complete the physical design. This becomes even more of a problem in commercial development since it often happens that an organisation has a very small set of recommended tools (possibly even just one) and that the system has to be built with this tool. This forces a greater divergence from the logical design than does the selection of languages for conventional systems.

The major principles of Physical Design defined by KADS are:

- Prevention of redundancy and inconsistency. This corresponds to similar design principles in database design where the use of data normalisation and a fully relational DBMS usually solve these problems. The same principles apply to KBS but there is not yet any KBS equivalent of normalisation.
- Uniformity in Reasoning and Representation. This principle simply tries to ensure that the minimum number of methods are used within the system.
- Modular knowledge base. This is simply a restatement of the principle that modularity reduces problems.

Although these principles are excellent in their presentation, KADS does not offer any significant help by defining how these can actually be achieved.

6.5 KADS and small systems development

6.5.1 Scalability

One of the major difficulties for the practical application of KADS on commercial projects is its complexity. While many of the individual ideas are excellent, potential users are often overwhelmed by the volume of the deliverables and their non-commercial language. Some books have been produced which provide a single source for most of the KADS-I material which are significantly more readable than the original documents, although these inevitably omit the more detailed aspects of the deliverables which could prove useful. A second major problem with KADS, once the developers have understood it, is the complexity of the individual models which KADS users are to produce. Like many commercial methods, KADS defines the models to a level of detail which may be appropriate for large complex projects, but creation of all of the detailed documents would place an intolerable burden on the developers of small systems. KADS appears not to be easily scalable.

The main principle of scaling methods is that the project manager should cause the developer to produce only those deliverables essential to the project, rather than all those defined by the method. This immediately also means that only those tasks that produce the required deliverables are carried out. These principles can be applied to a KADS method to reduce the number and detail of the documents produced. It is important to realise that a deliverable or document can be validly represented by a single sentence or paragraph in a larger report; it does not have to be a separate document. Removing the overhead of multiple reports immediately reduces the documentation time significantly. The early stage of feasibility can be reduced substantially in this way until it can be realistically carried out in a matter of days. Once the analysis phase starts, the developer comes up against the weight of the many detailed KADS analysis models.

6.5.2 *Building the knowledge model*

The Knowledge Model is central to the development of any KBS and this remains true for any system regardless of size.

Domain Layer. This is built up through the normal process of knowledge elicitation, typically using interviewing and through reference to appropriate documentation. It is often not necessary to use the more formal approach to modelling domain knowledge such as the Domain Description Language. Simpler techniques can be used. These are often graphical, such as classification hierarchies, composition hierarchies and semantic nets, backed up by English definitions of the items of significance in the domain.

Inference Layer. The Interpretation Model will often be built in parallel with the Domain Layer, each providing support for the development of the other. It is very important that the temptation is avoided to allow the Interpretation Model to evolve from a small simple diagram into a complex breakdown of all the tasks that are carried out and all of the information and expertise that is required. An Interpretation Model is not a data flow diagram. If the model does not fit on to one side of A4 then it is too detailed.

Task Layer. The Task Layer is essential to provide documentary backup for the use of the interpretation model that has been developed. Small systems will generally only operate in one mode, for example they will just be decision support for one type of user, thus requiring only one format of user interface, one type of explanation (if required at all), and so on. Where the system will be used by a number of different types of users, possibly in different modes, then the system will probably require more substantial analysis. For simple systems, a straightforward definition of the task structure, using all of the standard KADS

components - task name, goal, input and output, control terms, task structure –
can be developed for each task. This will usually be built in parallel with the
Model of Cooperation.

Strategy Layer. It is very unlikely that there will be a strategy layer. If this is
required then the problem being tackled is substantial and should be subjected to
a more rigorous and detailed use of KADS.

6.5.3 *Modality Analysis*

The task decomposition and identification of interdependencies are carried out
much as for conventional systems. Standard diagramming techniques such as
decomposition hierarchies and dependency diagrams can be used.

The third major element, the production of the Model of Cooperation itself,
should be considered but need not be actually developed. In simple systems, the
interface between the system and any external agents is likely to be
straightforward. In many cases it will be a question and answer session; in
embedded systems it may simply be the passing of parameters into and out of the
KBS. Under these circumstances, it can often be enough just to note the approach
to the interaction without going into any detail about the precise structure.

6.6 KADS-II

KADS-II provides a much more coherent attempt at the development of a KBS
method than does KADS-I. The two major features of KADS-II are:

- It addresses the major issues of project management through its definition of
  an approach that is risk driven and based on the spiral model of Boehm.
  Greater support is also provided for the project manager through the
  definition of a life cycle model.
- The definition of models is both more coherent and more comprehensive. It
  takes greater account of the environment, considers issues very similar to
  Business Process Reengineering although not by name, and defines ways in
  which model states can be defined. The way in which the models are related
  is also well defined.

The consortium is considerably larger than that for KADS-I and consisted of:

- Cap Gemini Innovation, France
- Cap Programator, Sweden
- Netherlands Energy Research Foundation ECN, Netherlands
- Eritel SA, Spain
- IBM France, France
- Lloyd's Register, UK
- Swedish Institute of Computer Science, Sweden
- Siemens AG, Germany
- Touche Ross Management Consultants, UK
- University of Amsterdam, Netherlands

- Free University of Brussels, Belgium

The description of KADS-II which follows is necessarily tentative and relatively sketchy. KADS-II has not yet achieved stability and there is as yet no single definition for the method. However, the sections which follow give some flavour of the way in which KADS-II is moving.

6.6.1 Life cycle

As in KADS-I, KADS-II takes the view that a fully specified design should be developed before the system is actually implemented. Although KADS-II does not forbid prototyping, it is seen as an activity which helps to reduce the risk of a project rather than as a development approach.

KADS-II makes use of a spiral model based on Boehm's original model which was described in Chapter 2. The KADS-II model has renamed the quadrants to Review, Risk, Plan and Monitor Development. This is shown in Figure 6.6.

The purpose of the spiral model is to provide a project management activity cycle which sits above the development of the models. The same sequence of tasks are used as are defined for GEMINI and this is described further in the next chapter. The main reason for this is that the consortium that developed GEMINI had a number of members who were also working on the KADS-II consortium. It is a sound, high level approach to defining the project management tasks and so has been adopted by both methods. However, considerably more work has gone into enhancing the KADS version of the spiral model and it now consists of a total

Figure 6.6
KADS spiral model.
Source: Adapted from
Porter (1992)

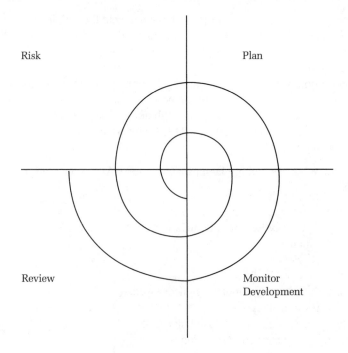

Risk

Plan

Review

Monitor
Development

of 14 segments rather than the original four. These enhance the level of detail that can be provided by the model and effectively provide sub-tasks within each of the top level quadrants. Although this increases the level of detail, it does tend to obscure the essentially simple but powerful ideas embodied in the spiral model.

6.6.2 KADS-II model set

Model development in KADS-II is not carried out in a fixed sequence but allows the project manager to configure the ordering of the models and gives the opportunity to develop two or more models in parallel. One consequence of this is that each model in the model set may be in a different state of development. Consequently, CommonKADS introduces the notion of 'Model States'. Three states are identified as being important:

> State 1: The first partially complete state is reached when the basic task decomposition and task descriptions are complete and the data input, output and transfers are defined.
> State 2: Initiative labour assignments have been described and agent interfaces are complete.
> State 3: Initiatives have been described for all agent interactions. This includes a definition of the cooperation that is required.

Two states not defined by KADS-II but considered to be implicit can be thought of as:

> State 0: No work has been done on the model.
> State 4: Model is complete.

The model set consists of six models, a slight reduction on the original set of KADS-I. These are the Organisational Model, Task Model, Agent Model, Expertise Model, Communication Model, and Design Model. Each of these is described below.

Organisational Model

The purpose of the Organisational Model is to support the identification of possible areas for KBS, facilitate assessment of the impact of a KBS, and provide information for use in other models. The model consists of two main parts – a definition of the organisational problems, of which part is a portfolio of possible KBS applications, and a set of organisational descriptions. These describe the organisation from five points of view:

- *Functional Constituent*. This is a breakdown by function of the organisation. This is carried out by defining the functions that the organisation actually does, not by the way in which the functions are split across departments. In effect this takes a Business Process Reengineering view of the functions.

- *Structural Constituent.* This represents the actual breakdown of the organisation into departments thus reflecting the way that the organisation is currently constituted.
- *Process Constituent.* The process constituent defines the process flows between elements of the organisation.
- *Power/Authority Constituent.* The definition of the structure of the power and authority hierarchies are placed in this model. This highlights the decision making process by making the hierarchies explicit.
- *Resource Constituent.* The final component simply defines the resources that are available within the organisation.

Much of the Organisational Model can therefore be mapped easily on to the high level business modelling which is already recommended as a starting point for IT strategy planning.

Task Model

The Task Model is confined to a definition of the tasks carried out in the area currently under scrutiny for the construction of a KBS and is therefore a subset of the tasks for the domain as a whole. The relationships between tasks are defined as are the data that are used. The major elements that are defined in the task model are:

- input;
- output;
- goals;
- environmental constraints;
- control;
- features;
- capabilities;
- ingredients.

Much that is in the KADS-II Task model was originally found in the KADS-I Model of Cooperation.

Agent Model

This is completely model. In this model, all of the agents identified are described in some detail. In KADS-I, although agents were identified, they were not defined formally as part of a model. Major elements of this model are the constraints under which agents have to act, such as who takes what decision; the abilities of each agent, for example definition of the competence of the human users and information about other computer systems and databases; identification of which agent is permitted to carry out which set of tasks; and so on.

Expertise Model

The Expertise Model corresponds largely to the Expertise model found in KADS-I although there are a number of significant changes to the four layer model of expertise. The principal area of change is that the four layer model has been split and is now a pair of models. The Strategy layer has been removed and the resulting three layers represent the 'Application knowledge'. The Strategy layer becomes Problem solving knowledge and is represented by Problem solving methods and Strategic knowledge.

One cosmetic but useful (although at times confusing) change applies to the two primitives found on inference structures. The *knowledge source* is now known as an *inference function*, and the *meta-class* has been renamed the *knowledge role*. Both changes are a significant improvement on the names used in KADS-I as they now mean more without extensive definitions.

The strategy layer is now seen as providing knowledge about tasks, inferences and the domain so in a way can be considered orthogonal to the new three layer structure. The strategy layer is, however, still not very well defined.

Communication Model

The Communication Model focuses on the communication required between agents carrying out the tasks and is an extension of the communications aspects of the Model of Cooperation. In addition to the ingredients, which are unchanged from KADS-I, four further components as defined:

- *Transaction*. This is a collection of the ingredients that flow between the agents, effectively the KADS-II version of data flow in conventional systems.
- *Information item*. This is formally defined as 'the specification in an admissible vocabulary and syntax of the ingredient(s)'. In conventional terms this is the data definition.
- *Capabilities*. The capabilities describe the knowledge and skills that are needed for the agents to partake in the transaction. This is not explicitly part of conventional analysis and can be an area when inadequate recognition of the skills of human agents can cause problems with implementing a new system.
- *Transaction plan*. This plan defines the context in which the individual transfers take place and puts an overall plan on to the transfers. This bears more than a passing resemblance to standard Transaction Analysis in conventional development.

Design Model

The Design Model encompasses both the logical and the physical design of the system. It is split into three major parts – the Application Design, the Architecture Design and the Platform Design.

The *Application Design* results from the decomposition of the domain into its components and remains in the sphere of Logical Design. KADS acknowledges that there are a number of different ways in which this can be carried out including functional, data-oriented and object-oriented. No specific support is given on which should be used and when. The Application Design also covers the specification of the individual programs within the system, typically using a Program Definition Language (PDL) or pseudo-code/pseudo-English.

The *Architecture Design* starts the move towards the Physical Design of the system although it is possible to complete this aspect keeping the design largely logical. It covers the definition of the interaction between the system and the agents, for example the way in which the user interface is configured (but still not specifying the details of the hardware implementation), and the computational approaches and representation techniques to be used for the knowledge.

Platform Design is the last part of the Design Mode. It requires a definition of the target environment so that the mapping of the logical design on to the physical aspects of the selected hardware and software can be carried out in detail.

Relatively little support is provided for these aspects. KADS-II still concentrates largely on the analysis and early parts of design.

6.7 Summary and conclusions

KADS is continuing to evolve, both through its further development in KADS-II, and through the use of many of the main KADS-I ideas within industry and commerce. The development of KBS has not yet become a sufficiently commonplace activity for any method to be taken up widely so there has not been a very high level of feedback about the practicality of any particular approach. KADS-I has delivered its results in a comprehensive set of deliverables. These are often, though by no means exclusively, academic in nature and so very off-putting to many in commercial development. The appearance of further texts giving details of the approaches is bound to increase the takeup of ideas, if not the whole approach, within IT departments. The availability of training on KADS in the UK also means that potential users have several different sources of training.

Many of the ideas seen as valuable contributions to KBS development, such as the knowledge and cooperation modelling, have been taken up by other methods. The principal approach that makes use of many of the KADS ideas and that is available from bookshops is GEMINI; this method is covered in detail in the next chapter. Other methods that have used parts of KADS include KBM (discussed in Chapter 4) and STAGES (see Chapter 3). There are also a number of commercial versions of KADS available as identified at the end of Chapter 5. Many in-house approaches also make use of the results of KADS-I.

All this indicates that while some of KADS has been taken up, it is relatively unusual for the whole method to be accepted. This is partly because of the fragmentary nature of the documentation for KADS-I. One of the objectives of KADS-II is to produce a document, called CommonKADS, which defines the core components of a KADS method. This will then ensure that there really is something identifiable as 'the KADS method'.

It is intended that CommonKADS will be widely available with most, if not all, of the deliverables from the project available. Commercial reasons have meant that there have been moves to restrict the availability of KADS material since the collaborators are partially funding the project and so want to see some sort of return on their investment. While this is quite understandable, it would be unfortunate if the most useful deliverables were only available through consultancy from the consortium members since this will inevitably reduce the commercial takeup of CommonKADS.

It is interesting to note that many of the additions in KADS-II have direct counterparts in conventional IT. Typical examples include many of the aspects of the Communications model such as the Transaction, Information Item and Transaction Plan. It is difficult not to read the definitions of these and wonder if aspects of the wheel are being reinvented, although the similarities do mean that it will be easier to integrate KADS with conventional IT.

In summary, KADS-I produced useful ideas but as a method it has needed considerable work on it to make it commercially viable. KADS-II, or CommonKADS, has the promise of significant improvements over KADS-I and could produce a good method definition which is more widely taken up. However, this relies on the creation of comprehensive, comprehensible documentation.

Table 6.5 lists the criteria given in Chapter 2 to support the assessment of methods and rates KADS against them.

Table 6.5 KADS assessment criteria

Criterion	KADS
Type of life cycle	Waterfall and Spiral
Availability	Freely available
Depth of knowledge analysis	Very deep
Scope of method	Analysis and design
Project Management	Poor in KADS-I, better in KADS-II
Links	None
Perspectives:	
Data	Poor
Process	Poor
Behaviour	Very strong
Knowledge	Very strong

7 GEMINI

GEMINI is the KBS guidance developed under the auspices of the CCTA (responsible for, among other things, IT methods for all government bodies) and forms part of their Information Technology Infrastructure Library (ITIL). SSADM, the most widely used conventional development method, is also part of the ITIL. This chapter looks at the background to the development of GEMINI, its contents, and the ways in which it is related to other methods. GEMINI differs from most KBS methods by providing a very solid basis for project control and management while supplying few of the low level technical details found in most of the methods already considered. It is the only comprehensive method that is in the public domain.

7.1 Introduction

7.1.1 Development of GEMINI

The project to develop GEMINI had its roots in a recognition during 1987 by the Advanced Technologies group at the CCTA that there was a need for a standard approach to the development of KBS. This was further emphasised at the first KB in Government conference held in November 1987. The development of such a method was planned to complement the guides that already existed for more conventional systems development, such as SSADM (the method for conventional systems development) and PRINCE (a project management method). By mid-1988, a project had been initiated by the CCTA to develop an outline method for KBS. This was being produced by a consortium of organisations which included Ernst & Whinney, ICL, Logica Cambridge, SD-Scicon and Touche Ross. The initial development work resulted in a slim document which was the Outline Method Definition. This was reviewed with a number of major organisations and a plan for the main development phase of the project was created. During this period, the CCTA reviewed the options for a KBS method development and carried out a detailed market assessment of the commercial requirements for a method. This included an extensive survey of the use of KBS within the top 300 UK organisations.

The initial phase was followed by the main development of GEMINI. This was put out to tender and won by a consortium consisting of BIS (now ACT),

Ernst & Young, Logica, SD-Scicon and Touche Ross. The overall project management was carried out by Ernst & Young and the technical management by Touche Ross. The main technical development by the consortium occured in the first few months of 1990. This took the Outline Method Definition and expanded it considerably, adding much detail and updating the contents. The main philosophy behind the development, as with the initial definition, was to integrate existing ideas rather than develop new ideas. The main sources of material for this were the methods that had been developed by the consortium members themselves, their experience in KBS development, published work on KBS, and software development in general. This was supplemented by significant work from the KADS-I project (described in Chapter 6). The project was not long, about 200 person-days in total, and delivered a handbook to the CCTA which was to provide the majority of the material for the final published GEMINI volumes. Although the whole of this work was funded by the CCTA, most of the technical detail was supplied by the consortium.

Once the document had been delivered in mid-1990, it went into an extensive review cycle. During this period the CCTA initiated a number of field trials for GEMINI. The experiences were fed back to the CCTA and the method definition was updated with some assistance from members of the consortium and a Project Managers' Handbook was developed. This was followed by further in-house work by the CCTA during which the method was made to conform more closely to PRINCE. It was also split into three volumes – *Controlling KBS Development Projects*, *Managing KBS Development Projects*, and *Technical Reference*. A number of additional projects were also run including a definition of the links to SSADM and the definition of a project to develop an intermediate representation.

During this review period, attempts were made to obtain further funding from industry to develop the handbook into a method definition to the same level of detail as, for example, SSADM. Unfortunately the economic climate meant that very few organisations were willing (or able) to raise sufficient funding to make the further development of GEMINI possible. Consequently the definition of the existing material was changed from a 'method' to a 'guidance'. The intention was that the guidance would provide significant support for KBS projects but would not provide the technical detail of the modelling itself.

The final output of the project was a set of three manuals for KBS projects. These supply a framework without providing the technical detail that is usually expected from a method. A major benefit with the relatively open definition of GEMINI is that it is easier to integrate into existing conventional approaches than it would be if it were a detailed method. The integration of the guidance into existing IT environments is one of the issues examined later in this chapter.

While GEMINI is primarily aimed at a government audience, it is expected that it will be taken up by industry in the same way as SSADM. If this is the case then the guidance should become the most popular of KBS development approaches. An essential element of this is the integration of GEMINI with existing methods so that it can be used by commercial organisations alongside, or fully integrated with, their current conventional method, and it is not always clear within the guidance how this can be achieved. Ways in which the integration can be achieved are considered with each part of the discussion on the guidance.

Another theme running through the chapter is to outline the areas in which GEMINI is deficient in terms of a comprehensive development method. It is only intended as a guidance rather than a method and so is severely lacking in some areas, most notably in the absence of detailed descriptions of techniques. Guidance is given on how the definition can be 'fleshed out' to provide a more comprehensive method.

7.1.2 *Consortium approach*

It was decided very early in the life of GEMINI that a consortium approach would be taken. This was mainly to ensure a wide spread of views and practical experience on the development of KBS. A consortium approach has these advantages but it also brings the major problem of compatibility and consistency with anything produced by individual members. This is one of the reasons that the release of GEMINI was delayed for so long beyond its initial consortium development in the first half of 1990. A consequent problem caused by the delay is that the area of KBS development has moved on since 1990 and although the basic material is still very relevant, it is not as up-to-date as it could be.

7.1.3 *Scope*

GEMINI places particular emphasis on the project management and control aspects – two of the three volumes are devoted to these issues. It also covers the quality aspects of KBS, provides a framework for them and discusses legal issues. In terms of the scope of the technical aspects it covers the phases from feasibility through to logical design as does SSADM. It provides definitions of the tasks which make up the phases, outlines the products and gives a list of the techniques and very brief definitions of some of them but without going into any detail. It outlines a knowledge model but does not define this in any depth.

7.1.4 *Product-driven*

A major difference between GEMINI and some of the other methods is that it takes a product-driven approach unlike most conventional development methods which tend to be task-driven. This means that the key objective of a GEMINI project is to create a specific set of products rather than carry out a set of tasks. One consequence is that the guidance defines a set of products in some detail but does not describe how they should be produced to any depth. It also means that the life cycle is slightly different since it must cope with this approach.

7.1.5 *Organisation of GEMINI*

The three primary functions identified by the guidance are controlling the project, managing it, and the development itself. These are the three volumes into which it is split, each targeted at a different audience. One consequence of this division is that some material is repeated in all three volumes. This is primarily a discussion on how the guidance is intended to be used and the way in which GEMINI projects are organised. The contents of the first two volumes, controlling and managing KBS projects, shows the most overlap and so these two are described together in the next section. The technical issues, described in the third handbook, are described separately in Section 7.3.

7.2 GEMINI to control and manage projects

7.2.1 Introduction

The Control and Manage volumes cover very similar ground, the main topics discussed being the organisation of the project, the way in which GEMINI projects are managed, the issues involved in the assessment of risk and the management of that risk, and the integration of GEMINI projects with other methods. This overlap means that the main ideas in the two volumes can be introduced and described together and this is done in this section.

The Control volume is aimed at the individuals responsible for controlling development within the part of the organisation that is commissioning the system. These people will probably have responsibility for a number of different projects at once and so, although needing a general understanding of how KBS projects are run, a detailed understanding is not necessary. Their knowledge needs to be appropriate both for projects run from within their own organisation and for those commissioned from external suppliers.

The management process is covered in the Manage volume. This discusses the major aspects of project management both for the project managers who have responsibility for supplying KBS developments for their own organisation and for those managers provided by an external organisation. The spiral model of project management is described in greater detail and the way in which this can be applied to conventional projects as well as KBS projects is outlined. The issues of quality and risk management introduced in the Control volume are discussed in the context of project management. The management deliverables a GEMINI project has to produce are described.

7.2.2 Project structure

The structure of a GEMINI project is very similar to most IT developments and is shown in outline in Figure 7.1.

The project structure is divided into two main components – the demand side and the supply side. The demand side contains those who are controlling the acquisition of the new system and are therefore (usually) employed by the company installing the system. The hub of this structure is the Project Controller; the role of this person is key to the success of a GEMINI project. The domain team contains not only the users, as is usually the case for conventional systems,

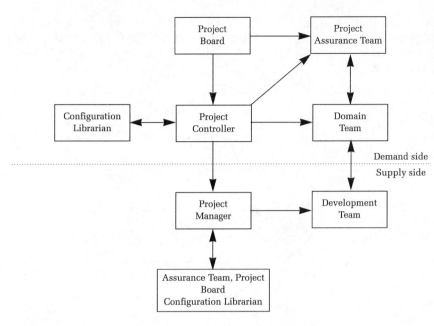

Figure 7.1
Project structure.
Source: Adapted from
Scarff and Fynn (1993a)

but also the expert. The difference between these two roles, even though they may be the same person, is critical to the development of KBS, and GEMINI makes a clear distinction between them. The Control and Manage volumes are addressed primarily to the demand side and the project manager on the supply side.

The second half of the project consists of the supply side – the individuals whose job it is to develop the system. This team may be resourced from the same organisation as the demand side, although usually from the IT department, but may be represented by an external organisation such as a software house. Good communication between the two sides is essential. The Technical volume is addressed mainly to the project team on the supply side.

7.2.3 *The spiral model*

The spiral model is key to understanding and using the whole of the guidance. It is based on the spiral model of Boehm (described in Chapter 2) and the GEMINI variant is shown in Figure 7.2.

The four quadrants identified in this version are Review, Risk Assessment, Planning and Development. All projects start in the Review quadrant with a review of the work that has been done to date. On a systems development project the main input will usually be a Project Initiation Document (PID) which has already been developed. Once the review has been completed and the document/work accepted, the project moves forward into the Risk quadrant. At this point, all the risks associated with the project are identified and assessed. These include the risks of continuing with the project and those associated with revising or abandoning the work. A decision is made on the next course of action.

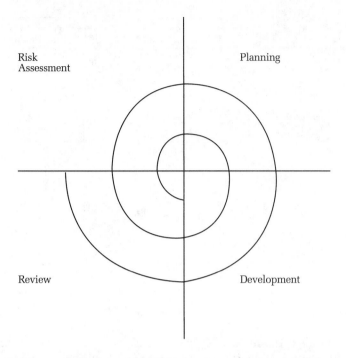

Figure 7.2
GEMINI spiral model.
Source: Adapted from
Scarff and Fynn (1993a)

Risk
Assessment

Planning

Review

Development

Assuming that the project is not abandoned, it moves forward into the Planning quadrant where the detailed planning for the next step is carried out. It is important that appropriate actions are identified to control the risks that emerged in the preceding quadrant so they can be minimised by appropriate planning. Once this has been completed, the project moves forward to the Development quadrant where the plan is executed. On completion, the project moves into the Review quadrant where the work carried out is assessed. The project continues around this spiral, gradually becoming more complete as time passes.

An important feature of the spiral model is that it is impossible to go backwards. The axes represent cumulative attributes such as cost and time and it not possible to reverse these (unfortunately), although it should be noted that the spiral is not to scale and does not imply that an equal amount of time is spent in each of the four quadrants. It is likely that the vast majority of time will be spent in Development.

If a review is carried out which finds that work has not been completed adequately then a sub-spiral is 'spun off' to deal with this. The main spiral, which has identified the problem, is effectively suspended temporarily (although if the axes are being interpreted strictly it could be said that the project continues to proceed around the Review quadrant of the spiral but at a much reduced speed) and the sub-spiral manages the reworking. As with the main spiral it starts by reviewing the work that needs to be carried out, an assessment of the risks involved, planning the work, its execution and then review. Once this has been completed successfully, with several circuits if necessary, the sub-spiral is terminated and control returns to the main spiral.

The spiral model is very easy to map on to the more conventional life cycle with each circuit corresponding to one phase of the project. Sub-spirals simply correspond to sub-parts of that phase, for example its division into activities.

The spiral model also has the benefit that it can be used to control parallel developments very simply. The main project spiral controlling the project as a whole, remains in place and 'spins off' two or more spirals during the development quadrant which are executed in parallel. The immediately preceding quadrants of review, risk and plan, prepare the ground for the parallel activities. The sub-spirals manage their own activities and the convergence of the completed (and therefore individually reviewed) sub-spirals is checked by the review quadrant of the main project spiral.

7.2.4 *Quality and GEMINI*

Quality is an aspect common to all production processes and the guidance is no exception. It assumes that a basic quality process is already in existence and provides support for the issues specific to GEMINI (and therefore KBS). It does not define the ways a quality function can be set up although it can be used as a basis for doing so if it does not already exist.

Problems which GEMINI identifies as being specific to KBS include:

- controlling parallel development;
- checking output produced iteratively and partially complete products;
- uncertainty about knowledge capture, applicability and use.

Controlling parallel development is not easy. However, the spiral model makes it easier as already outlined. Parallel development is most likely to occur when a system consists of both KBS and conventional components and each can be developed separately but simultaneously. The parallel development of aspects of a system is not usually part of conventional systems development and so requires additional control and quality aspects. At a high level this is provided by the spiral model.

Checking output produced iteratively and the existence of partially complete products are very closely related. Iterative development will result in partially complete products throughout the phases until the point when they are finally completed. Since GEMINI permits the iterative development of products, and as products are complete sets of information defined by common objectives rather than aligned to phases, it is inevitable that partially complete products will have to be reviewed. Prototyping and use of the spiral model also mean that products are generated iteratively and have to be checked for quality during their construction.

The difficulties of the uncertainty about knowledge capture, its applicability and use are very closely tied to the general problems of KBS development. Knowledge is inherently uncertain; its capture and use are therefore more difficult than for data which are usually fixed. This means that the quality assurance has to be carried out knowing that the items being checked will inevitably be incomplete and have an element of uncertainty in them.

Approach to quality

The Project Controller is the interface between the Project Board and the Project Manager and is a key person in the assurance of quality. The Project Controller is responsible for providing direction to the project and ensuring that control activities are being carried out appropriately. He or she needs to be aware of the risks to quality and GEMINI provides a set of checklists for this. The Project Assurance Team is responsible for ensuring that the quality process actually takes place. It is independent of the development team and the Project Controller for the project. The scope of the quality objectives must be defined at an early stage in the project life cycle. In general, the person responsible for a cycle of a spiral is responsible for the quality of all products and activities. That person is responsible for delegating responsibility to sub-spirals as appropriate and reporting to higher spirals.

When planning for quality, three main documents are involved – the Quality Assurance Statement, the Quality Plan, and the Product Definitions. The Quality Assurance Statement documents the quality approach for a project. It is developed principally by the Project Controller and is defined and documented at project initiation. The Quality Plan defines how the quality will be ensured through reviews and includes quality statements in Product Definitions. It provides details of the quality system and quality archivist role. In addition to the normal contents of a Quality Plan, GEMINI also includes definitions of issues such as:

- the standards and procedures to be used;
- life cycle configuration;
- deliverables and products and how they will be developed in terms of the life cycle;
- use of the spiral model - the entrances and exits to each spiral should be explicit;
- policy details for reviews at all stages;
- methods for design and development.

A major element of the Quality Plan is ensuring that each product definition contains statements about how that product should be assessed for quality. The Quality Strategy defines how the Project Controller will approach the quality process – the reviews that he will attend, the monitoring process for documents and activities.

The quality process itself is driven by the spiral model. The inspections take place largely during the Review phase of the spiral and check that the products generated by the previous Development quadrant are acceptable. If a review fails, a sub-spiral will be spun off which assesses the risk of continuing or not continuing, plans the reworking, carries it out and finally reviews the updated product. The review is carried out by a team including someone who is independent of the project to give an unbiased view. The process is often more difficult than conventionally because of the iterative nature of the development and it is often necessary to review or verify partially complete products. Final testing is usually carried out through user trials which may last some time.

Configuration management

A major aspect of the quality process in GEMINI is configuration management. This is again because of the inherent configurability of GEMINI and the iterations introduced by use of the spiral model. The major aspects of configuration management are the following:

- Identification and definition of items. The project should define all items forming intermediate or final products and then cross-reference to the activities which create and use the items.
- Version control. It is quite possible that the same product can be used on different concurrent spirals during the Development quadrant and so tight control is essential. Iterative development may mean that there can be several equally valid versions of one item at the same time – for example versions of a user interface. It also means that it may be necessary to go back one or more steps if a blind alley is entered, thus it is essential to know which version is the most appropriate to which to return.
- Traceability. Multiple versions and the origin of each must be traceable – particularly knowledge in an environment which could have legal implications.

7.2.5 Risk management

GEMINI looks at the issues of risk which are particular to KBS, identifies the main sources of risk, and discusses how the risks can be managed. In so doing it also provides a risk management method that can be used on any project. Risk assessment occurs mainly in the Risk quadrant of the spiral model.

Typical risks associated with all software projects include:

- not meeting a business need and so not providing the expected business benefit;
- failure to assess the technical and organisational feasibility adequately;
- not meeting time and budget constraints.

There are, however, many risks that are particularly important for the control of KBS. These include:

- Less well defined specifications because the knowledge acquisition process is less well understood and it is difficult to elicit all the relevant information from the expert. It is possible that the expert may be uncooperative or, more likely, that they will be unable to verbalise their expertise adequately. The requirements for KBS are also often less well defined.
- The uncertainty that tends to be inherent in all knowledge. The knowledge may not be fixed and accurate. There is also the explicit use of uncertainty to consider.
- The tendency for KBS to be developed using an iterative development process, so making it more difficult to manage, estimate and control. There are also far fewer metrics available for this type of development than for conventional systems.

- Decreased familiarity of the technology to the systems developers when compared with conventional development. This means that selecting the right applications and following through the development process is much more prone to risk.
- Organisational issues can present similar problems to conventional systems in that KBS can be seen, often wrongly, as taking away and/or deskilling jobs. There can be some resistance to this although if presented properly the deployment of KBS can be accepted enthusiastically. It is also essential that someone in the organisation is prepared to take responsibility for decisions, particularly where there are professional or legal implications.

Risk management process

GEMINI identifies four main stages to the resolution of risks – identification, quantification, resolution, and impact. The identification stage requires the risk to be, not surprisingly, identified. This is often very difficult and is based largely on experience. However, GEMINI offers support through the extensive set of potential risks that it lists. Once identified, the risk needs to be quantified. The two aspects to this are an assessment of risk probability (the likelihood of the risk occurring) and the risk severity (the impact that the risk would have on the project if it actually occurred). Both are essential since it is not uncommon to find a low probability risk which is so catastrophic that it kills the project instantly. Such risks need to be identified. Similarly risks which have a small impact but are very likely to happen also need to be planned for and managed. An outline plan for the way in which the risk can be managed is drawn up. Once this has been completed, the impact of the plan on the project is considered. It may be that the project plan has to be changed significantly to cater for potential risks and that this changes the overall timescales and budgets significantly. In this case a decision has to be taken as to whether the risk management procedures planned are too draconian and can be reduced, or whether the project is genuinely too risky to continue with.

7.2.6 Legal issues

Legal issues are not often covered in methods; however, with the world becoming increasingly litigious, legal issues are becoming more important. GEMINI covers a wide range of legal issues, not just the contractual issues of delivering what has been requested, but also potential legal risks in the KBS development itself. The legal aspects can be put into four main categories – Constraints, Obligations, Ownership rights and Liabilities.

Constraints limit what you can do. The most obvious example is the limitations imposed on activities by UK law. Perhaps less obvious are the restrictions which appear because of European law and GATT agreements. A typical example of a UK restriction is the Data Protection Act which limits the type of data that may be held about an individual. An example where GATT agreements may be relevant is a KBS designed to assist in the freighting of goods around the world.

An agreement assumes *obligations* – for example the provision of services, goods, payments and so on, and also the avoidance of damage, etc., as a result of executing the agreement. These are all on the supply side. Obligations are also placed on the demand side, for example to provide the services of an expert at the level required to build a KBS. This becomes particularly important when the KBS is being built by an external supplier such as a software house or consultancy.

Ownership rights of topics such as Intellectual Property Rights, copyright, trademarks, confidentiality, etc. It is essential that the rights to the knowledge being captured are clearly defined as belonging to the demand side. It may be appropriate to insert a clause into the contract stating that this is the responsibility of the demand side.

Liabilities exist for the breach of formal regulations, damages for acts or omissions (leading to failure and loss), and compensation for breach of agreements. A liability may arise where professional advice causes economic loss. A good example of this is the provision of advice about investments or pensions: if advice is given by a person and is wrong there are professional bodies with whom the matter can be raised. If the advice is given by a KBS the liabilities are the same but the recourse for the injured party is much less clear.

GEMINI does not provide specific guidance on how each of these legal issues can be tackled but simply proposes that well drawn contracts are a very important way of setting out rights, obligations, and limits of liability. In particular GEMINI recommends that getting proper legal advice early on in a project can save a lot of time and money if things do go wrong. Legal issues could also have a significant impact on the cost/benefit analysis of a system, not only because of the cost and time implications of getting legal advice, but also in the management of the risks identified by this process. It is also important to ensure that all documentation is kept up to date – particularly for areas such as rule traces where legal or professional advice is given by a system.

7.2.7 Integrating GEMINI

The business is not interested in the technologies used to provide an answer to problems – it just wants solutions. There is a clear requirement here for being able to provide systems regardless of technology by an approach which the users see as seamless.

Different methods have different focuses – SSADM for data and process, GEMINI for knowledge – each covering its own aspects. But which method should be used if a system requires more than one focus? Everything described so far for GEMINI has been oriented specifically towards the development of KBS; there has been no mention of possible conventional aspects. This is because GEMINI only considers the KBS aspects. It does not cover topics such as data and process analysis or database design; it assumes that there is a conventional method in place to model these.

The major issues of importance in integrating GEMINI with a conventional method are:

- GEMINI is product-driven;
- GEMINI uses the spiral model and permits iteration and prototyping;
- GEMINI does not define the products, tasks and techniques to the same level of depth that most conventional methods do.

Against the background of these major differences, the GEMINI approach to integration is described in the following paragraphs.

Achieving integration

The Project Controller effectively sits at the top of the hierarchy and has the project managers working for him; this means that he will have charge of one or more project managers who are responsible for the conventional and KBS components. This is a key role in the top level of integration. The four levels identified by GEMINI to describe the degree of integration of the conventional and KBS components are Strategic, Project Planning, Development Approach and Tools/Technology.

Integration at the Strategic level. At this level, the conventional and KBS elements are independent and consequently are run as separate projects. Each has a separate spiral and is initiated through the development and use of separate PIDs. The coordination of the projects is by Project Board and Project Controller. At this level the Project Controller must ensure that both projects have compatible PIDs and that they cross-refer to each other. Even though the level of integration is simply management at the top levels, the lower levels of integration must not be forgotten. It is important that the same approaches and techniques are used for both the conventional and KBS elements so ensuring a degree of consistency and making possible future integration more realistic.

Integration at the Project Planning level. The conventional and KBS elements are not independent at this level although they may be run as separate projects. They have a common top level spiral with parallel lower level spirals. The common spiral ensures that the two elements are coordinated and synchronised effectively. There is considerable interaction between the plans for the two elements of the project and the delivery schedules of the components, reviews, sign-offs, etc., need to be synchronised.

Integration at Development Approach level. The third level describes the integration necessary when a single project is building both the KBS and conventional components. One method is in overall control, and generally it will be the conventional method. It will therefore be necessary to split the work into the conventional and KBS streams. This is usually carried out on a phase-by-phase approach with common planning points at the beginning of each phase and common review points at the end of each phase. Mapping this on to the spiral model, each phase represents one circuit of the spiral. This corresponds exactly to the statements of how the spiral model operates in GEMINI, and it is not difficult to map on to a phase in a conventional method. Most conventional methods start by reviewing the current situation, revising plans for the phase and end with a review of the work carried out. Usually the only omission is an explicit examination of the risks involved and this can be added to the early planning activities very easily. Within each phase, procedures are required to start off the conventional and KBS components as separate tasks, to ensure their coordination during the parallel development, and to merge the two streams for review at the end of the phase. The development approach should be common wherever possible, with techniques and documentation also being common as far as the different requirements of the KBS and conventional streams permit.

Integration at Tools/Technology level. This is the bottom level of integration and is concerned with ensuring that:

- common data are stored appropriately for access by both components;
- interfaces between the conventional/KBS components are both possible and practical;
- implementation tools should be common wherever possible, although it is relatively unlikely that the same tools can be used for both the conventional and KBS components.

It may be possible to use the same method of accessing data, for example SQL calls from both the KBS and conventional software. It may also be possible to employ a similar approach by, for example, both elements making use of Object Oriented software.

7.3 GEMINI Technical reference

7.3.1 *Products*

GEMINI identifies three types of products in the Technical reference volume – Management, Quality and Technical. Management products generally emerge from the Risk and Planning quadrants and cover topics such as the Project Initiation Document (PID), risk assessments, spiral model plans, records of meetings, progress reports, and so on. Quality products are both generated and used within the review quadrant and typically include review requirements and results, and testing information. Both the management and quality documents may be passed up to the higher level spiral which is controlling the current spiral. They may also be passed over the supply/demand boundary. Relatively little detail is provided for these types of products in this volume.

Technical products are generated within the Development quadrant and are concerned with the creation of the system itself. They also provide the support for the system once it has been implemented, therefore also covering topics such as user documentation and Service Level Agreements. The technical products are the subject of most of the rest of this section.

GEMINI requires the project manager to define the set of products needed for a project and for these to be assembled into a Product Breakdown Structure. The full

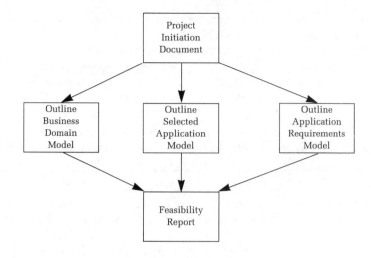

Figure 7.3
Product
dependencies:
Feasibility.
Source: Adapted from
Scarff and Fynn (1993c)

complement of products defined by GEMINI is not necessary for every project; this represents a comprehensive list of potential products and may be expanded or contracted depending on the needs of the project. This is the first stepping stone to producing a detailed project plan. The product definitions supplied by GEMINI are consistent in themselves but do not provide nearly as much detail as, for example, SSADM. One consequence of this is that additional material needs to be added to the GEMINI definitions before the products can be built.

The product definitions given below are in the sequence dictated by the dependencies between the products; this is also shown in Figures 7.3, 7.4 and 7.5. The input to the project, and therefore the first set of products, is the PID. This is used to define the scope and objectives of the Business Domain Model and the Application Requirements Model. These are defined in outline during the Feasibility study.

The *Business Domain Model* (BDM) is an organisational model. The whole of the relevant area of the organisation is modelled, not just that of immediate and obvious concern. If a complete organisation model is available then the BDM is a subset of this and can be created on this basis very quickly. The idea of building this model is to provide a basis for assessing the impact that the system will have on the organisation. In particular it needs to contain the structure, objectives and problems of the target area, all defined from the business point of view.

The *Selected Application Model* provides the initial description of the application of the domain and so in a sense is a subset of the BDM. It represents a first pass at the feasibility and will contain a cost/benefit analysis. Interfaces with other systems and user interfaces will be identified (but not defined at this stage).

The *Application Requirements Model* provides a first pass at the user requirements and an initial clarification of the scope identified in the PID. As well as the requirements for functionality and performance from the user, this model also describes the constraints to be applied to the development. The requirements are documented as either mandatory or desirable. These are then taken into account when completing the cost/benefit analysis and may be subject to negotiation with the users.

The *Feasibility Report* output from this stage represents only an initial assessment. With KBS it is possible that the feasibility will change as work progresses – hence the need for the spiral model so that the risk can be constantly reassessed. This report is compiled from the results of the three models outlined. Three aspects to the assessment of feasibility are identified: technical, business and organisational. The technical feasibility covers the technical aspects of the proposed project; can the problem be addressed using KBS techniques, are the skills required actually available? The business feasibility refers to the classic requirements of cost/benefit analysis: can a system be built which provides the necessary benefits for the business? The third aspect, organisational feasibility, refers to the assessment of whether the organisational structure is appropriate for the proposed system; will it be possible to incorporate the system into the organisation, what organisational reengineering will be required, will there be any opposition and if so how will it be countered, is the required expertise readily available?

Once these assessments have been completed and documented, the Feasibility Report is complete but the other three models which feed into it are not. This is where the version control starts to become important as it is essential to know which versions of the incomplete models have supplied input to the Feasibility Report. One reason for this is that the Feasibility Report is a deliverable and will be passed from the supply side to the demand side of the project structure.

The three models developed for the Feasibility study are then expanded further and completed (see Figure 7.4). These provide the input to the Expertise and Modality models and during this process the scope is defined very much more clearly. The construction of these models may also result in a need to revisit the feasibility assessment for the project.

The *Expertise Model* contains four types of knowledge – Domain, Inference, Tactical and Strategic. These are effectively the layers of the KADS four layer model although the guidance does not say so explicitly. A description of this model can be found in Chapter 6. Reasons for this overlap include the presence of KADS project members in the consortium and the absence of any other freely available knowledge model of an adequate depth at the time the guidance was originally developed.

The *Modality Model* shows how the system interacts with the rest of the world. This therefore contains not only the user interface but also interfaces to other systems and also describes the way the system interacts with them. Task lists are put into a structure, the data required for each task are documented, and the agents that are involved are defined. The interactions between the tasks and the agents are defined, including the nature of the interactions, for example the system acts as decision support, tutor, etc. This also bears more than a passing resemblance to KADS, in this case to the Model of Cooperation.

These are then brought together in the *Logical Analysis Model*. This simply contains a validation of the Expertise and Modality Models against each other and does not define any new material. For example, the tasks and data identified

Figure 7.4
Product
dependencies:
Analysis.
Source: Adapted from
Scarff and Fynn (1993c)

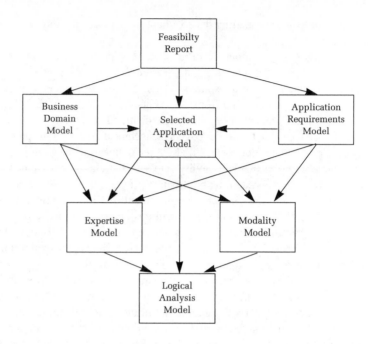

in the Modality Model are checked against the Expertise Model to ensure that all the requirements can be met. This is an iterative process since the Modality and Expertise Models are validated against each other as they are built rather than as a one-off exercise at the end. This ensures that the models are built consistently.

The next model, the *Functional Design Model*, is built from the Logical Analysis Model (see Figure 7.5). It adds in the necessary additional information which surrounds the Logical Analysis Model while still remaining logical rather than physical. It includes definitions of the data to be stored, the interfaces with other systems, definitions of the way in which the knowledge is to be represented, the user interface, performance and so on.

The *Technical Environment Description* contains the requirements for the implementation environment so that it meets the design definition contained in the Logical Analysis Model. It therefore includes hardware and software requirements and constraints, interface details (both user and to other systems), performance requirements, impact on the organisation, constraints such as budgets and corporate policies, hardware and software usage and so on.

The final model to be built is the *Physical Design Model*. This takes the design defined in the Functional Design Model, the tool selected as a result of the requirements defined in the Technical Environment Description, and contains a definition of the physical implementation of the system. This is used as a basis for coding. GEMINI does not define this model in any detail.

7.3.2 Tasks

One of the consequences of the product-driven rather than task-driven approach

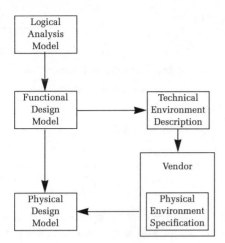

Figure 7.5
Product
dependencies: Design
Source: Adapted from
Scarff and Fynn (1993c)

is that the tasks are not defined in any great detail. An example set of tasks for a set of phases is provided but these are clearly stated as being exemplars rather than a fixed set of tasks for all projects. This has also been done deliberately to try to ensure that GEMINI is not treated as a KBS cookbook.

The tasks are configured according to the requirements of the project and are based on the products selected from those described above. The task configuration is then used with the spiral model to ensure that all the essential procedures of reviewing, risk analysis and planning follow each other in the correct sequence and that they are always present. The use of the spiral model is straightforward. At the top level there is one spiral for the project with each circuit of the spiral corresponding to one phase of the project. As it becomes necessary to break the project down then this main spiral spawns sub-spirals for each individual set of tasks. Where these tasks are carried out in parallel, the spiral model is used to control this as already described.

At the top level, the set of phases defined by the GEMINI task structure is:

- Feasibility
- Requirements Analysis
- System Modelling
- Logical Analysis
- Logical Design
- Technical Environment Definition
- Physical Design

Mapping the Feasibility phase on to the spiral model could give a set of tasks such as is shown in Table 7.1. This can be done similarly for each of the phases.

Table 7.1 Feasibility to spiral model mapping

Spiral	Actions
Review	Review the current situation and the Project Initiation Document
Risk	Assess the issues and risks involved in moving/not moving to a Feasibility Study
Plan	Plan the Feasibility Study
Develop	Do the Feasibility Study according to the plan
Review	Review the results of the Feasibility Study

The precise sequencing of the tasks is based on the products to be developed and the dependencies between the products. This in turn depends on the products selected for the current project. Consequently it is not possible to provide an absolute mapping between the phases and the products; products are frequently created in one phase and updated in several subsequent phases. Each project has to be configured separately using the guidelines provided in GEMINI. The approximate relationships between the products already defined and the phases are shown in Table 7.2.

Table 7.2 GEMINI products and phases

Product	Phase
Selected Application Model	Outline in Feasibility, detail in Requirements Analysis
Application Requirements Model	Outline in Feasibility, detail in Requirements Analysis
Business Domain Model	Outline in Feasibility, detail in Requirements Analysis
Expertise Model	System Modelling
Modality Model	System Modelling
Logical Analysis Model	Logical Analysis
Functional Design Model	Logical Design
Technical Environment Description	Logical Environment Design
Physical Design Model	Physical Design

It cannot be stressed too strongly that the precise relationships need to be determined for each individual project and project plans drawn up on that basis.

Moving down one level within the feasibility phase, GEMINI gives a suggested list of tasks of:

- FS.10 Outline Requirements Analysis
- FS.20 Outline System Modelling
- FS.30 Provisionally Plan Project
- FS.40 Assess Feasibility
- FS.50 Produce Feasibility Report
- FS.60 Review Feasibility

The product dependencies given in GEMINI show that activity FS.20 can be carried out in parallel with activities FS.10 and FS.30. There is therefore no reason why they should be carried out strictly in numerical sequence. The way in which they can be carried out in parallel is, as before, by spinning off two sub-spirals, one to control activity FS.20, and one to control activities FS.10 and FS.30. Once both spirals are complete, they can be brought together and the next activity, FS.40, carried out.

In this way the whole project can be planned using the very simple basic principles of the spiral model and the product-driven approach. This helps to ensure that the project is carried out as quickly as possible, by permitting parallel activities, while ensuring that all the necessary quality and risk procedures are carried out, driven by the spiral model.

7.3.3 *Techniques*

Of the three elements in the Technical manual – Products, Tasks and Techniques – the Techniques are the least well defined. In accordance with the principle of a product-driven approach, the techniques are linked to products rather than to the tasks. This is achieved through a large grid which cross-references potential techniques with each product definition. Each possible use of a technique is further qualified by an indication whether it can be used extensively, moderately, in a limited fashion, or not at all. An extract of the Product/Technique cross-referencing table is shown in Figure 7.6.

The techniques themselves are outlined in one chapter but relatively little guidance is given on their use. The technique descriptions can act as useful reminders of their contents but it is not generally possible to learn how to use the techniques from the descriptions given. For this, reference must to made to one or more of the many books on KBS development techniques. While this is not a major omission, it is a limitation on the immediate usefulness of GEMINI. Since the guidance does not define techniques in any detail, it is inevitable that it does not provide standards for the construction of KBS diagrams (such as semantic nets) in the same way that SSADM provides standards for data flow diagrams. It is left up to the individual organisation to supply these. While this is a relatively straightforward matter it is nevertheless time-consuming to carry out comprehensively. One of the biggest omissions is that GEMINI does not provide

Figure 7.6
Product/Technique
cross-references.
Source: Adapted from
Scarff and Fynn (1993c)

Techniques \ Models	Business Domain	Selected Application	Applications Requirements	
Knowledge Acquisition				
Exploratory Interviews	●	●	●	
Structured Interviews	●	●	●	
Case Analysis	◐	●	●	
Simulated Work		◐	○	
Training		●	◐	
Questionnaires	○	◐	◐	
Card Sorts		○	○	
Repertory Grid		○	○	

● Extensive use
◐ Moderate use
○ Limited use
  No use

any sort of unified approach to the representation of knowledge. The models that are built as part of the Expertise and Modality Models must follow either KADS or some in-house representation. Some initial work has been carried out by a number of the consortium members in conjunction with the CCTA to tackle this major area but nothing has been published.

Within the description of techniques in GEMINI, four types of techniques are identified:

- Knowledge acquisition
- Knowledge representation
- Validation
- Others

The contents of each of these is described briefly below.

Knowledge acquisition is concerned with the extraction of knowledge from three main sources – Experts, Documents, and Data. Elicitation from experts briefly covers the standard interviewing approaches and some of the more formal structured approaches such as card sorting and Kelly grids. Extraction from documents outlines the problems that can be encountered with this approach and gives some tips on the types of documents that can prove useful. The extraction from data covers techniques that are used more often as development approaches rather than simply knowledge elicitation such as rule induction.

Knowledge representation looks briefly at ways in which the extracted knowledge can be documented. The definitions of typical approaches include rules, frames, logic, contexts/worlds, semantic nets and conceptual graphs.

While these can be very useful for relatively small systems, they can easily get out of hand when a system contains many hundreds, if not thousands, of rules/frames, etc. Since this is not a problem which has been solved with these approaches elsewhere, it is not surprising that GEMINI does not address these issues.

Validation in GEMINI is defined as determining whether the system meets the requirements defined for it. This has two aspects – objective and subjective. The objective validation includes checking the knowledge base for conflicts and inconsistencies by inspection and checking the inferencing processes operate as specified. It also includes checking completeness. Subjective elements include the validation of the knowledge base against subjective criteria, for example checking the knowledge by the expert, ensuring the competence of the system, and demonstrating the operational quality.

The general bucket term of *Others* contains everything that would not fit easily into the other three categories. These include the use of prototyping, task analysis, structured English, and Data Flow Modelling. The use of prototyping is mentioned very briefly simply to say that it can be used as part of the spiral model to support some activities. There is no significant discussion on when and where prototyping can be used, its control, and so on. The other techniques mentioned are largely those found in conventional systems development which can be of use in KBS development.

7.4 GEMINI in action

GEMINI is a very new method and as such has not been used extensively. However, a number of conclusions about its usefulness on commercial KBS development projects can be drawn from general KBS methods experience.

7.4.1 Benefits and difficulties

GEMINI provides a structured approach to the development of systems in a KBS-oriented framework and so it is preferable to the relatively common 'fudged' life cycle and very much better than nothing at all. It uses conventional terminology whenever it can and this makes it easier for people with a conventional IT background to integrate it with a conventional approach. It also makes it much easier to understand. In particular, its use of a (more or less) standard approach to project management through its use of PRINCE ensures that it is relatively easy to integrate into IT departments.

It has sound backing via the CCTA – it has not been developed by an organisation that is likely to disappear overnight. This is of major importance in a world where smaller companies seem to come and go at a rate of knots. As it is supported by the CCTA it is easily available and can be bought off-the-shelf. The main consequence of this is that support in the form of training can be obtained from any one of a number of different sources.

However, a key element of a KBS method is the way in which the knowledge is actually analysed and documented and this is not defined in GEMINI. Similarly, the techniques that can be used are identified but not defined in any detail. These require significant work to be done to make GEMINI usable as a method rather than a guidance. To be fair to GEMINI, this has been deliberately excluded as it is available elsewhere.

An iterative approach to development is used through the spiral model and the product-driven approach. While appropriate for KBS development, it does not sit immediately with the more conventional approaches, although with a little work they can coexist reasonably well.

Estimating is difficult as the method is new and no metrics have been built up yet – but then estimating is difficult for conventional systems even though there is now a considerable body of widely used and accepted metrics.

7.4.2 Installation

GEMINI is a stand-alone approach as defined in the three manuals although an SSADM interworking guide is available. It needs to be integrated with the methods currently used by an organisation for systems development. Integration is not a trivial task at the best of times and needs a thorough understanding of the principles of all of the methods elements. The general task of integrating a KBS approach (or method) into an organisation is considered at some length in the next chapter. The key issues that are pertinent to GEMINI include:

- Elements of KBS need to be integrated into the phases before feasibility so that they form part of the strategy – not 'we must use KBS' but 'we must expand the use of IT into all available technologies appropriate for the business'.
- KBS development does not end at design. Physical design can be very difficult using advanced tools because they do not work in the same way as conventional languages; for example with some KBS tools there is no such thing as a program listing. The roll-out of KBS can be very difficult because of the 'acceptability of solutions' problems and ensuring that the system knows its own boundaries.

7.4.3 Additional material

The consequence of GEMINI being a guidance rather than a method is that it needs to be supplemented with significant additional material to produce a reasonably detailed working KBS development method. The principal areas in which this needs to be done are in knowledge modelling and techniques.

The area of *knowledge modelling* is difficult since there is relatively little that is freely available. If it is to be supplemented from currently available material then KADS probably provides the best source. The GEMINI models map easily on to the KADS models and there are a number of books available on KADS as well as the original documents. Chapter 6 on KADS provides sufficient detail to get started.

Techniques are not defined in GEMINI so they need to be gathered from elsewhere – at least to form a core set of documentation techniques so that everyone uses the same standards and can pick up other people's work. These can be found in many of the books on knowledge engineering which are available from bookshops.

The alternative to do-it-yourself is to obtain outside support from one of the many organisations now offering support in KBS development and methods. This is likely to bring a more comprehensive solution but will inevitably be very much more expensive in the short term.

7.4.4 *Training*

An understanding of the basic principles is essential for everyone concerned in a GEMINI project, from the Project Controller down to the programmer, in particular the use of the spiral model and the product-driven approach. Although actually relatively straightforward, they can appear daunting from just reading the manuals. A GEMINI project can easily lapse into an imitation of a simple waterfall project or degenerate into an endless series of iterations if not properly controlled. QA is significantly different because of the way in which the products are created across phases – a consequence of the product-driven approach.

It is very important to realise that the manuals do not provide a 'KBS starters' handbook' – they were never intended for this. An understanding of the issues involved in KBS development is essential and therefore general training in this technology is required. Similarly an appreciation of the ways in which knowledge can be modelled is essential because the guidance does not provide any details of this.

7.4.5 *The future*

There are no plans to extend GEMINI further in the immediate future; development will depend on its success over the next year or two. The strength of the guidance is that it provides a framework for the development of KBS in the same mould as SSADM which is currently the most widely used conventional development method in the UK. It is sufficiently specific to provide a very useful high level framework for the development of KBS while still allowing the incorporation of detailed techniques from many different areas of KBS development. If GEMINI follows in the footsteps of SSADM then its future is assured.

7.5 Summary and conclusions

The GEMINI guidance differs from all the other KBS methods described because it was deliberately created as a public domain method from pre-existing material rather than being proprietary or based on its own extensive research. It is not described as a method because it does not go into the same level of detail as similar conventional methods such as SSADM. It largely provides support for the project controller and project manager rather than the technician building the system. As such it is very comprehensive and it provides a sound detailed structure for the development of KBS.

Table 7.3 lists the criteria given in Chapter 2 to support the assessment of methods and rates GEMINI against them.

Table 7.3 GEMINI assessment criteria

Criterion	KADS
Type of life cycle	Waterfall and Spiral
Availability	Freely available
Depth of knowledge analysis	Shallow*
Scope of method	Analysis and design
Project Management	Very strong
Links	SSADM through a separate guide
Perspectives:	
Data	Poor*
Process	Poor*
Behaviour	Poor*
Knowledge	Poor*

Note: * GEMINI scores badly in these categories because it is intended to be supplemented with detailed technical methods and standards from outside.

Part III Methods in action

8 Integration and configuration issues

KBS are rarely the only type of IT system built by an organisation and so any KBS method needs to be integrated with whatever approach is currently used. This chapter looks at the issues associated with taking on (at least) one additional method for KBS and integrating it with the existing IT development approach.

8.1 Why integrate ?

The development of KBS demands approaches which differ from current software engineering practice. As a result, many organisations and academic institutions are developing methods specific to KBS. One consequence of this is that the number of KBS methods under development is increasing, each with its own approach and usually with its own terminology. This burgeoning of KBS methods leaves many IT departments in a quandary – should one method be decided on and, if so, how will it fit into their current working environment? If a KBS method is selected, what happens when new versions of it appear? What degree of compatibility can be expected between the KBS method and existing practices?

As well as these organisational integration issues there are the problems of combining the two technologies on a single development. How can software be built which incorporates both conventional and KBS aspects for which there is no comprehensive KBS + conventional development method? Two commercial projects typifying the increasingly close relationship between KBS and conventional systems that would benefit from an integrated approach are:

- A manufacturing company with one principal product theme but several thousand variations had difficulty in matching the precise product to customer requirements. A KBS advisory system as part of the sales order processing would advise on the most appropriate product depending on the customer's needs, product cost and availability. It would then log the appropriate order information, passing it on to the existing sales order processing system.
- A credit assessment module embedded in a financial control application. The module takes the information on individual customers from the database and recommends changes to their credit limit.

Projects such as these could potentially be carried out by separating the KBS elements, treating them as small development sub-projects and developing them separately using a KBS method.

This chapter sets out to address some of these issues and describe a way in which they have been either resolved or eased.

8.1.1 Difficulties with methods adoption

Methods explosion

Over the last fifteen years there has been an explosion in the number of conventional development methods available to IT departments. The original development methods have spawned numerous offspring, each claiming to have advantages over its rivals. Many organisations have difficulty in selecting a method which is most appropriate for their needs because of the differences in scope of methods and the varied claims by their vendors. It is not unusual for IT departments to use more than one conventional method, for example Information Engineering for the strategic level view and SSADM for the detailed system development view.

KBS methods appear to be evolving in a similar way with different vendors producing apparently different methods often with common roots. The 'granddaddy' of many KBS methods with academic origins is KADS and this has spawned at least half a dozen variations which are available from organisations throughout Europe. Many organisations, most notably the consultancies, have developed their own brand of KBS methods for internal use and for their clients. Other large organisations in the UK have developed methods for in-house use, some of which have also borrowed from KADS. The result is a plethora of KBS methods that individually cover widely differing ground, therefore demanding that more than one is used if comprehensive coverage is required.

Methods applicability

Different methods usually have different focuses. Some conventional methods have been developed for the typical batch/on-line transaction processing systems that characterised the systems development of the 1970s and 1980s. These tend to rely heavily on the analysis of the data stored and the processes which manipulate the data. Other methods are aimed more at the development of real-time systems, such as process control in factories. These tend to have greater emphasis on the behaviour of the system – such as what happens when event x occurs. The very wide ranging nature of these systems means different methods are essential to enable the matching of the most appropriate method to the required system.

The focus of KBS methods is different again. While conventional methods lay their emphasis on data, processes, and occasionally behaviour, KBS lay greater emphasis on the knowledge required to solve problems and the ways in which that knowledge can be used.

Many KBS which could solve real business problems need to be embedded in existing applications or require access to data already available electronically, for example on corporate databases or on datafeeds. Most current KBS methods are able to cope with such commercial systems as long as the KBS components can be separated from the conventional components. In some cases this is possible and successful systems are written. However, in others this is not possible and it becomes necessary simply to regard the potential computer system as a system which may (or may not) incorporate both KBS and conventional components. In these situations, a method which encompasses both aspects and permits the seamless development of both the conventional and KBS components is invaluable, if not essential. Very few methods take this approach; most KBS methods are for KBS alone. One widely available method that attempts to provide hooks for this integration is the government sponsored method GEMINI which links with SSADM. However, this still requires the use of a separate integration guide.

New approaches

New types of computer systems are now being developed, of which KBS is just one. Others include the continuing rise of Management Information Systems and the relatively recent appearance of Executive Information Systems. The production of both of these differs significantly from conventional batch/transaction processing systems development. The increasing power of PCs and the rise of window-based systems are also having an impact on the ways systems are developed. The use of client–server architectures, distributed processing and Computer Supported Cooperative Working, Document Image Management and multimedia, all change the approach to computer systems design. All of these are finding their way into mainstream IT and require specific approaches to developing systems incorporating them. This could cause an even greater proliferation of methods and add-ons to methods if each is to be designed and developed efficiently and effectively.

Cost of new methods

New methods are expensive to take on. The process of adopting a new method often includes hiring staff from the methods vendor to install the method, the provision of new documentation, and the sending of staff on training courses. These are just the visible sources of expenditure. Less visible to the accounting procedures, but equally, if not more, costly is the disruption caused to existing work and the inevitable learning curve. The use of existing methods is therefore not only cheaper in terms of direct expenditure, but also in the learning necessary. Reuse of existing skills ensures the minimum possible disruption when taking on additional technologies.

Methods configuration

Methods are frequently viewed as prescriptions for building computer systems and have been followed rigorously with the consequent excess of documentation, much of which is irrelevant for the project in hand and will never be used. The experienced and successful systems developer has known for many years that methods can only be used as descriptive guidelines; no method can provide everything required for a particular project *and only* that which is required. Methods should be used as guidelines that capture some (certainly not all) of the expertise required to build successful systems. This has the consequence that methods need to be tailored to the requirements of individual projects. This methods configuration tends to be carried out very badly, if at all, and yet is of vital importance to project planning and consequently the success of the project.

Feedback of expertise

A major difficulty in the use of current methods is that they inhibit the feedback of expertise developed on projects. Using an identical method on successive projects which certainly will not be identical means that the second project cannot be developed in a more efficient way than the first, even if the mistakes of the last project are avoided. A more flexible approach is required which will allow the feedback of expertise into a method so that it can be used by all future projects.

Scalability

Scalability of methods – their application to projects of very different sizes – is a very major issue in KBS development. While the same basic analysis techniques can be used for all conventional IT projects, the same is not true for KBS projects. Simple KBS demand simple techniques; the comprehensive knowledge modelling of, for example, KADS, is not appropriate on a 20-day project building a small system. It is more likely to be appropriate to large complex projects.

This issue means that different projects have very different requirements for products; the conventional approach of using one fixed method is often not appropriate.

8.1.2 Solutions?

Universal method

One solution suggested is the development of a 'Universal Method' that caters for all aspects of systems development. While this may solve, at least temporarily, the problems associated with developing hybrid KBS/conventional systems, it raises another set of problems:

- To cover all the ground currently encompassed by all existing methods, the Universal Method would have to be huge, probably impossibly large.

- It would have to be constantly rewritten to cater for new technologies.
- It would require extensive training both in its use and in the configuration and management of the method. Given the probable size of this method, this would present enormous problems of time and cost.

There is also the problem that the more generally applicable something becomes, the less specific detail it contains and the more abstract it becomes. Therefore the volume of work needed to make it usable on specific projects increases. It seems highly unlikely there will ever be anything approaching a single Universal Method.

Integration

An alternative approach is to integrate existing methods as required from a *toolset* or *repository* of methods to produce a single method that is project-specific and which has the characteristics required to develop the target system. In this approach, each of the individual components of a method – the life cycle, tasks, techniques and products – are documented as separate independent units. Methods are then configured from this repository as required by individual projects. This overcomes many of the problems outlined above:

- The type of method required for a particular system can be configured from the components of a repository. This is likely to be based on a single method or a combination of two, thus retaining the benefits provided by methods that are aimed at specific types of systems.
- The repository contains only the methods relevant to the organisation for which it has been developed. It is therefore a fraction of the size of the Universal Method.
- New approaches can be loaded into the methods repository without having to rewrite substantial parts of existing methods to incorporate the new aspects.
- The cost of taking on new methods is substantially reduced since the basic contents of the methods repository remain unchanged, they are simply supplemented by new elements as necessary.
- The feedback of expertise is made easier since each component is described separately. There is therefore no need to update an entire method definition.

In addition to creating a repository of methods, a structure is necessary to support the use of the repository and allow the integration of methods in a consistent fashion. This structure can also be used to assist in the configuration of methods to the requirements of specific projects.

8.2 The repository concept

The notion of a repository, at least as far as systems development is concerned, has been around for a number of years. The concept is simply to store everything of interest in a single place so that systems development is made easier. One type of repository would ideally be held in a CASE tool so that all the data and processes within an organisation are documented in a uniform format. All systems development can then be based on the contents of the repository. While this is a very good idea in theory and many organisations are attempting to put it into practice, it has yet to be widely achieved.

The same idea can be applied to system development methods. It has already been seen that there are a very wide range of methods that may be applicable to an organisation: project management methods, conventional waterfall development approaches, rapid development methods, KBS development methods. If these are all documented separately, each in their own format, it becomes very difficult to apply the methods uniformly across an organisation. If the concept of a methods repository is used then all these different methods are documented to a similar format, all are easily available, and each can be used as appropriate to meet the requirements of a development project.

The structure of a methods repository is relatively simple with three main components:

- life cycle definitions;
- product, task, technique, role and guideline definitions;
- guidelines on the use of the repository.

These are each described below.

8.2.1 Life cycles

The methods repository makes the same important distinction between the life cycle and the method that has already been defined – the life cycle describes the overall approach and flow through the project development, and the method defines the details. Example life cycles are the waterfall approach and a rapid development approach. The life cycle definitions describe the overall philosophy of the method such as the amount of iteration allowed and where it is allowed. A life cycle definition will usually contain a set of typical phases the project goes through.

There are now two major accepted life cycle philosophies in conventional IT – waterfall and rapid development. These are applicable to projects under different circumstances. A waterfall approach is more appropriate to large complex systems with much new data, systems that do not change rapidly, batch systems, and particularly safety critical systems. The step-by-step approach gives a greater degree of assurance that the system will perform the required operations accurately and consistently. Rapid development (RD) is more appropriate to systems where the user requirements are not clear, the business is changing quickly, and where much of the data is either already held (perhaps in the corporate database) or is local to the new system. However, it is notable that some organisations now prefer to adopt a rapid development approach for all systems development.

Once a life cycle has been selected, it needs to be configured to the requirements of the project. This will usually not be possible until some investigatory work has been carried out during the project planning. Typical operations to configure the life cycle include the setting of objectives, and hence identification of typical products that will be required, and the identification of major tasks to be carried out; for an RD approach this will include the initial identification of timeboxes. This stage will usually also involve the identification of the roles required in the project, on both the supply side and the demand side, and the initial identification of the role of the users in the development.

8.2.2 *Component definitions*

The second major element is a set of definitions for the individual methods components. While there can be many different formats for the methods components, the major elements fall into five categories – Products, Tasks, Techniques, Roles and Guidelines. These are each described below.

Products are items generated by the project. They are usually either documents or software. They may be used internally by the members of the project team or passed from the development side of the project to the demand side – the users or management. In the latter case they are often known as deliverables.

Tasks are definitions of the activities carried out to create the products. A task will often take one or more of the products as input and create one or more products as the output. They may also take documentation external to the project or simply update existing products.

Techniques define how individual tasks may be carried out. They are often applicable to more than one method; for example many KBS interviewing techniques can be used successfully in all systems development.

Roles define the set of skills, authorities and responsibilities required to carry out tasks. For example the project manager role needs a set of management skills, the authority to take decisions and the responsibility for taking those decisions. A set of roles is often defined at a relatively high level and frequently sits across all development methods.

Guidelines defined for a method provide backup information such as the way in which projects using the method are organised and run. They usually define the philosophy of the approach.

The methods repository is product-driven. This means the products to be delivered are defined first and then the tasks to generate the products are identified. This is in contrast to task-driven methods which define a largely fixed set of tasks that should be carried out where the products are almost side effects of the tasks. Taking a product-driven approach ensures that only the necessary products are generated, and only essential tasks are carried out. There is a tendency with task-driven methods simply to carry out all the tasks 'just in case' they are useful; the result is usually significant wasted time and irrelevant product creation.

The process of the configuration of the components is therefore:

1. Identify the products required for the life cycle selected based on the

requirements of the users and management.

2. Identify the tasks required to generate the products. As well as the tasks which directly generate the products, there will almost certainly be a number of intermediate tasks, such as interviewing the users, which do not directly generate a product.

3. Identify the techniques to support the selected tasks. This may be possible in detail, for example selecting the data modelling techniques, or only relevant at a higher level, for example identifying the general type of interviewing techniques that are more likely to produce the required output given the nature of the proposed system.

8.2.3 Repository guidelines

The third major component is the set of techniques or guidelines which tell the user how the repository is actually used. These could be simple directions as to how the repository can be configured to the requirements of an individual project, or could contain more detailed models of methods to guide the process. A set of suggested models are described in detail in Section 8.3.

8.2.4 Uniform documentation

The repository concept apparently demands that all methods are redocumented according to the repository standards. While this is certainly very helpful and can make the process of configuring a method very much easier and quicker, it is not essential. The most important factor is the development of a 'repository mindset'. Once methods are viewed as product-driven and consisting of a number of discrete components, which have relationships, then it is much easier to reconfigure methods to specific projects. This approach of decomposing methods into their constituent parts and viewing them as separate entities has foundations in both KBS/AI and Object Orientation. The basic component can be viewed as either a frame or an object. The way in which each of these is defined is described in much more detail in the following section.

If the methods are not to be redocumented then it is useful to have at least a skeleton repository with appropriate references to the existing documentation providing a cross-referencing mechanism. This creates a sophisticated index for the methods without going to the lengths of redocumenting them, thus reducing the clerical aspects of the repository creation substantially. The cross-reference consists of the five major elements already described (Products, Tasks, Techniques, Roles, Guidelines), cross-references between the elements, and references to a set of abstract methods models. The content of the cross-reference is defined in more detail in Section 8.3.

However, if redocumentation is deemed necessary then the scale of the task should not be underestimated. Each method tends to be documented differently, particularly if the individual methods have been obtained from different sources as is often the case. There is no instant solution to this problem since the only way in which to document methods uniformly is to re-document the whole set. Where the methods are not already in word-processed format, technology is now such that scanning documents and converting them into the appropriate word-processing format is a relatively straightforward, though time-consuming, task, once any copyright issues with the material have been resolved. The subsequent restructuring to ensure all methods follow the same format can be more problematic. It is not unusual for commercial methods, which one would expect to be absolutely consistent, to have errors in their cross-referencing and relation of tasks to products, for example in identifying tasks that create, update and refer to products. These are difficulties that need to be solved by reference to the methods developer. There are now tools available which permit the restructured methods to be delivered to every project manager, ranging from simple hypertext which may require significant effort to be useful, to sophisitcated software often linked to CASE tools.

8.2.5 Benefits

The main benefits to be gleaned from a repository approach include:

- the integration of components of different methods, both KBS and conventional (and possibly for other technologies as well), thus creating a method which covers multiple technologies;
- the tailoring of methods components to the requirements of individual projects while maintaining the integrity of a methodological approach to systems development;
- maximising the speed of development by ensuring that only the essential methods components are incorporated in a project plan;
- the use of a common set of products, tasks and techniques on projects of a wide range of sizes and types, therefore minimising the learning curve;
- the development of a set of core skills which can easily be used on a wide range of projects;
- the feedback of expertise gained on projects into the relevant methods components;
- a uniform approach to the documentation of all aspects of KBS methods which facilitates the methods delivery both on paper and electronically through hypermedia;
- the provision of a methods framework that can incorporate new components as they appear.

Although the repository approach provides a significant improvement over the conventional methods approach, it does not reduce the degree of project management necessary; if anything, it increases the need for competent project management.

8.3 Repository structure

The structure of the methods repository was initially developed as part of the methods modelling research project introduced in the Preface. This has been significantly enhanced as a result of practical experience in building and using methods repositories. Three complementary models have been developed to allow methods to be described uniformly and integrated consistently. These are the Structural Model, the Perspectives Model and the Methods Process Model. These form the major part of the guidelines for the use of the repository. The Structural Model describes the contents of the methods themselves, the Perspectives Model describes the elements of the world which methods attempt to model, and the Methods Process Model describes the relationships between the individual components of a method. These three are described in turn; the way methods themselves are modelled is then described.

8.3.1 Structural Model

The purpose of the Structural Model is to provide a definition of the contents of methods in general. The model was compiled through an extensive survey of over a dozen of the most widely used methods, both conventional and KBS, and reflects the contents of current methods. It is important to note that this is not an attempt to produce a supermethod but simply models the contents of current development methods. The model takes the form of a hierarchy of 'Generic methods components'. The top level of the model is:

> Structural Model
>   Products
>   Tasks
>   Techniques
>   Roles
>   Guidelines

A more detailed fragment of Products hierarchy is:

> System description
>   Objectives
>   Existing system
>   Context
>   Description
>   System model
>   Users
>   Glossary
>   etc.

Each element is referred to as a 'Structural Model component'. A full version of this hierarchy can be found in Appendix B.

The contents of each of the components and their relationships to other components are described in some detail. The key part of the Structural Model for the purposes of methods integration is the set of Products since it is the products that must be integrated initially; the tasks and techniques which assist in the creation of the products follow on once the products are defined. The full model contains definitions of over 100 different methods components.

One of the main uses of the Structural Model is to act as a reference point on to which the methods to be integrated can be mapped. This enables the methods to be verified in terms of their coverage of the development process, therefore allowing gaps and overlaps between the source methods to be identified easily. If gaps thus identified are believed to be significant in terms of the type of system to be developed, they can be resourced from other development methods. This is most likely to occur if a complex KBS is to be built and the integration is between a conventional method and an SE-based KBS method. There will clearly be no KBS elements in the conventional method, and the knowledge modelling in the KBS method is likely to exist only at a relatively high level. This may be suitable for simple KBS but is not appropriate for the construction of deep knowledge models. The Structural Model can thus help pinpoint areas where the methods need to be supplemented by components from more complex KBS methods. While this is a trivial example, the same process can be used to identify much less obvious gaps.

Potential overlaps between the methods can also be identified simply by seeing where a single Structural Model component is represented by elements from both of the methods. One approach to resolving this would be simply through inspection of the overlapping components. A more rigorous way would be to use a model which defines the things in the real world that methods components attempt to model. This is one of the uses of the Perspectives Model which is described next.

8.3.2 *Perspectives Model*

This model has already been introduced in Chapter 2 where the structure was described in some detail. It has also been used as the basis for the KBM knowledge model described in Chapter 4. The model consists of four parts – data, process, behaviour and knowledge – which are related as shown in Figure 8.1.

This describes all of the components that can be modelled in both conventional and knowledge based systems. It subsumes the various knowledge models that have been described which are part of other methods. Part of the top two levels of the decomposition of the Perspectives Model are shown in Table 8.1 to give a flavour of its contents. The full hierarchy can be found in Appendix B.

Figure 8.1
Perspectives model.

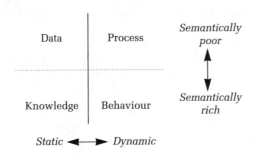

Table 8.1 Example perspectives hierarchy

Data	Process
Data entities	Task definition
Entity relationships	Task decomposition
Knowledge	Behaviour
Object definitions	Event definitions
Object relationships	State definitions
	Strategies and tactics

One of the main uses for the Perspectives Model is to resolve overlaps identified by the Structural Model. This is achieved through a detailed examination of which perspectives components are modelled by each of the methods components. It shows where the apparently overlapping components are genuine overlaps, where they are complementary, and where they represent totally different aspects of the same product. Three general rules can be followed during this process:

1. If they model identical perspective components, one of the methods components can be removed.
2. If they model completely different perspective components, they are complementary and both need to be retained. For example, the conventional methods component may represent the data, the KBS component may represent the knowledge.
3. If they model overlapping perspective components, they probably provide a valuable cross-reference between the methods. For example, the conventional methods component may represent components of the process and behaviour perspectives, the KBS methods component may represent components of the behaviour and knowledge perspectives.

8.3.3 Methods Process Model

The last of the three models is concerned with looking at the way the various elements of the Structural Model and the Perspectives Model are put together to form a complete method. The Methods Process Model is very close to a high level life cycle model in that it describes the way in which the various methods components are related to each other. However, it does not name phases in the way a waterfall model does but looks at the ways in which more generic tasks, products and techniques, are related to each other.

The Methods Process Model (MPM) has been developed through a detailed study of sound software engineering practices, development methods, project management methods, and research on software engineering. Its four principal activities (shown in Figure 8.2 as boxes) are Review, Decide, Plan and Develop, representing the four main types of activities which occur in software development. It is interesting to note that these bear more than a passing resemblance to the quadrants of Boehm's spiral model. This is not surprising as Boehm's model was one of the influences on the MPM and both were developed

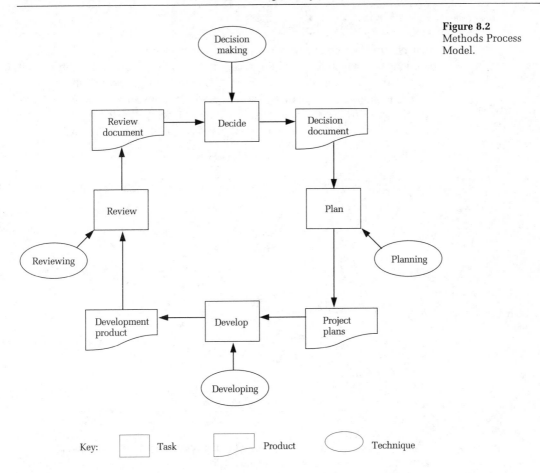

Figure 8.2
Methods Process
Model.

from best practice. The MPM differs in that it explicitly also relates together the top classes of products, tasks and techniques defined in the methods repository. The only missing element is roles. This is because the roles define the characteristics of those individuals who actually carry out all of the tasks defined on the model and it is not practical to show how roles relate to each of the other components without obfuscating the essential simplicity of the diagram. The purpose of this model is to provide support during integration and configuration so that the resulting method contains all the different types of products, tasks and techniques required for good SE practice, and to ensure they are in the correct sequence. In particular, it helps ensure that regular reviews are carried out and that these are followed by a decision as to the next step in the project.

8.3.4 *Methods modelling*

The sections above have described the essential models that depict methods in a way that allows them to be mapped on to each other. What has not yet been covered is how the methods themselves are modelled. This is in fact very simple. The principal components that need to be modelled to carry out integration are the products, tasks, techniques and roles. These are almost invariably given in methods descriptions as hierarchies and this makes the modelling process straightforward. Each individual component is taken as a separate entity and its relationships to other components are described, including where it fits into the Structural and Perspectives Models. This is effectively taking an Object Oriented approach to the methods. As an example, part of the KBM product hierarchy is shown in Table 8.2.

Table 8.2 KBM product hierarchy

System Specification
   System Description
   ...
   Data model
     Project dictionary
     ...
   Process model
     Extended activity diagrams
     Functional decomposition
     ...
   Behaviour model
     Event definitions
     ...
   Knowledge model
     Object definitions
     ...

Each component is then documented in the repository format with all products following the format shown in Table 8.3.

Table 8.3 Product component

Name	Contents
Product name	The name of the product (unique within a method)
Parent product	A larger product which this product is a part-of
Structural Model	The place the product occupies in the Structural Model
Perspectives Model	Perspective components modelled by this product
Description	A short textual description of what the product contains
Document Support	Documents defined by the method to support the product, i.e. must be available for the product to be created
Tasks	References to tasks which create this product. The value of this slot is generated dynamically when the method is loaded
Techniques	References to specific techniques within the method which may be used in the creation of this product

Again taking KBM as an example, the component 'Process Model' would be defined using this format as shown in Table 8.4.

Table 8.4 KBM Process Model

Name	Contents
Product name	Process Model
Parent product	System Model
Structural Model	\Development\System description\Existing System\System Model
Perspectives Model	\Process
Description	The Process Model fully defines all of the processes which occur in the target domain
Document support	Process Model Definition
Tasks	Define Process Model
Techniques	Functional Decomposition, Functional Definition, Dependency Diagrams, Process Charts

Note that the position of the product in the hierarchy of the Structural and Perspective models is indicated by the use of a \ for each level. The complete path to the specific component is therefore defined.

Similar component definitions can be created for tasks, techniques, roles and guidelines. Definitions of the formats for each of these methods components can be found in Appendix B. The documentation of methods in this way represents the first step towards the creation of a methods repository. If this is not to be followed by a redocumentation of the methods, each component can simply be annotated with the source of the full textual description. This then provides a comprehensive indexing system. If the methods are to be redocumented, then this frame/object-based description can be expanded so that the complete details are put into the object definition.

Once similar hierarchies have been built for a number of methods and each entity has been mapped on to the two methods models, the integration process is made significantly easier. This approach also makes the electronic delivery of methods through, for example, Hypertext much more straightforward, since the structures required to make this possible are made explicit through the modelling process.

8.4 Using the repository

Methods integration and the subsequent tailoring of the method to the requirements of an individual project can be summarised in five steps:

1. Selection of the methods to be integrated.
2. Selection of an appropriate life cycle model.
3. Construction of an integrated product breakdown hierarchy.
4. Configuration of the integrated products to match the requirement of the project.
6. Configuration of the appropriate tasks and techniques.

This process is illustrated in Figure 8.3. There are three major outputs from this sequence of steps:

1. The initial output is the life cycle model which is identified in the first two steps.
2. The second emerges from the fourth step and is a single product hierarchy developed from the selected methods and configured for the current project.
3. The final output is a project plan from step 5 which is tailored to the requirements of the individual development project.

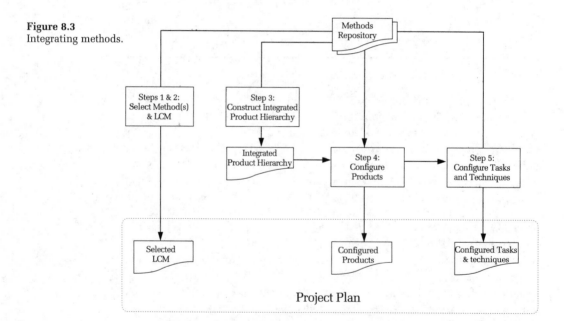

Figure 8.3
Integrating methods.

8.4.1 Steps 1 and 2: Selection of methods and LCM

The methods selected will depend on a number of factors, not least of which is the methods found in the repository. It is always possible the repository is perceived as inadequate and needs additional methods but if this is the case then it should be supplemented accordingly before continuing.

The selection of a method and a life cycle model are intimately connected. The

LCM required should be present in one of the methods to be integrated for any reasonable degree of success. This method is then used as the base and all other methods are integrated into it. It is likely in most organisations that there will be little choice over which method is used as the base since this will often be a matter of company policy. However, it is always worth considering whether an alternative method would be more appropriate. Although this may require significant additional work to put it into the repository it may prove more effective on projects and therefore be quicker in the longer term.

8.4.2 Step 3: Product integration

The product-driven approach ensures only the products required for the development of a system are selected. The tasks carried out to develop the products follow on from the identification of the products, and the techniques to support the tasks can then be identified. It is not sensible to attempt to integrate or configure a method in any other sequence.

The product integration process has two main tasks corresponding to the use of the Structural and Perspectives Models.

The first task consists of mapping all of the components of the selected methods on to the Structural Model and identifying gaps and overlaps. Gaps are Structural Model components with no matching method component and signify that neither method covers the area. This may be acceptable since the Structural Model describes a very wide range of components, not all of which are relevant for every project. A decision has to be made as to whether the gap is acceptable or whether it needs to be sourced from another method.

Once all gaps have been resolved, the overlaps need to be considered and this forms the second task. Overlaps are Structural Model items represented by more than one component from the methods being integrated. These are resolved by detailed examination of the perspectives components modelled by each of the methods elements as already described.

When the overlaps have been resolved, the Perspectives Model can be used to check that all of the perspectives are modelled by the integrated hierarchy. If there are gaps to be filled these can then be sourced from other methods.

The result of this exercise is a product breakdown structure which contains all of the products required for the subsequent tailoring of the method for individual projects.

It is then possible to use the product breakdown structure on subsequent projects without repeating this exercise every time. The only occasions it will be necessary to revisit the integration are if the initial method definitions are supplemented or updated and this needs to be reflected in the integrated product breakdown structure. If the repository is supplemented as a result of the feedback of experience from projects or with new/enhanced techniques, it is usually sufficient to update the individual repository components and ensure the changes do not violate the mapping on to the Structural and Perspectives Models.

8.4.3 Step 4: Product configuration

The MPM can be used to ensure all the required types of products are identified and sequenced correctly. The products required for each of the four sections of the MPM are identified. It is very likely that for three of these, Review, Decide and Plan, the products are going to be the same as for conventional development methods.

It is worth paying additional attention to the risk assessment element of the Decide tasks since the risks involved in the development of KBS tend to differ from those in conventional development. For example there are more parties involved – as well as the IT department, the user department and the appropriate senior management, there are also experts. The technology is likely to be less familiar, thus increasing the risk, as so on. These are particularly well highlighted in GEMINI.

The final task is to define the integrated set of products needed for the development phase. The products required will depend on the nature of the project being undertaken. For example, if the system to be built is purely batch, there is little point in including the products which describe the user interface. This process of deleting unwanted products can be guided by the Perspectives Model.

8.4.4 Step 5: Task and technique configuration

Once a complete set of products has been identified, the tasks required to construct them can be identified and configured. The first pass can be carried out by using the product–task dependencies. The only tasks required are those which create the products selected. Where no physical product is developed, as may be the case for some of the decision tasks, care needs to be taken to ensure that appropriate tasks are included. The dependencies between the tasks and products (a task cannot reference a product before it has been created) will guide the identification of tasks, leading ultimately to the generation of a project plan. The techniques required to support each of the identified tasks can then be added in. It is important generally to try to use a core set of techniques for all projects to ensure it is not necessary to learn how to use different techniques for every project.

8.5 Methods modelling in practice

This section describes how the methods models have been used on a number of projects.

Conventional + KBS + OO

A significant project involving methods integration required KBS and OO to be merged with a conventional Rapid Development method. This was achieved through using the steps described in Section 8.4. The life cycle required for the organisation was Rapid Development and a standard RD method was taken off the shelf. This was then subjected to tailoring to meet the precise needs of the company. The products to be created for conventional developments, KBS developments and OO developments were identified, described and linked into the appropriate parts of the life cycle definition. The tasks and techniques required to support all of the products were then adapted as required.

The entire exercise, from no method to a complete integrated RDM + KBS + OO manual tailored to meet the requirements of a particular IT department, and including briefings to the IT department and senior management, took a matter of weeks. The development of such an integrated and coherent method based on three separate approaches by any other process would have been extremely difficult.

Hypertext

Methods delivery has become a significant problem because of the size of methods and the need to tailor them to the requirements of individual organisations and then to specific projects. This is very difficult to achieve successfully when methods are delivered on paper. An alternative way of delivering methods is electronically, possibly as simple word processing files, or with more sophistication through the use of hypertext. This permits each person working on a development project to have their own copy of the method and for the project manager to feed experience directly back into it very easily. The updated method can then be made available to the next project.

Attempts have been made simply to transfer the text of methods into hypertext systems. This is not usually very successful without substantial additional work since text needs to be significantly reformatted if it is to appear as a coherent hypertext system. It then needs to have the links hard-coded into the method descriptions so that the user can navigate around the method. An alternative approach is to use the methods models already described. Methods can be decomposed into their component parts along the lines of the Structural Model and each method component defines its relationship to the others. Since the three methods models define the structure and contents of methods, and the method definition itself has the relationships between the individual components, these can be used to allow the user to navigate around a hypertext-like system without the need to hard-code any of the links. This means the method can be edited easily without the need to reconstruct large numbers of links manually.

Checking completeness

Methods that have been integrated unaided contain errors, often because of the size of the methods themselves. The methods models have been used to check the contents of manually integrated methods, and indeed unintegrated methods. This has often revealed significant gaps that were not apparent, or at least had not been made explicit.

Database designers' toolkit

A major development of a hybrid KBS/conventional system was the production of a toolset to support database administrators to design, refine, tune and monitor relational databases. The system required a substantial amount of information describing the data the database is to handle, definitions of the environment in which the database operates, definitions of the characteristics of the particular database being used (Oracle, DB2 etc.), and the knowledge and procedures required to carry out the DBA functions. The substantial volumes of data and significant elements of procedural processing demanded that a uniform representation for all aspects of the system was developed. An Object Oriented approach was selected that would permit the representation of data and facts within a class structure, and the procedures and problem solving strategies as methods within the classes. KBS elements were also developed to manipulate the classes and instances. The result was a relatively seamless representation of all four aspects of the systems – data, process, knowledge and behaviour.

9 Installing integrated methods

The final chapter looks at the issues surrounding the selection and installation of a KBS method. This process does not only have an impact on the IT department but affects the organisation as a whole. The major challenges the installation provides are considered and some pointers given on the best way to approach this significant task.

9.1 Methods implementation

Methods implementation is one of the most difficult areas to execute successfully. It is unlikely that the IT department will have much, if any, experience of implementing new methods and poor implementation can cause far more damage than bad systems development. The implementation process can be split into a number of stages as outlined below.

Requirements

Implementing a method can be viewed in a similar way to the development of a new system: both need a set of requirements. These define the expectations of the organisation for a new or additional method in a measurable way. Typical requirements for installing KBS methods are:

- Current situation : Only a small group of people understand how to build KBS.
  Goal : Everyone in the IT department must understand how to build KBS.
- Current situation : KBS are not well documented.
  Goal : KBS must be documented to the same level as conventional systems developed in the IT department.
- Current situation : QA is a problem because there is no method.
  Goal : KBS development must conform to QA processes at the same level as conventional systems.

Once a detailed set of requirements are in place they can be used to select the method and any support deemed necessary. After the implementation of the method the results can be checked against the requirements to see if the method has achieved the objectives set out.

Method selection

Selecting a method is the next step. This is a complex task and needs very extensive consideration. The main issues to be considered were introduced in Chapter 2 when considering the ways in which methods could be compared. This was then carried forward into the summary tables at the end of each of the chapters describing the methods. When deciding which method is the most appropriate, these guidelines and tables can be used to support the decision process.

Method integration

Once a method has been selected it needs to be integrated into the organisation. This process can have a significant impact on more than the IT department. While it will inevitably change their working practices, it will also affect users, particularly if a method is to be installed which requires greater input from outside the IT department, such as a Rapid Development Approach. This typically requires the involvement of users and experts for as much as 50% of their time for the duration of the project. There clearly needs to be a high level of commitment to the selected approach.

The details of the technical issues involved in integrating a method have already been covered in Chapter 8. The organisational and technical issues involved in this process are described in more detail in Sections 9.2 and 9.3.

The first project

The way the first project is selected is usually through a standard opportunities evaluation suitably extended for KBS. It is preferable that this is regarded as a pilot project and treated as such. The developers will not only have the usual problems of developing a system, but will also have to learn a new method. Guidelines for an opportunities evaluation and the selection of a pilot project are given in Sections 9.4 and 9.5.

9.2 Organisational issues

An initial question often asked when discussing the installation of a KBS method is whether the process is any different from that for a conventional method. The answer is that it is different and there is one main reason for this. Organisations considering the installation of a KBS method clearly believe methods are 'a good thing' (otherwise why bother with a KBS method?) and so will usually already have a method in place for conventional systems. This means that the KBS method will be a supplement to the existing approach. In the case where a site is considering the introduction of methods for the first time and one of the required components is KBS, the same issues generally apply although the approaches will be installed simultaneously. The KBS method will have to be integrated with the conventional methods in such a way that projects which contain elements of both can be developed using a single coherent approach.

9.2.1 *Impact of KBS*

KBS have the potential to affect every part of the operation of an organisation in the same way as the introduction of more conventional computer systems has done. KBS are best viewed as a major extension to the power and abilities of computer systems, increasing the scope of information systems and widening the range of problems that can be solved. This can be seen by looking at how data are used within an organisation. At the lowest levels, the majority of the work is concerned with the manipulation of data and is often supported through conventional systems. As higher levels in the organisation are explored so the use of raw data diminishes and the need for summary information increases. The need to have decision support, and hence KBS, also becomes greater. KBS are therefore often implemented across a very broad spectrum of users throughout the organisation. There are relatively few conventional development methods, and even fewer KBS methods, which take such a broad view of the issues of IT. It is, however, important that the full impact of KBS are realised and that the issues arising are appreciated and explored. It will often be the case when implementing a KBS method that the high level IT strategy and impact issues are not covered within the method and so have to be developed as an adjunct.

9.2.2 *Organisational awareness*

There is little point in introducing a KBS method into an organisation where there is no real awareness of the potential uses of the technology. It is necessary to cultivate an environment which supports the identification and development of KBS.

There is currently little awareness of the real capabilities of this technology in the way that there is for conventional computer systems. This is largely a result of the length of time for which conventional systems have existed compared with commercial KBS. It is also partly a problem of the excessive hype over the last 10 years about the potential of KBS. There are probably as many people with unrealistically high expectations of the technology as there are people with little or no idea of its capabilities. The introduction of KBS has therefore to include an increase in the general level of awareness of its practical potential. This ensures that business problems which can be helped through the use of KBS will be identified by the individuals in the organisation who have to address those problems on a daily basis. It is important that this awareness is spread simply as an increase in the potential solutions that the IT department can provide rather than through details of the technology itself. The business is interested in the solutions, not the technology.

Raising awareness

Several different approaches have been used to raise the profile of KBS depending on the nature of the organisation. Those described here have all been employed successfully.

The first is to explore the organisation for a business problem suited to a KBS solution (either wholly or partially KBS – quite possibly an extension to an existing system). The proposed system should not be excessively large or complex but it is essential that it solves a real business problem and that its success is visible to as large a part of the organisation as possible. Once the system has been developed and implemented, it can be used to demonstrate that the technology is capable of giving real benefits. The key part of the publicity is that it has solved a real business problem and provided measurable benefits.

A second approach is to deliver a series of high level seminars to senior managers. The purpose of these is not to go into the detail of the technical issues but to give an understanding of the potential of the technology and to put the initiative into the hands of the people who actually have the problems which need to be solved. It is very important that the potential business benefits are clearly described. Too often in the past KBS have been identified and built by a member of the IT department as a demonstrator which had no practical value to the organisation. All this proved was that KBS techniques could be used to build useless systems.

A very low profile approach has been used successfully by some organisations where KBS have been oversold in the past or where there is a suspicion of 'new' technologies. This has involved identifying areas of systems currently being built, or extensions to such systems, which could benefit from KBS elements and incorporating them without any mention of the technology employed. The users simply see an extension to computer systems without any awareness of the changes in the underlying technology. Having seen the new abilities of a system, it is much more likely that they will ask for similar features to be built into existing and new systems.

9.2.3 IT department awareness

Many of the skills required to build good conventional computer systems are also essential in the development of KBS. There are a number of additional areas of knowledge which are needed to extend the capabilities of the IT department into KBS.

Conventional development

A general awareness within the IT department of the way KBS are developed can have significant benefits for the way conventional systems are built. Many of the interviewing techniques used to elicit knowledge from experts can be used very productively in the analysis of all computer systems whether or not they include elements of KBS. An appreciation of the technology may reveal areas of systems

already in existence or currently being built which could benefit from the
addition of KBS components.

Knowledge engineering

One of the key areas of skills is in the elicitation of knowledge from experts and
the subsequent analysis of that knowledge. Although this has many elements in
common with conventional analysis, there is a whole battery of additional
interviewing techniques used in the knowledge elicitation process available for
use. Many of these have been brought in from other disciplines involving
discussion and interviews between people such as psychology, personnel
management, negotiation, and sales. Others have been developed specifically for
the elicitation of knowledge from experts for the construction of KBS. These
additional interviewing techniques are essential if the knowledge is to be elicited
from experts effectively.

Once the knowledge has been elicited it needs to be documented and
structured. At present there is no single set of knowledge engineering techniques
that is universally accepted; each method generally has its own approach to the
problem. Some methods are very thorough in their description of knowledge
engineering, for example KADS. Its drawback in commercial terms is that the
full set of the original KADS documentation runs to many volumes and is
extremely complex. At the other end of the spectrum, in terms of technical
documentation at least, is GEMINI. This method describes many of the
management issues in detail that are not covered by KADS but makes no attempt
to describe knowledge engineering issues in depth, preferring instead simply to
make detailed cross-references to existing techniques.

It is not necessary to have a deep understanding of the intricacies of complex
methods such as KADS to start building small, commercially viable KBS. A
general understanding of interviewing and knowledge structuring techniques is
sufficient, gained either through training on the KBS method being used or
through more general KBS training courses. It is possible to gain experience in
knowledge engineering through untutored practice in real knowledge
engineering interviews but this has some major drawbacks. The process is
inevitably slow and it runs the significant possibility that the experts being used
become alienated through the use of inefficient techniques.

Technical skills

A thorough understanding of the basic concepts of KBS is essential. Most
methods do not provide such an overview; they assume that the reader is familiar
with the technology. If there has not been any serious work in KBS before the
installation of the method, then a grounding in the basic concepts is essential
both to understand what is involved in building a KBS and also to understand the
method itself. This can be obtained through reading some of the many
introductory texts to the subject. The main drawbacks to a self-teach approach,

as is always the case, is that it is relatively slow and that it is possible to miss one or more major elements without realising. Another potential problem is that relatively few of the introductory texts have been written by commercial KBS practitioners.

KBS are often, through not necessarily, implemented in special languages or through the use of shells and development environments produced specifically for KBS. This often demands a very different approach from the conventional programming activity and generally necessitates training in the tool being used. This can usually be gained most effectively from the tool vendors.

9.2.4 Business Process Reengineering

Business Process Reengineering (BPR) is an approach to the reorganisation of businesses in ways that will make them more efficient. This usually involves looking at the tasks executed in a business to carry out the principal functions, and then looking at ways in which these can be reorganised to make the business more efficient, often with the support of information technology. This is a very different approach from that taken in many organisations where the function of the IT department is often simply to automate the processes that already exist. KBS have become a very important technology in the implementation of BPR. This is because KBS are able to provide automation for processes that had previously been rejected as too complex for conventional IT approaches. KBS can often supply the solution, particularly in areas where the key issue is not simply in automating an existing process, but in automating a process to give the organisation a competitive advantage.

9.3 Management issues

9.3.1 Project management

KBS projects can demand greater flexibility from the project manager than conventional projects. This can be unsettling to a project manager used to conventional systems. This occurs for a number of reasons. One is that it can be much more difficult to determine the technical feasibility before commencing on the development and it is sometimes necessary to explore technical options in much more detail than conventionally. It is also not unusual for an organisation to embark on a KBS development only to discover that the solution to the problem is simply an improvement to existing manual or computer procedures. If this provides business benefits the work can be considered a success. However, some project managers may feel that the termination of a project before any system has been built is a sign of failure.

The need for greater flexibility extends to the project life cycle. A prototyping approach to both the production of the system design and the code can often be an appropriate way to develop a KBS although this is also more difficult to control than a waterfall project. Whatever development approach is taken it is likely that there will be a need for tight control over the versions of documents and software release, often to a greater extent than for conventional systems particularly if prototyping is used.

9.3.2 Quality management

The application and management of quality control procedures can be made more difficult because of the flexibility required in the project management. Additional problems are also introduced as a knowledge base is very rarely complete and because it can be acceptable for a KBS to give the wrong answer occasionally, just as it is acceptable for a human expert to be wrong. Appropriate quality management and assurance procedures have yet to be defined in detail in any method although GEMINI does provide a good grounding through its definition of QA guidelines. The best approach at present is simply to take what little is offered, add this to existing quality procedures, and keep a watch for advances in the quality management of KBS.

9.3.3 Use of experts

An additional category of individuals appear within KBS development on the demand side of the project: these are the experts. As with conventional projects there is a management structure within and above the development team, and a set of users and their management structure; in addition for KBS there are the experts and their management structure. The existence of this additional group of people who need to be involved in the project is vital to the success of the development. The expert (or experts) need to be committed to the project and be prepared to cooperate fully by being interviewed, often frequently, and by getting involved in any prototyping and testing. Equally important is that the expert's managers need to be committed to the project. Experts are usually very busy (if not busy, why is a system being built to support their work?), and important to the organisation. This can often mean that they are difficult to contact and can spare very little time. Full agreement from the expert and the appropriate managers is essential if sufficient time is to be committed to the project. The failure of the expert to be sufficiently available is likely to doom the project to failure.

9.4 Opportunities evaluation

When starting to build KBS, businesses often have a number of problem areas already targeted for automation but where technology has not existed to provide the necessary support. Where this is the case, the candidate applications need to be screened thoroughly for their suitability for KBS. It is not unusual for areas apparently suitable for KBS, such as scheduling, to be very complex and not appropriate for the first steps. While a successful system may provide very substantial business benefit, the risks involved in tackling a major project as the first exercise in KBS are usually too high for it to be a satisfactory choice. A better alternative is to explore the organisation through an opportunities evaluation to identify candidate problems for automation or support.

The evaluation process generally involves investigating one or more business areas, selecting the most promising potential applications and carrying out a limited feasibility study. This also provides an opportunity to bring an awareness of the type of business problems KBS can address in the organisation.

The main objectives of an opportunities evaluation are:

- to determine where KBS techniques can provide worthwhile benefits;
- to identify the most promising application areas and determine their priority for further study;
- to educate and stimulate interest in KBS so that additional applications may be identified in the future.

The process of identifying opportunities can be divided into a number of tasks. These are outlined below.

Project Orientation and Planning

This task is concerned with setting the objectives and constraints, defining the plans for the study, and carrying out orientation in the business area. The main output is a Terms of Reference for the phase.

Orientation

The orientation task is concerned with making initial contacts with the parts of the organisation to be involved in the study. The organisation as a whole is examined, its structure is defined and the Critical Success Factors identified. This assists in identifying areas where IT solutions are likely to have the greatest impact. Once a high level view has been obtained, the study focuses on one (or possibly more than one, but only a small number) individual department. A familiarity with the objectives is gained and the main players in the department are identified together with their principal responsibilities and authorities.

Applications Survey

The objective of the survey is to gather basic information on business problems where knowledge based solutions may be applicable. This involves discussions with various sections of the department. Depending on the level of awareness of the people being interviewed, discussions on the basic benefits of KBS (not the technical issues) may also be appropriate. Interviews are held with the principal members of the department to identify any tasks causing problems.

Evaluate Applications

The evaluation process defines, in more detail, the main characteristics of all the potential applications and identifies and documents the possible benefits of developing a system using a KBS approach. At this stage, potential problems with the development of a KBS are also identified.

Select Applications

The applications survey will probably have revealed a number of areas in which KBS techniques could be applicable. Having defined the main characteristics of each, the decision is now made on which ones to pursue. A brief evaluation of the technical feasibility of each area is carried out and the likely development costs and benefits are assessed.

A business case for the development of a KBS is drawn up and presented to the decision makers. It is usually more appropriate to concentrate on the costs and benefits of a development than the technology. If these do not sell the proposed development then the technology is irrelevant.

9.5 Pilot project

The optimum approach to testing a new method is through its use on a pilot project selected through an opportunities evaluation. The people involved in the project will have both to learn the method and to carry to out the task of building a new system. This is very challenging and not to be underestimated. A suitable project needs to be selected for the pilot and will generally have the following characteristics:

- It should solve a real business problem so that the completed system can be installed and provide significant benefits.
- It should preferably not be a key business project that has very pressing budgets and time constraints. It is inevitable that using a new method for the first time will take longer than future developments because of the learning curve.
- The development team should be committed to the objectives of the project.
- The management of all departments involved must be committed to the project.

It is important that all the members of the development team are committed to both the project and the new method. If training is available then this should be taken up for everyone involved. A training course will generally provide the basics for the approach and give an opportunity for the team to try out techniques away from the demands of the normal office environment. However, this will only provide an introduction; the real learning always takes place when solving real problems 'on the job'.

9.6 Conclusions

Selecting, integrating and installing a KBS method is not a task to be undertaken lightly, any more so than the similar process for a conventional method. Taking on a KBS method can only be carried out successfully where there is an initial understanding of the technology; the method supports the development of systems – it does not tell you 'everything you always wanted to know about KBS'. The key points are summarised below.

Prerequisites:
- commitment that KBS are worthwhile for the organisation;
- commitment that a KBS method is worthwhile for the organisation;
- commitment of significant expenditure for taking on a KBS method;
- an understanding of the basic difficulties in the development of KBS, preferably through personal experience.

Major decisions:
- What should be the overall approach: Waterfall, Rapid Development, Repository?
- Should the method be developed in-house or bought in?
- Should the method be proprietary or freely available? If proprietary, should it be from the same organisation as the existing conventional method?
- What depth of knowledge analysis is required?
- What should be the scope of the method?
- How closely should it be integrated with current in-house methods?
- Should it provide project management support?
- Which KBS method should be used?

One of the key decisions is whether to develop a method in-house or buy in a method. Whichever option is selected, it demands considerable input from the organisation, initially in determining the precise requirements, and subsequently in the installation, training and use of the method. When it is carried out entirely within an organisation, the daily cost of the individuals may be significantly less than from outside, but will the inevitable difficulties simply result in a reinvention of solutions that exist elsewhere?

Whatever route is taken to exploiting this exciting technology, the path is bound to be difficult and not without its problems. However, in the long term, the ability to solve business problems effectively and efficiently through the use of KBS technology is the ultimate goal.

Appendix A: Bibliography

This appendix provides a set of references for much of the material used in the preparation of this book. This has also been supplemented by references to appropriate texts which are 'easy to get at' through bookshops or libraries. It is hoped that one of the problems frequently encountered with references, that of not being able to obtain the paper/book required, will at least be partly circumvented in this way.

Chapter 1: Introduction

Diaper, D. (ed.) (1989) *Knowledge Elicitation: Principles, Techniques and Applications*, Ellis Horwood, Chichester.

This book and the next are two of the many that are available on knowledge acquisition.

Hart, A. (1986) *Knowledge Acquisition for Expert Systems*, Kogan Page.

Hayes-Roth, F., Waterman, D.A. and Lenat D.B. (1983) *Building Expert Systems*, Addison-Wesley.

This text is one of the classic books of KBS. The 'methods' section however, is very small, consisting of only a few pages near the beginning of the book.

Jacobs, S. (1992) 'What is Business Process Automation?', *Expert Systems Applications*, August.

This provides a very simple introduction to Business Process Automation and relates it to the 'enabling technologies' with particular emphasis on KBS. It uses McDonnell Douglas as one example.

Keraunou, E.T. and Washbrook, J. (1989) 'What is a deep expert system? An analysis of the architectural requirements of second generation systems.', *Knowledge Engineering review*, Vol 4, No. 3.

This discusses first and second generation systems.

Kosko, B. (1992) *Fuzzy Thinking: The new science of fuzzy logic*, Hyperion.

A book which provides a popular view of fuzzy logic. While some of the details are disrupted by other fuzzy logic exponents, it provides a sound basic understanding of this approach to using uncertainty in KBS.

Ringland, G.A. and Duce, D.A. (eds) (1988) *Approaches to Knowledge Representation: An introduction*, Research Studies Press/John Wiley.

Provides an introduction to many of the knowledge representation approaches used for KBS.

Schreiber, G., Weilinga, B. and Breuker, J. (eds) (1993) *KADS: A principled approach to knowledge-based systems development*, Academic Press.

Chapter 13 of this book describes the use of KADS in developing the Barclays Fraudwatch system.

Chapter 2: Software Engineering and KBS

General

Avison, D.E. and Fitzgerald, G. (1979) *Information Systems Development: Methodologies, techniques and tools*, Blackwell Scientific Publications.

Bennington, H.D. (1956) 'Production of large computer programs', *Proceedings of the ONR Symposium on Advanced Programming Methods for Digital Computers*, June.

The first paper to describe a waterfall life cycle.

Boehm, B.W. (1986) 'A spiral model of software development and enhancement', *ACM SIGSOFT Software Engineering Notes*, Vol. 11, No. 4, August.

The describes the first appearance of the spiral model. This is worth looking at if the spiral model, in particular as described in GEMINI and KADS, is to be used seriously.

Boehm, B.W. (1988) "A spiral model of software development and enhancement", *IEEE*, May.

Further developments on the spiral model. Also worth looking at.

Hayes-Roth *et al.*, *op.cit.* under Chapter 1 references.

Holloway, S. (1991) 'Methods, bloody methods!', *Proceedings of the Data Management Specialist Group Conference*.

A lively discussion on, amongst other things, the derivation of many of today's methods. Interesting and fun but not worth trying too hard to find.

Partridge, D. (1992) *Engineering Artificial Intelligence Software*, Intellect Books, Oxford.

Partridge, D. (ed.) (1992) *Artificial Intelligence and Software Engineering*, Ablex Publishing Corporation, New Jersey.

Wilson, M., Duce, D. and Simpson, D. (1989) 'Life cycles in software and knowledge engineering: a comparative review', *Knowledge Engineering Review*, Vol. 4, No. 3.

Discussion on the various life cycles used for KBS.

CRIS conferences

This is a series of papers and books related to the CRIS conferences. From a practical point of view only the last is of interest in modelling methods. It is also the most up-to-date, having gone through two editions.

Olle, T.W., Sol, H.G. and Verrijn-Stuart, A.A. (eds) (1982) *Information System Design Methodologies: A comparative review*, North-Holland, Amsterdam.

Olle, T.W., Sol, H.G. and Tully, C.J. (eds) (1983), *Information System Design Methodologies: A feature analysis*, North-Holland, Amsterdam.

Olle, T.W., Sol, H.G. and Verrijn-Stuart, A.A. (eds) (1986) *Information System Design Methodologies: Improving the practice*, North-Holland, Amsterdam.

Olle, T.W., Verrijn-Stuart, A.A. and Bhabuta, L. (eds) (1988) *Computerized Assistance during the Information Systems Life Cycle*, North-Holland, Amsterdam.

Olle, T.W., Hagelstein, J., Macdonald, I.G., Rolland, C., Sol, H.G., Van Assche, F.J.M. and Verrijn-Stuart, A.A. (1990) *Information Systems Methodologies, a Framework for Understanding*, 2nd edition, Addison-Wesley.

This book describes the results of the modelling carried out under the banner of the CRIS conferences. It also contains a discussion on the first three perspectives – data, process and behaviour.

Methods modelling

Glasson, B.C. (1989) 'Model of system evolution', *Information and Software Technology*, Vol. 31, No. 7.

Harris-Jones, C., Barrett, T., Walker, T., Moores, T. and Edwards, J. (1992) 'A methods model for the integration of KBS and conventional information technology', *Research and Development in Expert Systems IX*, ed. M. Bramer and R. Milne, BCS SGES Conference Proceedings, Cambridge University Press.

This volume contains the most easily accessible of the papers which describes the methods modelling used as a basis for the Perspectives and Structural models described in this book.

Loucopoulos, P., Black, W.J., Sutcliffe, A.G. and Layzell, P.J. (1987) 'Towards a unified view of system development methods', *International Journal of Information Management*, Vol. 7, pp. 205–218.

A description of AMADEUS.

Ould, M.A. and Roberts, C. (1988) 'Defining formal models of the software development process', in *Software Engineering Environments*, ed. P. Brereton, Ellis Horwood, Chichester.

Chapter 3: Conventional methods adapted for KBS

Booch, G. (1994) *Object-Oriented Analysis and Design with Applications*, 2nd edition, Benjamin/Cummins.

Graham, I. (1993) *Object Oriented Methods*, 2nd edition, Addison-Wesley.

Hares, J.S. (1990) *SSADM for the Advanced Practitioner*, Wiley.

Hares, J.S. (1991) *Information Engineering for the Advanced Practitioner*, Wiley.
Hares' books contain sections on how SSADM and IE relate to KBS using STAGES as the KBS method.

Inder, R. and Filby, I. (1991) 'Survey of knowledge engineering methods and supporting tools', *Proceedings of the BCS SGES Knowledge Based Systems Methodologies Workshop*, December.
A survey of some of the currently available KBS methods. While not complete, it does provide good coverage.

Keller, R. (1987) *Expert Systems Technology: Development and Application*, Yourdon Press, Englewood Cliffs, NJ.

Martin, J. and Odell, J.J. (1992) *Object Oriented Analysis and Design*, Prentice Hall.

Chapter 4: KBM – The ACT KBS method

Harris-Jones ., *et al.*, *op.cit.* under Chapter 2 references.

Southwick, R.W. (1988) 'Topic explanation in expert systems', *Research and Development in Expert Systems V*, BCS conference proceedings.
Describes use of topics and landmarks.

Chapter 5: KBS methods

See sections on Chapters 6 and 7 for KADS and GEMINI references.

Keats

Brayshaw, M., Domingue, J. and Rajan, T. (1989) 'An integrated approach to monitoring the performance of inference systems', *HCRL Technical Report No. 47*, Human Cognition Research Laboratory, Milton Keynes.

Domingue, J. and Eisenstadt, M. (1989) 'A new metaphor for the graphical explanation of forward chaining rule execution', *HCRL Technical Report No. 52*, Human Cognition Research Laboratory, Milton Keynes, September.

Motta, E., Rajan, T. and Eisenstadt, M. (1989a) 'Knowledge acquisition as a process of model refinement', *HCRL Technical Report No. 40*, Human Cognition Research Laboratory, Milton Keynes, UK.

Motta, E., Rajan, T., Domingue, J. and Eisenstadt, M. (1989b) 'What should knowledge engineers do? The Keats approach to knowledge engineering', *HCRL Technical Report*

No. 54, Human Cognition Research Laboratory, Milton Keynes.

Valtorta, M. (1989) 'KADS vs. Keats', *IJCAI-89 Workshop, Knowledge Acquisition: Practical Tools & Techniques*, August.

KEMRAS

BHRA (The Fluid Engineering Centre), ERA Technology Ltd, The Building Services Research & Information Association, The Research Association for the Paper & Board, Printing & Packaging Industries, The Welding Institute, The University of Liverpool, Loughborough University of Technology, and University College London (1989) *KEMRAS: Knowledge Elicitation Manual for RAs, Part I.*

EDESIRL

Watson, I. (1992) 'Project management for the evolutionary development of expert systems', *Research and Development in Expert Systems IX,* ed. M. Bramer and R. Milne, BCS SGES Conference Proceedings, Cambridge University Press.

Chapter 6: KADS

Breuker, J., Wielinga, B., van Someren M., de Hoog, R., Schreiber, G., de Greef, P., Bredeweg, B., Wielemaker, J. Billault, J-P., Davoodi, M. and Hayward, S. (1987) *Model Driven Knowledge Acquisition: Interpretation Models*, ESPRIT P1098, deliverable D1 (task A1), University of Amsterdam and STC Technology Ltd.

de Hoog, R., Martil, R., Wielinga, B., Taylor, R., Bright, C. and van de Velde, W. (1992) *The CommonKADS Model Set*, ESPRIT P5248, document KADS-II/WP I-II/RR/UvA/018/4.0.

Hesketh, P. and Barrett, T. (eds), Anjewierden, A., Schreiber, G., de Alberdi, M. and Tansley, S. (contributors) (1990) *An Introduction to the KADS Methodology*, ESPRIT P1098, deliverable M1, STC Technology Ltd.

This is an introduction to the method written at the end of the KADS-I project by members of the project. It is probably the most comprehensible of all of the original KADS documents and, since it contains an extensive KADS bibliography, provides an excellent starting point for accessing the original KADS-I documents.

Hickman, F., Killin, J., Land, L., Mulhall, T., Porter, D. and Taylor, R. (1989) *Analysis for Knowledge-Based Systems: A Practical Guide to the KADS Methodology*, Ellis Horwood, Chichester.

The first book to appear on KADS. It reflects the status of KADS in 1988 so does not contain a complete view of the KADS-I project. Good, given its timing but largely superseded by subsequent books and developments on KADS.

Kingston, J. (1993) *Pragmatic KADS 1.0*, University of Edinburgh report AIAI-IR-13.

A brief description of how KADS can be used on smaller projects. Report available from the AIAI at the University of Edinburgh.

Porter, D. (1992) *KADS-II: Towards the CommonKADS method*, ESPRIT P5248, document reference KADS-II/T5.1.2/PP/TRMC/001/1.0.

Schreiber, G., Weilinga, B., Hesketh, P. and Lewis, A. (1989) *A KADS Design Description Language*, ESPRIT P1098, deliverable B7, University of Amsterdam and STC Technology Ltd.

Description of the Design Description Language (DDL).

Schreiber, G., Weilinga, B. and Breuker, J. (eds) (1993) *KADS : A principled approach to knowledge-based systems development*, Academic Press.

This provides a detailed description of the principal results of the KADS project, written largely by the members of Amsterdam University. This is not really a method definition in the conventional sense but is probably the nearest text to a 'vanilla-flavoured' KADS that is available.

Tansley, D.S.W. and Hayball, C.C. (1993) *Knowledge-Based Systems Analysis and Design: A KADS developers handbook*, BCS practitioners series, Prentice Hall.

An excellent book which provides a good commercial practical view of this important method.

Chapter 7: GEMINI

Montgomery, A. (1988) 'GEMINI – Government Expert Systems Methodology Initiative', *Research and Development in Expert Systems V*, BCS conference proceedings.

GEMINI reference manuals

Scarff, F. and Fynn, J. (1993a) *GEMINI: Controlling KBS development projects*, CCTA IT Infrastructure Library, HMSO.

Scarff, F. and Fynn, J. (1993b) *GEMINI: Managing KBS development projects*, CCTA IT Infrastructure Library, HMSO.

Scarff, F. and Fynn, J. (1993c) *GEMINI: Technical reference*, CCTA IT Infrastructure Library, HMSO.

Chapter 8: Integration and configuration issues

Harris-Jones *et al.*, op.cit. under Chapter 2 references.

Appendix B: Repository models

1 Structural Model

The Structural Model defines the set of Products, Task.s and Techniques that are typically found in development methods. The way in which this model is used is defined in some detail in Chapter 8.

1.1 Products

The products can be divided into four groups – Plan, Review, Decision and Development. Each of these is defined in turn.

Plan
  Terms of reference
    Project plans report
    Development plan
    Phase plans
      Business analysis
      External design
      Internal design
      Programming
      Testing
        Unit testing
        System testing
      User acceptance
      Cut-over
      Maintenance
    Standards
    Resources

Review
  Phase products
    Walkthrough checklist
    QA review
    Monitoring

End of development products
  Project evaluation review
  Post-implementation review

Decision
  Reporting
    Risk analysis
    Management summaries
  Meeting records

Development
  Phase report
  Feasibility assessment
    Business feasibility
    Technical feasibility
    Organisational feasibility
  Business background
    Structure
    Objectives
    Problems
    Constraints
    Other systems
  System description
    Objectives
    Existing system
      Context
      Description
      Users
      System model
      Glossary
      Bibliography
      Volumes and frequencies
    Requirements
    System options
      Area of change
      Alternative solutions
      Costs
  Proposed system
  Description
  External design
    Domain activities
    System activities
      I/O formats
        Security and control

    Internal design
      Domain activities
      System activities
        Interfaces
        I/O formats
        Security and control
        Program/module specifications
  Physical environment
    Hardware environment
    Software considerations
  Prototypes
    Prototype definition
    Prototype results
    Prototype software
  System
    Program documentation
    Testing documentation
      Link testing
      System testing
      Acceptance testing
    Development standards
    Implementation
    Operational documents
      Operations
      Users
      Support
      Training

1.2 Tasks

Task
  Plan
  Develop
    Gather information
    Abstract
    Check
    Convert format
  Review
  Decide

1.3 Techniques

Technique
  Planning
  Development
    Information gathering

Abstraction
Checking
Format conversion
Reviewing
Decision making

2 Perspectives Model

2.1 Hierarchy

The decomposition of the perspectives can be defined under each of the four perspectives – Data, Knowledge, Process and Behaviour.

Data
    Entity
      External
      Internal
    Data structure
    Physical file/table
    Entity relationship
    Attribute
    Logical data item
    Column/field
    Data store
    Data flow
    I/O structure
    Protocol

Knowledge
    Object
    Logical object
    Physical object
    Object relationship
      Object hierarchy
      Object sibling
    Logical slot
    Physical slot
    Object role

Process
    Task
    Function
    Process definition
    Task relationship

Task hierarchy
Task sibling

Behaviour
  State
  Event
  Task structure
   Processes
   User dialogue
   Screen design
   Screen sequences
   Explanation/help design
   Internal process
   Procedure definition
  Goals
  Goal definition
  Strategies
   Control
   Logical rules/processes
   Procedure/ruleset definition
   Tactics
   Inference structure
   Inference mechanism
  Task role
  Role definition

2.2 *Cross-references*

There are a large number of potential cross-references between the Perspective entities. The Perspectives model does not contain definitions of all possible cross-references but just indicates the most common. These are:

Entity # Attribute
Task # Entity or Object
Task # Event
Event # State
Object # Object Role
Task # Task Role
Object role # Task role
Task # Task structure
Task Structure # Task role

3 Methods Definitions

The five major elements of methods are the Products, Tasks, Techniques, Roles and Guidelines. The cross-reference elements of these components in a methods repository are defined in the following sections.

3.1 *Products*

Table B.1 Products

Name	Contents
Product name	The name of the product (unique within a method)
Parent product	A larger product which this product is a part-of
Structural Model	The place the product occupies in the Structural Model
Perspectives Model	Perspective components modelled by this product
Description	A short textual description of what the product contains
Document support	Documents defined by the method to support the product, i.e. documents which must be available for the product to be created
Tasks	References to tasks which create this product.
Techniques	References to specific techniques within the method which may be used in the creation of this product

3.2 *Tasks*

Table B.2 Tasks

Name	Contents
Task name	Name of task in the method
Parent task	Name of the task which this task is part-of
Structural Model	The place the product occupies in the Structural Model
Description	Description of the task
Trigger	Event which causes the task to be executed
Product(s) output	Product(s) which are generated by the task
Product(s) updated	Product(s) which are updated by the task
Product(s) referenced	Product(s) referenced by the task
External products required	Products required which are not part of the method
Techniques	Names of techniques which can be used to carry out this task
Roles	Names of roles which carry out this task
Resources required	Names of the resources required by the task

3.3 *Techniques*

Table B.3 Techniques

Name	Contents
Technique name	Name of technique in the method
Parent technique	Name of the parent technique
Structural Model	The place the technique occupies in the Structural Model
Description	Description of the technique
Perspective	Perspective in which the technique is used
Trigger	Circumstances which cause the technique to be used. May be a set of potentially complex circumstances
Skills required	Types of skill required to carry out the technique
Skills consulted	Other skills required to complete the technique
Resources required	List of the resources required to carry out the technique

3.4 *Roles*

Table B.4 Roles

Name	Contents
Role name	Name of role in the method
Parent role	Name of the parent role
Description	Description of the role
Skills required	Types of skill required to carry out the role

3.5 *Guidelines*

Table B.5 Guidelines

Name	Contents
Guideline name	Name of the guideline in the method
Parent guideline	Name of the parent guideline
Description	Description of the guideline
Guidelines	Cross-references to relevant guidelines
Products	Cross-references to relevant products
Tasks	Cross-references to relevant tasks
Techniques	Cross-references to relevant techniques
Roles	Cross-references to relevant roles

Index